A Life Worth Living

Series in Positive Psychology

Christopher Peterson
Series Editor

A Life Worth Living: Contributions to Positive Psychology
Edited by Mihaly Csikszentmihalyi and Isabella Selega Csikszentmihalyi

A Life Worth Living
Contributions to Positive Psychology

Edited by
Mihaly Csikszentmihalyi
and
Isabella Selega Csikszentmihalyi

OXFORD
UNIVERSITY PRESS

2006

OXFORD
UNIVERSITY PRESS

Oxford University Press, Inc., publishes works that further
Oxford University's objective of excellence
in research, scholarship, and education.

Oxford   New York
Auckland   Cape Town   Dar es Salaam   Hong Kong   Karachi
Kuala Lumpur   Madrid   Melbourne   Mexico City   Nairobi
New Delhi   Shanghai   Taipei   Toronto

With offices in
Argentina   Austria   Brazil   Chile   Czech Republic   France   Greece
Guatemala   Hungary   Italy   Japan   Poland   Portugal   Singapore
South Korea   Switzerland   Thailand   Turkey   Ukraine   Vietnam

Published by Oxford University Press, Inc.
198 Madison Avenue, New York, New York 10016

www.oup.com

Oxford is a registered trademark of Oxford University Press

Library of Congress Cataloging-in-Publication Data
A life worth living : contributions to positive psychology / edited by Mihaly Csikszentmihalyi and
Isabella Selega Csikszentmihalyi.
p. cm. —(Series in positive psychology)
Includes bibliographical references and index.
ISBN-13 978-0-19-517679-7

1. Positive psychology. I. Csikszentmihalyi, Mihaly.   II. Csikszentmihalyi, Isabella Selega.
III. Series.
BF204.6.L54 2006
150.19'8—dc22   2005027911

9 8 7 6 5 4

Printed in the United States of America
on acid-free paper

THIS BOOK IS A PRODUCT OF
The Gallup International Positive Psychology
Summit (GIPPS) established in 1997 by The Gallup
Organization to convene the world's most highly
committed, world-class researchers who study,
measure, and report on "what is right with people,
workplaces, schools, communities, policy, etc."

We are extremely grateful to Mihaly Csikszentmihalyi
and Isabella Selega Csikszentmihalyi, editors of this
volume; to each of the chapter authors; to Mike
Morrison, Dean of the University of Toyota (an
ongoing sponsor of GIPPS); to the GIPPI board; to
Gallup clients and associates; and especially to
Sheila M. Kearney, the Executive Director of the
Gallup International Positive Psychology Institute.

High regards,
Jim Clifton. Chairman & CEO
The Gallup Organization

Contents

Contributors

Jochen Brandstädter
University of Trier
54286 Trier
Germany

Isabella Csikszentmihalyi
Writer and Editor
Claremont, CA 91711

Mihaly Csikszentmihalyi
The Claremont Graduate University
Claremont, CA 91711

Antonella Delle Fave
Medical School of the University of
    Milan
Milan, Italy

Robert A. Emmons
University of California
Davis, CA 95616

Barbara L. Fredrickson
University of Michigan
Ann Arbor, MI 48109–1109

Daisy D. Grewal
Yale University
New Haven, CT 06520

Jane Henry
Open University
Milton Keynes MK76AA
United Kingdom

Tim Kasser
Knox College
Galesburg, IL 61401

Dmitry Leontiev
Moscow State University
Moscow, Russia

Jari-Erik Nurmi
University of Jyvaskyla
FIN-40014 Jyvaskyla
Finland

Christopher Peterson
University of Michigan
Ann Arbor, MI 48109

Csaba Pléh
Budapest University of Technology
    and Economics
Budapest, Hungary

Katariina Salmela-Aro
University of Jyvaskyla
FIN-40014 Jyvaskyla
Finland

Peter Salovey
Yale University
New Haven, CT 06520

Martin E. P. Seligman
University of Pennsylvania
Philadelphia, PA 19104

Kennon Sheldon
University of Missouri–Columbia
Columbia, MO 65211

A Life Worth Living

Introduction

MIHALY CSIKSZENTMIHALYI

T he volume you are about to read is a collection of essays from some of the foremost scholars from around the world who identify them- selves with the new direction in the discipline called "positive psychology." This direction is distinguished by an interest in the more desirable aspects of behav- ior—what used to be called the "virtues"—as opposed to the recently more preva- lent focus on pathology. If we imagine human experience as following along a bell curve with illness and despair at the left tail of the slope, joy and creativity at the other end, and the great majority of experiences around a middle neutral point, one could say that for the past half century or so psychology in the United States has been focusing almost exclusively on the left-hand tail of the curve. The goal of most psychologists has been to bring people whose lives were spent in regions of misery far below the mean back into a semblance of normalcy. Yet increasing numbers in the profession have begun to feel that without under- standing what happens on the right slope of the curve, the best we have been able to do for people was not good enough. Even "normal" people need to grow, to hope for a better life, to change themselves into what they consider to be bet- ter persons. It is in response to this realization that positive psychology started to take shape in the last decade of the 20th century as a loose confederation of thinkers and practitioners with overlapping interests in positive psychological states.

Given the tenor of the contributions to this volume, I took the risky step of characterizing its content as dealing with *a life worth living.* For many scientists, this amounts to raising a red flag. After all, it is widely held that statements of value are outside the purview of science. So, if psychology is to be scientific, it should avoid dealing with issues such as what might or might not be worthwhile.

And even if we were somehow to agree on what a valuable life is, one could still argue that examining one's life is not the way to reach it. Recent insights into the functioning of the mind suggest a conclusion opposite to the one attributed to Socrates: Introspection, reflection, and attempts at understanding ourselves are just side effects of having a hyperdeveloped frontal cortex, a dubious boon for a species that survived because of its relatively exceptional rational capacities. The subtext of evolutionary psychology is often that the most authentic way to live is in accordance with the ancient genetic programs we have inherited and to discount the more recent developments of the human species as "cultural" accretions of dubious standing and value.

Both of these critiques, however, are based on a parochial perspective on the human condition. When trying to understand what it means to be human, we cannot ignore what we value, and why. Nor does it make sense to conclude that the emergence of new capacities, such as that for reflection, is less important for the destiny of the species than the more ancient genetic programs that control so much of our mind and behavior.

Let us take the first of these two issues. It is an incontrovertible fact that, in every human culture that is known to us, certain outcomes of development have been considered more valuable than others. Some of these outcomes are universal—everywhere, for instance, a "good life" would involve health, freedom from need, the feeling that one has contributed to the well-being of one's family, the respect of one's peers. Other outcomes are more tied to the unique prescriptions of the culture, for instance, in a Hindu Brahmin's life, after a man has provided enough resources for the comfortable existence of his spouse and progeny, the prescription for a worthy life includes retiring from the world to become a contemplative monk who has to beg for food at the edges of civilization. Whatever the understanding of a good life might be, it is not possible to understand the thoughts and emotions of people without knowing what they value about their own existence.

Of course, Western psychologists—especially developmental ones—have always held, explicitly or implicitly, to some version of an optimal life. For example, Erikson (1963), Loevinger (1976), Levinson (1980), and Vaillant (1993) all posit as the most desirable outcome of development a final stage of psychological integration—a point at which a person comes to accept his or her past, no longer seeks to change or achieve the impossible, yet is vitally connected to the immediate environment. Others have proposed the concept of *wisdom* as the culmination of personal development (e.g., Baltes, Glück, & Kunzman, 2002), or the achievement of a universalistic morality (Kohlberg, 1984), or of mature faith (Fowler, 1981). But the notion of a good life is not restricted to a single final outcome. It is even more important to realize that at each stage of life one can choose to live fully and well, or choose to indulge in self-pity and despair instead (Csikszentmihalyi & Rathunde, 1997). All developmental theories from Erikson on have tried to describe age-linked turning points when physical or social maturation presents specific challenges and opportunities for a person; depending on the choice made at these points, the quality of a person's life is likely to take a new direction for better or for worse.

These usually implicit views of desirable developmental outcomes are being much more explicitly voiced since the inception of "positive psychology." The perspective of positive psychology is intended as a corrective both to the value-free stance of experimental approaches, on the one hand, and to the exclusively pathology-oriented views that have permeated much of clinical psychology, on the other. It is a loosely knit "movement" that was catalyzed by Martin Seligman in the year he became president of the American Psychological Association, with the help of several colleagues, present company included (Seligman & Csikszentmihalyi, 2000). Positive psychology could be described as an effort to revive some of the agenda that had mobilized humanistic psychologists in the middle of the 20th century. At the same time, it does not share Maslow's and Rogers's suspicion of abstraction and quantification, but tries instead to extend the scientific method to deal with aspects of experience that had been ignored during those decades of what has been characterized as the "dust-bowl empiricism" of the mid-20th century. The historical antecedents of positive psychology have been recently debated in various venues (e.g., Lazarus, 2003; Rathunde, 2001). Given how few years have passed since the inception of this movement, it seems pointless to ask whether it is just a fad or a permanent shift in the study of humankind (Lazarus, 2003). Every new field of inquiry could be mistaken for a fad at its inception; only in retrospect does its success seem inevitable.

Whether we are dealing with only a temporary blip in the progress of knowledge or a genuine sea change depends on whether the ideas advanced by positive psychologists will be found useful by at least some members of the next generation of scholars; whether the concepts they advance will enter the vocabulary of the human sciences; or whether the results they find are convincing enough to be accepted as part of what defines our understanding of reality. If positive psychology passes these tests, it will become a genuine paradigm shift in the human sciences (Kuhn, 1970). While it is clearly too early to pass judgment on the final outcome, the initial signs are more than encouraging. In barely a half dozen years, scholars who have identified themselves with this perspective have produced a prodigious number of articles and books. And while the quality of this scholarly outpouring is understandably varied, on the whole it is surprisingly high. Among the volumes that have appeared recently one should certainly single out the encyclopedic handbook edited by Snyder and Lopez (2002), which all by itself should validate the legitimacy of positive psychology as a subdomain within the discipline; the excellent textbook by Carr (2004); the rich collections by Aspinwall and Staudinger (2002) and Keyes and Haidt (2003); and the path-breaking biography cum history cum theory written by Seligman (2002). In addition, there is the slightly earlier volume edited by Kahneman, Diener, and Schwartz (1999), which could be seen as sig-naling the transition into the new paradigm. Other books inspired at least in part by positive psychology include investigations of the effects of materialism and materialistic goals (Kanner & Kasser, 2003; Myers, 2000; Schmuck & Sheldon, 2001) and studies of the ethics of professional behavior (Csikszentmihalyi, 2003; Gardner, Csikszentmihalyi, & Damon, 2001).

All well and good, a critic might say, but what do these disparate contributions add up to? Positive psychology is apparently an attractive perspective for many scholars, but it lacks theoretical coherence. It is not unified by a central concep-tual apparatus. In fact, the many contributions are not even linked in what one might call a nomological network—they remain discrete ideas or findings that share only a common attitude toward what matters about human experience and behavior. This lack of unifying theory might be remedied with time. For instance, the recent volume by Peterson and Seligman (2004) provides, if not a theory, then at least a theoretical framework in which most approaches to positive psychology can find their place. In my opinion, however, the main contribution of positive psychology to the understanding of human thought and action does not hinge on whether it will or it will not become a unified theoretical system.

Even in its present exuberantly centrifugal phase, the perspective of positive psychology is enormously generative. First of all, it encourages young scholars to explore vitally important areas of human experience that until now were con-sidered to be unreachable, if not unimportant. In the middle of the 20th century, for instance, Norman Bradburn wanted to entitle the book that contained the summary of the results of his years of study of life satisfaction "the psychology of happiness." But he and his publishers concluded that, in the intellectual cli-mate of the times, serious scholars would ignore a book with such a lightweight title, so it was eventually called *The Structure of Psychological Well-Being* (Bradburn, 1969). This kind of self-censorship is no longer necessary. Thanks in large part to what positive psychology has already accomplished, the useful-ness of such "soft" concepts as happiness, hope, courage, gratitude, or enjoyment is recognized. They are no longer beyond the pale and can be actively studied, thereby adding to knowledge and to human well-being. If nothing else, this con-tribution alone amply justifies the existence of positive psychology.

Second, the idea behind the label of positive psychology acts as a catalyst for bringing together individual scholars who otherwise may have done their work in obscurity, at the margins of the discipline, unaware that many potentially stimulating peers were also laboring in the same vineyard. The sociology of sci-ence is clear about the enormous contribution that a supportive network can make to the development of a domain of study. Being able to exchange ideas, to validate each others' findings, or just to be cheered on often makes the difference between abandoning a field that seems fallow and persevering until success is obtained. Even such an independent genius as Galileo kept up his resolve in part because he was able to correspond across the continent with supportive colleagues such as Johannes Kepler, receive curious visitors from all over Europe, and attract bright students like the mathematicians Torricelli and Viviani. That was 400 years ago. It could be argued that now all one has to do is turn to the Web and find out immediately who belongs to one's network of interests, worldwide. Yet the very abundance of this information has its own drawbacks. How can one sort out a promising colleague from the many who are not serious? In the 16th century, many worthy persons may have been ignored, but the ones whose names traveled far were likely to be worth visiting, even if it took a fortnight on muleback. In any case, by creating the label of positive psychology, a common forum was created, and researchers and practitioners from all over the world were able to get together and exchange ideas.

Finally, positive psychology, by providing a variety of financial supports, has made it possible for young scholars to pursue research in areas that a few years ago would have been completely underfunded. Thanks to the vision and energy of Martin Seligman and to the generosity of a few farsighted sources, such as the John Templeton Foundation, the Atlantic Philanthropies, and the Gallup International Positive Psychology Center, it has been possible to organize meetings and workshops, support small studies, and recognize with substantial prizes some of the best work done by junior scholars in the field. No matter how idealistic a group of talented people might be, without free time, work space, equipment, and clerical support, it is very difficult to produce research that will pass the muster of scientific journals. And all of these prerequisites depend on access to money.

These contributions to positive psychology—a common set of ideas and approaches, a network of social connections, and the first seeds of financial support—are necessary for any new advance in science to take hold. But of these three the most essential one, the one without which no movement can be called a science, is the first: a set of ideas and findings that adds to our understanding of how human life unfolds and what makes it worth living. It is to this first task that the present volume speaks.

This book collects a number of essential writings that are based on presentations given at the First International Positive Psychology Summit sponsored by the Gallup organization in Washington, DC. Of the many important papers presented at that meeting, a small number was selected to represent the variety of ideas and approaches, and their authors were invited to rewrite their texts in a format more suited to the general reading public. It is this selection that I now have the pleasure to introduce. Before each set of chapters, I have provided an executive summary describing how the chapter fits with the rest of the volume and what its main points are—at least in my opinion. While such a procedure might seem a bit presumptuous, its advantage is that it provides continuity to what otherwise risks being a too richly diverse set of perspectives.

Will these chapters add up to a complete and convincing argument about what kind of life is worth living and how one might go about it? Certainly not. That question is likely to remain open for as long as humans continue to reflect on their existence. But it is a question that needs to be asked again and again during each generation, to prevent our understanding of life from becoming outdated. What gives value to existence changes from one epoch to another. The Greeks believed that life should be dedicated to achieving immortal fame, which in turn resulted from committing heroic deeds. The Christians introduced the notion that worldly existence is just a preparation for eternal life thereafter and required a completely different set of virtues from those of classical antiquity. In China and India, exquisite forms of self-contained, harmonious conduct were developed as models for how a sage gentleman—the epitome of human achievement—should behave.

And behind the subtleties of such cultural inventions, there throbs always and everywhere the rhythm of biological life, which needs no external value or speculation to justify itself. The body knows that life is worth living. It is programmed to always seek out whatever outcome promises to maximize the probability of its survival—and the survival of the copies it makes of itself through reproduction. Living things do not seem to question the value of their existence—with one exception. That exception is us—modern men and women who sometimes wonder if struggling on is worth it and who always seek some larger purpose to add value to who they are.

Why we are like this, we do not know. A likely explanation points to the development of the prefrontal cortex in our ancestors tens of thousands of years ago. This new feature of the brain was a great boon to humankind: It allowed a person to collect, compare, and prioritize information from all of the other parts of the brain and then to decide which course to take. The old brain was built on simple stimulus-response principles: If an apple smelled good and you were hungry, you ate it; if you saw a serpent, you either fled or you attacked it; if the serpent appeared next to the fruit, you got confused. Sensory inputs that were relevant to the survival of the organism had specific pathways to areas in the brain that told the organism what to do, but these parts of the brain did not communicate much with each other. Chances are that if you live with a dog or a cat, you have noticed that the animal has definite opinions about its likes and dislikes and ignores everything else—even its own image reflected in a mirror.

The old brain is still active in our skulls. Much of what we experience and what we do is controlled by programs cobbled together by the selective forces of evolution. The way we respond to hunger, sex, threats, and other basic elements of life are just as stereotyped and "natural" as those of our animal companions. But the latest additions to the brain—the most recent layers of the temporal cortex and the prefrontal lobes—have brought some enormous changes to how we experience the world. Some of these changes have been liberating and have made us the most powerful organism on earth. But this power has its dark side.

The new areas of the brain are not directly connected to the senses that bring us information from the surrounding world. Their function is not to tell us what happens outside but rather what is happening inside in the other, older parts of the brain. We have evolved a metabrain, an organ that can integrate the contents of the single-purpose modules of the nervous system and that can manipulate, interfere with, and override the old connections between stimulus and response. This new organ—which is responsible for what philosophers have been calling "self-reflective consciousness"—has emancipated humans from strict genetic programs. With its help, we can make plans, we can postpone action, we can imagine things that do not exist. Science and literature, philosophy and religion could not have taken shape without it.

But an inevitable consequence of this new ability has been that we are also able to consciously deceive others about our intentions, to plot and to lie, to compare ourselves to others and to feel envy, and to experience greed. These undesirable consequences were largely the result of the realization of selfhood brought about by the operations of the metabrain. As the prefrontal lobes took on more and more of the task of synthesizing information from the rest of the nervous system, there slowly arose a corresponding datum of metainformation, the realization that there is an independent agent at work, making all of the important decisions, the center of the known universe. This agent, the outcome of our brain becoming aware of its own existence, eventually became identified with the essence of our self. It gave us a unique identity, separate from the flow of life. We became self-conscious, aware of our individuality.

The realization of individuality made possible by self-reflective consciousness is often considered the most precious achievement of our species. At the same time, some of our worst traits follow from it. Having realized that we are unique, distinct from conspecifics and other life forms, each human tends to conclude that the preservation of his or her individual existence is the ultimate priority. Selfishness and cruelty, which formerly existed mainly as tools for biological survival, now have become extended to protect the psychological needs of the self, for the metabrain cannot help but conclude that its own existence is the most precious thing in the world, and all other goals pale in importance compared to its preservation. The terror of nonexistence, the fear of death, has become one of the ruling motives of humans. Instead of getting the most out of living, we spend more and more energy in hoarding resources, in escalating desires, and in futile attempts to prevent the dissolution of consciousness.

Paradoxically, self-reflection also ushers in the possibility of self-doubt. As humans realized that they were independent individuals with a short lifespan, the question of what choices would lead to a meaningful life became increasingly urgent. After all, if the spark of consciousness only lasts a few heartbeats in the cosmic darkness, is there really any point in hanging on to life, when so much of it involves suffering? To answer this question, our ancestors—freed and unmoored from the implicit meaning provided by biological existence—had to come up with credible reasons that life was indeed worth living. The myths, religions, and philosophies of every culture have been in large part directed toward answering that question.

Until quite recently, these explanations for what made life worth living naively accepted the evidence of the senses, including the information provided by the new brain. Just as our ancestors believed quite reasonably that the earth was flat and at the center of the cosmos, they continued believing as recently as the 20th century that consciousness gave a fairly accurate account of reality and that it was under the control of rational thought processes. Some took heart in the belief that inside their bodies there resided a soul which connected them to an immortal divinity. Others took comfort in the perspective voiced by Blaise Pascal, to the effect that humans might be a feeble reed in the immensity of the universe, but we are a thinking reed—and thus the unique masterpiece of creation. The realization of individuality brought about a sense of isolation and finitude, but it also gave the impression of autonomy and freedom. Trusting the creative independence of the mind, from the Age of Reason to the Atomic Age our ancestors could be at least somewhat confident that they could resolve the riddle of existence. But even this support was to be removed in time.

As the human sciences began to focus inward and examine the mechanisms of thought and choice, the innocent picture of the mind as a faithful mirror of reality began to change. When the objective glare of systematic analysis was turned toward investigating mental processes, one after the other the assumptions buttressing the autonomy of the mind began to crumble. For example, Karl Marx argued convincingly that "false consciousness" rules our perception of the world, distorting our judgments to fit our material interests. Sigmund Freud made us aware that supposedly rational decisions are often manipulated by unconscious needs. John B. Watson and B. F. Skinner demonstrated how much of what we do and believe is the result of random associations to pleasant and aversive stimuli. And these ideas were put forth even before the mighty wave of deconstructionism washed over the last remnants of our comfortable Victorian belief in reason, progress, and universal human values. Not many of the familiar props to human self-confidence have been left standing.

Even more recently, neuropsychology and behavioral genetics have come up with new and more systematic evidence that undermines a naive belief in the objectivity and autonomy of thought. The chemical basis of moods suggests that how happy or sad we feel does not depend on the operations of the mind but is determined at a lower level by molecular processes impervious to consciousness. Studies of twins suggest that the jobs we take, the kind of partner we marry, our political preferences, even the names we give our pets, are all substantially determined by genetic heritage. Given this flood of evidence, it is difficult to see how the human race could make its way out of a paper bag, let alone resolve the ultimate riddles of existence. Could it be that we are missing something when we apply the scientific method to understanding ourselves?

In the effort to reduce all human action to causes of a lower order—genetic programs, chemical impulses, economic interests—most investigators steadfastly ignore or discount any evidence to the effect that the mind can develop its own agenda independently of the various inputs it receives. If a man or woman does anything deserving praise, whether it is an act of courage or compassion, it is dismissed as due to circumstances external to the will or character of the seemingly virtuous person. This tendency is then reinforced by an opposite argument—that robbers and murderers are victims of circumstances who should not be accountable for their actions. Even though the currently prevailing victimology is grounded in a noble sympathy for the downtrodden, when applied wholesale it can result in a denial of responsibility that reduces human actors to the status of puppets manipulated by two strings: the genetic program and the forces of society.

As the 20th century wore on, concerned observers began to complain that the social sciences, into which the human sciences had morphed, were undertaking their debunking of naive anthropocentrism too gleefully. It was a great contribution to the understanding of who we are to trace and document the various ways our judgment is steered and clouded by factors originating outside consciousness and against which we are usually helpless because we do not even suspect their existence. But is it going too far to assume that men and women can be fully understood by prejudging in advance their nature? After all, chemists would be handicapped if they had to assume that molecular bonds obeyed the same rules as subatomic particles. And despite the recent flourishing of molecular biology, our understanding of living organisms would be severely restricted if we assumed that chemistry explained all that is worth knowing about animal life.

Caught in spasms of physics envy, many social scientists joined the mechanistic, reductive approach to understanding human beings. Against them, as a natural backlash, there has arisen a highly vocal and sophisticated cadre who takes pride in an anarchic rejection of any claims to objectivity. Between these two extremes, there is an almost empty ground, upon which those scholars should stand who believe that a rational, empirically grounded investigation is still our best bet in reaching knowledge, but who also understand that in moving from one level of explanation to another, the most relevant questions might have to change.

This means, in the study of humans, that the effects of self-reflective consciousness must be taken seriously. For example, even if free choice cannot be proven to exist, a person who believes in its existence—for whatever reason—is going to behave differently from one who does not. When confronted with overwhelming pressures to cheat, a businessperson who believes in strict determinism is more likely to submit to pressure, compared to a colleague who believes that when everything is said and done a person is free to take a stance opposite to whatever forces have conditioned her behavior.

In this sense the idea—or meme—of "freedom" becomes an agent in its own right, distinct from its biological or social origins. The memes of justice, equality, human rights, and so on evolved in the minds of individuals reflecting on their experiences, were passed down from one generation to another, and were slowly adopted by increasing numbers of people so that by now they seem to be part of human nature. Of course, having forged such concepts as brotherly love does not mean that we actually implement the meme in which we believe. None of the fruits of consciousness determines entirely what we think or do—but none of the commands of genes or of society do so either. It is always a probabilistic process in which different and often contradictory impulses vie with each other for the command of our actions. But certainly any approach to human behavior that ignores entirely the new reality emerging in consciousness misses what is perhaps the most important part of what makes men and women human.

Positive psychology has emerged as such a strong and vital alternative because many psychologists, young and old, felt that if they followed the traditional paradigms they would miss the essence of this grand story. In the first chapter of part I of this volume, Csaba Pléh reminds us of the intellectual roots of positive psychology in Western thought and highlights how important the concepts of freedom, autonomy, and intrinsic motivation have been in several of the previous narratives of human nature. Christopher Peterson presents a classification of strengths as a starting point for mapping human potentialities. Dmitry Leontiev proposes a dynamic perspective for evaluating the course of a person's life in light of positive principles of development. Finally, Robert Emmons reviews research on spirituality, arguing for the importance of this dimension, which is so often neglected by the field. Together, these four chapters provide a varied yet interconnected introduction to how positive psychology differs from previous paradigms and to the range of theoretical issues it confronts.

Part II is focused on the nature of positive experiences. Barbara Fredrickson suggests an evolutionary explanation for why it is advantageous to be happy, while Daisy Grewal and Peter Salovey describe the benefits of emotional intelligence. Jane Henry rounds out this section of the book with a survey of therapeutic interventions and with suggestions for how positive psychology might revitalize the mental health profession.

The authors of the chapters in part III take a more long-term perspective and look at the developmental implications of positive psychology. Jochen Brandtstädter describes how learning to adjust goals leads to satisfaction later in life. Antonella Delle Fave presents cross-cultural data showing that objective hardships need not prevent subjective well-being. The team of Jari-Erik Nurmi and Katariina Salmela-Aro report on studies confirming the long-term benefits of personally constructed goals. The ill effects of materialistic goals are detailed by Tim Kasser. Kennon Sheldon suggests how our notions of declining capacities as one ages can be reversed if we look at later years from the perspective of positive psychology. And finally, the concluding chapter by Martin Seligman clarifies the contribution of positive psychology to therapeutic practice and to psychology in general.

These chapters provide a powerful counterpoint to a mistakenly reductionistic psychology more impressed by objective measurement than by meaning. They show that subjective experience can be studied scientifically and measured accurately. Moreover, they make a convincing case for the importance of subjective phenomena, which often affect happiness more than external, material conditions do. If psychology is to be first and foremost a science that seeks to understand the inner workings of consciousness—as opposed to behavior, performance, and achievement—then these chapters inspired by positive psychology will make a much-needed contribution to the discipline as a whole.

References

Aspinwall, L. G., & Staudinger, U. M. (Eds.). (2002). *A psychology of human strengths.* Washington, DC: American Psychological Association Books.

Baltes, P. B., Glück, J., & Kunzman, U. (2002). Wisdom: Its structure and function in regulating successful life-span development. In C. R. Snyder & S. J. Lopez (Eds.), *Handbook of positive psychology* (pp. 327–250). New York: Oxford University Press.

Bradburn, N. M. (1969). *The structure of psychological well-being.* Chicago: Aldine.

Carr, A. (2004). *Positive psychology: The science of happiness and human strengths.* New York: Brunner-Routledge.

Csikszentmihalyi, M. (2003). *Good business: Leadership, flow, and the making of meaning.* New York: Viking.

Csikszentmihalyi, M., & Rathunde, K. (1997). The development of the person: An experiential perspective on the ontogenesis of psychological complexity. In W. Damon (Ed. in Chief) & R. Lerner (Vol. Ed.), *Handbook of child psychology: Vol. 1. Theoretical models of human development* (pp. 635–685). New York: Wiley.

Erikson, E. (1963). *Childhood and society.* New York: Norton.

Fowler, J. W. (1981). *Stages of faith.* New York: Harper & Row.

Gardner, H., Csikszentmihalyi, M., & Damon, W. (2001). *Good work: When excellence and ethics meet.* New York: Basic.

Kahneman, D., Diener, E., & Schwartz, N. (Eds.). (1999). *Well-being: The foundations of hedonic psychology.* New York: Russell Sage.

Kanner, A. D., & Kasser, T. (Eds.). (2003). *Psychology and consumer culture: The struggle for a good life in a materialistic world.* Washington, DC: American Psychological Association Press.

Keyes, C. L. M., & Haidt, J. (Eds.). (2003). *Flourishing: Positive psychology and the life well-lived.* Washington, DC: American Psychological Association.

Kohlberg, L. (Ed.). (1984). *Essays on moral development: Vol. 2. The psychology of moral development.* San Francisco: Jossey-Bass.

Kuhn, T. S. (1970). *The structure of scientific revolutions.* Chicago: University of Chicago Press.

Lazarus, R. (2003). Does the positive psychology movement have legs? *Psychological Inquiry, 14*(2), 93–109.

Levinson, D. J. (1980). Toward a conception of the adult life course. In N. Smelser & E. Erikson (Eds.), *Themes of work and love in adulthood* (pp. 265–290). Cambridge, MA: Harvard University Press.

Loevinger, J. (1976). *Ego development.* San Francisco: Jossey-Bass.

Myers, D. G. (2000). *The American paradox: Spiritual hunger in an age of plenty.* New Haven, CT: Yale University Press.

Peterson, C., & Seligman, M. E. (2004). *Character strength and virtues.* New York: Oxford University Press.

Rathunde, K. (2001). Toward a psychology of optimal human functioning: What positive psychology can learn from the "experiential turn" of James, Dewey, and Maslow. *Journal of Humanistic Psychology, 41,* 135–153.

Schmuck, P., & Sheldon, K. M. (2001). *Life-goals and well-being.* Gottingen: Hogrefe & Huber.

Seligman, M. E. P. (2002). *Authentic happiness.* New York: Free Press.

Seligman, M. E. P., & Csikszentmihalyi, M. (2000). Positive psychology: An introduction. *American Psychologist, 55*(1), 5–14.

Snyder, C. R., & Lopez, S. J. (Eds.). (2002). *Handbook of positive psychology.* New York: Oxford University Press.

Vaillant, G. (1993). *The wisdom of the ego.* Cambridge, MA: Harvard University Press.

PART I

HISTORICAL AND THEORETICAL PERSPECTIVES

The ideas that have fueled the development of positive psychology are certainly not new. It is probably the case that all cultures, with time, come to a consensus as to what the ideal life should be like and what steps one should take to reach it. In the great Eastern civilizations, the models for a life worth living converged on notions of self-discipline achieved through the control of attention and ritual observance. Although in some places and periods Eastern sages were involved in advising rulers and taking on administrative and political roles, thereby contradicting the generalization to follow, it is probably true that in the West, the *vita activa*—based on virtuous action—was held in greater esteem than the contemplative life.

The strands of European thought that feed into the psychological tradition of optimal experience and optimal development can be traced at least as far back as Aristotle's concept of *eudaimonia,* or the theory that the goal of individual life is to achieve happiness by fulfilling one's potential—a perspective that over twenty centuries later was revived by Jeremy Bentham and his school of utilitarian philosophy. Csaba Pleh takes up this story by looking at the influence of J. S. Mill on European psychology. Mill departed from Bentham's utilitarianism in realizing that some of the central contributors to happiness, such as love and knowledge, are not zero-sum and thus not dependent upon the roles of an economy of scarcity. Freedom, self-actualization, and the intrinsic rewards of knowledge are other central ideas in Mill's thought as well as that of two other precursors of positive psychology reviewed in this chapter: William Stern, who stressed the uniqueness of each individual forged by nature and nurture; and Karl Bühler, who in contrast with the more mechanistic psychoanalytic and behaviorist approaches, focused instead on the autonomous, self-initiated aspects of human behavior.

Christopher Peterson provides the first step toward systematizing positive psychology with the VIA (Values in Action) Classification of Strengths. The idea for this rubric first occurred to Martin Seligman when he was involved in revising the fourth edition of the *Diagnostic and Statistical Manual* (*DSM-4*), the master reference list that clinical psychologists use to determine, for example, whether a patient's depression is chronic or merely transient. As the *DSM-4* has an almost biblical authority in the field, it tends to imbue all human behavior with the taint of pathology. It provides excruciatingly elaborate descriptions of every hue of mental lapse, while saying next to nothing about the aspects of human functioning that represent the unique strengths of men and women—the autonomy, freedom, and self-actualization described by Pleh in our preceding chapter. So Seligman's idea was to develop the "Un-*DSM-4*," a list that complemented the pathology of the *DSM-4* with an enumeration of strengths and virtues.

Christopher Peterson spent several years leading a team that researched, reviewed, and tested a variety of traits that might qualify as the components of mental health. The criteria of selection and the reliability and validity of the constructs are described, as are their implications for the enrichment and deepening of psychology in general and clinical psychology in particular.

While the VIA leads to a theory of positive psychology grounded in classification, Dmitry Leontiev argues for the necessity of a theory based on processes and regulatory mechanisms rather than on traits or emotional states. His candidate for a leading construct in the domain is that of the multi-regulation of personality. This approach assumes that human behavior is regulated by a set of seven increasingly complex "logical" structures, starting with the logic of need gratification, and ending with the logic of ultimate understanding. The basic progress through the stages is that of increasing autonomy from natural causation (i.e., from genetically encoded programs) and socially learned habits. Leontiev's view, which presents interesting parallels to the Buddhist notion of the evolution of consciousness through nine successive states of emancipation from instinctual and cultural controls, is that positive psychology should encourage the development of the specifically human capacities and potentials rather than the more basic, instinctive ones.

The chapter by Robert Emmons explores what by all accounts ought to be one of the most uniquely human capacities, that for spirituality. Emmons distinguishes between spirituality, defined as a spontaneous and universal sense of belonging to the infinite, and religion, which he defines as a faith community rooted in spiritual traditions that seeks to enhance morality and the search for the sacred. According to the research reviewed by Emmons, spirituality helps to improve existence in two major ways: by adding meaning to personal goals and thus elevating the significance of a person's experiences; and by providing specific "spiritual emotions," such as gratitude, awe, or forgiveness, which in turn add positive experiences to the ebb and flow of daily life.

The reader might find that some of the ideas advanced by these four authors contradict one another—for instance Peterson's emphasis on classification appears to be challenged by Leontiev's concern with process. At this point, of course, it is impossible to tell which direction positive psychology will take in the coming decades. Will one or the other approach prevail? Or will they be combined in a more inclusive synthesis? Time will tell. What currently appear to be contradictions should serve as useful indications of alternative routes to the future.

The four chapters in this section illustrate some of the main concerns that are developed in more detail in the rest of the volume. They introduce the contrasts between science that claims neutrality vis-à-vis values, and science that takes values seriously; between autonomy and determinism; between positive, momentary emotions and enduring, life-long well-being; between pathology and health—just to mention a few topics that will recur over and over again. Of course, there are some approaches that could not fit between the covers of this book. In the future, neuropsychology, behavioral genetics, psychological anthropology, and a few other important perspectives are bound to contribute to the depth and scope of positive psychology. In the meantime, however, the themes introduced in this first section should provide ample food for thought to anyone interested in what men and women are like and what they can become.

1

Positive Psychology Traditions in Classical European Psychology

CSABA PLÉH

T he purpose of this chapter is to show the insights of 19th- and 20th-century European psychology that can be regarded as predecessors of present-day positive psychology. To see this in context, I will present an overview of some modern European epistemological predecessors of positive psychology. Basically there are four topics to be highlighted:

- self-rewarding motivational systems versus utilitarianism
- the theory of John Stuart Mill on the significance of knowledge and love
- the personalism of William Stern and the integrative value of personality
- early ethology research on the complexity of behavioral organization

I will anchor my points around specific heroes, such as John Stuart Mill, William Stern, and Karl Bühler. Yet these persons should be understood as representatives of entire streams of thought. During the long prehistory of positive psychology, many central issues emerged at various times. We can consider the tradition of positive psychology as one whose roots are based in an opposition to a passive, hedonistic, and at the same time helpless image of man. This opposition is shown in Table 1.1.

John Stuart Mill: Guided by Two Lights, Bentham and Coleridge

John Stuart Mill lived under the impact of two stars, Bentham and Coleridge. As he described it, both were looking for solid foundations, but one was looking for this in the reduction of every complicated human feeling to its elementary moments, while the other looked for it in the striving for spiritual meaning. The

Table 1.1. Opposition of Points Emphasized by Trends Toward Positive Psychology and by Those of Traditional Psychology

Positive psychology trends	Traditional trends
Central role of non utilitarian motivations	All motivations are of a homeostatic nature
Knowledge has a positive value in itself	Knowledge's only value comes from its usefulness
Self-initiated activities	Reactive organization
Curiosity and boredom are key aspects in human life	Basic human motivations are fear and anxiety

first was utterly utilitarian and honest in trying to reduce all aspects of life to pleasure and pain, while the other was romantic to the bone (for these influences, see his autobiography and his collection of essays; Mill, 1962).

John Stuart Mill started off on his road to investigate human nature armed with the notions of empiricism and comprehensive utilitarianism. The taken-for-granted model of the mind for him was utilitarianism. The concept of utilitarianism was introduced by Jeremy Bentham (1789/1948), who presumed that people are rational and selfish "*economic* men." His aim was to describe human nature with as few parameters as possible: In our heads, there are ideas, which combine with each other in obeying a small number of associative laws. The father of Mill, James Mill (1829/1967), even insisted that there was but a single law of association, which is *contiguity.* According to utilitarian thinking, human motivational forces are kept in motion by a small number of tendencies; these are the pursuit of happiness and the avoidance of pain. Values are created by the association of ideas and representations with this small number of basic tendencies. Thus, social life and our entire complicated social structure are a result of the contingent connection of these tendencies, much the same way as money gets its value: through satisfying our basic needs. Accordingly, the entire social structure is going to be conceived of as an associative construct, as a secondary alignment of originally separated individual entities.

This approach had a certain moral undertone as well. The utilitarian human being, stripped of all considerations based on an outdated moral authority, would merely follow the calls of interest. Therefore the aim of moral analysis would not be to condemn these tendencies in humans. Rather, our aim would be to build a society without illusions, which would comply with these principles. Unnecessary human suffering is a result of not observing the general laws of human nature. Thus, a social structure based merely on interest seems to be immoral for old-style moralists but indeed, it is the one that reduces overall suffering; therefore, it is moral for the new school.

Nature has placed humanity under the governance of two sovereign masters, *pain* and *pleasure.* It is for them alone to point out what we ought to do, as well as to determine what we shall do. The *principle of utility* recognizes this subjection and assumes it for the foundations of that system, the object of which is to rear the fabric of felicity by the hands of reason and of law. Systems which attempt to question it deal in sounds instead of sense, in caprice instead of reason, in darkness instead of light. (Bentham, pp. 1–2)

John Stuart Mill (1859, 1962) recognized that utilitarian thinking with its reduction of human motivation to a few principles seemed to be right when considering its adversaries, those contemporary systems that operated using speculative internal forces and moral feelings or other intangible entities to explain the complexities of human motivation. Yet he also realized that human mental life does have aspects that simply do not operate in the usual distributive way.

In this conceptual transformation, the young Mill undeniably had a personal inspiration. As he described vividly in his autobiography (Mill, 1873/1969), he was touched by romantic love himself. But a few newly discovered ideas also played a role in his change of mind: in particular, romantic poetry and humanistic philosophy. The ideas of Mill regarding the moving forces of the mind can be summarized in four basic points:

- *Knowledge is not a distributed property.* If we gain knowledge, no knowledge is taken away from somebody else. Using modern terms, one could say that knowledge for him was not an economic property of a zero-sum game.
- *Love should not be interpreted in a utilitarian way either.* Love is not distributed. If I love more people, I do not take away any love from other people—a slightly romantic thesis.
- *Self-perfection must be considered a life goal in itself.* A human being does not only strive to find pleasure and to avoid pain, but also tries to improve him- or herself.
- *Human life has a nonutilitarian, romantic aspect too.*

Nineteenth-century German philosophy, particularly the work of Wilhelm von Humboldt (1827), played a crucial role in Mill's questioning of the principles of utilitarianism. Humboldt's vision of human personality, which has become the cornerstone of knowledge-based but liberal educational systems, presented the cultivation of personality and a refining of individuality as a self-sufficient goal in itself. Under the impact of these German Romantic ideas, the cultivation of individuality, personality, and their enrichment became self-sufficient goals for Mill. The cultivation of individuality, of the individual who would be different from anyone else, was to become a balance against the mechanical features of his own intellectual system.

According to Mill, the cultivation of individuality is a balancing factor against the simplifying forces of associative mechanics. From a historical point of view, another of Mill's important conclusions (1859) is the cultivation of freedom: Considering freedom as the most important value helps us to clear those barriers that restrict the cultivation of personality as an end in itself.

All of this was clearly related to the internal events of the life of Mill. John Stuart Mill was a precocious genius. His father forced him into serious intellectual work before he was even 10 years old. His autobiography is an excellent psychological resource. He explained in it, among other things, how he came to give up the exclusive use of utilitarianism. His personal crisis was the crisis of a bookish youngster who theoretically saw through the futility and emptiness of all of our efforts. Two questions were raised in his mind during this rather early "midlife crisis." One of them is related to the necessity and compulsion for analysis. If, following associationist and utilitarian principles, we trace everything back to its origins and sources, then the authenticity of the feeling seems to vanish. Mill felt that to regard himself as a domain of mental and motivational mechanics meant that his feeling of individuality was lost. His second personal problem had to do with the aims of life: Does the entire struggle for an overwhelmingly and strictly rational world have a meaning? Does it give meaning to life to fight for the victory of utilitarianism? His personal crisis led to a general conclusion: It showed the impossibility of a scientific, mechanistic lifestyle as a personal program for life. Sigmund Freud, who as a young man translated Mill's autobiography, commented on his artificial life to a considerable extent.

As for the motivational aspect, Mill in his later works emphasized that there are certain aspects of life in which the shortage economy is not valid. *Shortage economy* implies the idea that the actors are involved in a zero-sum game structure: If A gets more of commodity X, then B necessarily has less of X. According to Mill, *knowledge* and *love* are exceptions to this economic balance. They can increase in each individual without taking from others. If I know more, that does not take away anything from your knowledge. Knowledge for Mill does not mean equating the function of knowledge with instrumental uses, as the famous slogan of Bacon's that "knowledge is power" implied. The cultivation of these aspects of life, together with a cultivation of the idea of a patterned personality and individuality, taken over from Romanticism and from the German Enlightenment, gave him a chance to overcome the static model, as well as the egoism of an all-around utilitarianism. It is true, from a strictly naive consideration, that these two factors are the ones that can only be achieved and accomplished by the given individual: I can do tasks instead of you, but I cannot know instead of you. I can help you to find someone to love, but I cannot love for you.

Present-day decision theories would label Mill's concept as an attempt to emphasize the non-zero-sum aspects of life. Knowledge and love do not belong to the realm of a scarcity economy. This is far from being trivial: *Knowledge is power* is a concept that from Francis Bacon to Lenin contradicts the idea of nondistributed knowledge. They were right in a way, considering the fact that in real societal contexts knowledge can become an economic power. For Mill, however, this aspect was not the only one to be considered; rather, he was concerned about the aspect that knowledge—regardless of its use—makes one's personality richer.

According to Mill, self-motivated—or, in other words, more playful—factors in life, such as love and knowledge, lead to the cultivation of personality. The mind, because of its curiosity, can be regarded as a self-motivated/self-explaining knowledge-generating system. And personality as well seems to develop in a *l'art pour l'art* fashion. In the later conceptual system of Darwinism, this would be interpreted by claiming that a greater behavioral or reaction potential implies greater evolutionary potentials.

From the point of view of the philosophy of history, one might treat these as poor or weak proposals. It is worth highlighting, however, that they are not in discord with some present-day ideas regarding the importance of nonregulative elements in the organization of human societies. In psychology proper, the ideas of Mill prepared the field for the so-called *self-actualization* theories of motivation and personality, and they continue in positive psychology trends that criticize the underlying shortage-economy principles of the regulative views on motivation. Mill also has some affinity with the theories and educational practices related to cognitive motivation, to the idea that the quest for knowledge for its own sake is not something that should be played down.

Mill's 19th-century thoughts were transformed and became part of an elaborated tradition thanks to the translating mechanisms of early 20th-century professional psychology. One of these is the cult of personality, and the other one is the emphasis on motivation systems that are based on self-actualization. I would like to introduce two lesser known representatives of these streams, who advocated these ideas decades before the advent of the modern positive psychology movement. One of these trends is the transformation of the cultivation of personality into actual research on personality and the other is a unique interpretation of ethology in the works of Karl Bühler.

William Stern: Integration and Internal Meaning in Personality

William Stern has more importance in the history of modern psychology than just as the "inventor of the IQ" (see Lamiell, 2002). From the beginning of the 20th century, Stern tried to develop an impressive program emphasizing that personality should be one of the most important integrating factors of psychology and a related program about the constructive nature of human development. In his first synthesis, calling for differential psychology (Stern, 1911), he declared that essentially there are two basic possible approaches to personality psychology. The first of them presupposes and analyzes traits and discusses those "formal regularities that are entailed in the very fact of mental variation" (Stern, 1911, p. 8). A basic Darwinian idea in his approach to personality is the necessary variety of humankind underlying these personality traits. This would be the essential core of differential psychology. The second task is to analyze, after examining all of the human varieties, correlations among the traits. In both of these approaches, however, the emphasis is on the features rather than on the individual as such. Another, less nomothetic approach, closer to the followers of Dilthey (1894), relies on a more ideographic description in dealing with personality. According to Stern, in order to fully understand human personality, we also have to approach it starting from the unique and original, i.e., from the individual. The two main methods for this latter purpose are psychography—a description of individual personal profiles, where biography is compared to individual profiles (which reminds us of contemporary psychohistorical approaches)—and comparative studies, where different particular individuals are compared in their totality.

The desire for another, ideographic pole had already appeared in Stern's early work. Essentially, that was a desire to attribute an independent meaningful globality to personality, like in his pioneering case study of Helen Keller (Stern, 1905). The individual-centered approach was present not only in the ambitious theoretical projects of Stern (1938) but also in his practical dealings: For him, intelligence testing also was an issue of idiosyncratic profiles. He believed that no two persons with the same IQ can actually have the same underlying profile when engaged in the same performance (see a modern analysis of this attitude in Smith, 1997).

In the domain of developmental psychology, Stern together with his wife (Stern & Stern, 1907) was a pioneer researcher of child language. He claimed that when acquiring language, children are recreating it, in line with the German romantic ideas about mental activity. However, the Sterns not only emphasized this very modern idea, which was later rediscovered by followers of Chomsky (1968) such as Blumenthal (1970), who inserted their approach into a nativistic framework of development; they also formulated ways to identify symptoms of this activity in the error patterns of children. They differentiated between *immanent* errors like *goed* instead of *went*, which do not change the rules, only apply them to wrong domains, and *transgradient* errors like *hand-socks* for *gloves.* Both imply, from the perspective of present-day psycholinguistics (see Pinker, 1997), that children are struggling with rules and are not merely acquiring associative habits. For the early German developmentalist, this was a self-evident issue. We have to remember how long it took other developmental researchers to rediscover relationships between rules and creativity in the individual re-creation of language.

Stern also developed a characteristic theory concerning the development of individuality, the often-quoted *convergence theory* (e.g., Stern, 1936; Stern &

Stern, 1907). The central point of this theory is not merely that our personality is determined by both genetic and environmental factors, but that these permanently and mutually presuppose each other and somehow have a converging causal impact on behavioral development. For Stern, development is much more than just the realization of a genetic plan. It has *epigenetic laws*, we would say today—as stated by Oyama (2000) and Karmiloff-Smith (1998), even though they do not cite Stern. Environment and, as we see it today, the very epigenetic process have an influence on the realization of these internal programs. In line with this, according to Stern, the whole personality is influenced by both genetic and environmental factors, and these are not merely additive but rather operate on the same internal structures. It is not accidental that 40 years later, in the 1960s, David Krech (Krech, Rosenzweig, & Bennett, 1960) rediscovered Stern while studying environmental and genetic determinants of animal learning performance. Selective breeding and early experience in rodents seem to have the same target: The same cortical chemical and metabolic factors operate under genetic and experiential influence, and they are not complementary but rather have an effect on the same underlying mechanism, on the relations of subcortical/cortical reactability and increased metabolism.

After a few purely philosophical excursions that are referred to as "personalism" (see Stern, 1936), in his later works Stern arrived at the conclusion that the entire human psychology should be approached from the aspect of personality (Stern, 1938). Personalism as an integrative discipline is the study of the entire person, and personality psychology—or even psychology—is simply a part of this broader enterprise. The mind goes beyond the differentiation into the mental and the physical realms, and it represents the original unity of the individual. This unified personality is the joint interface, we would say today, that makes any investigation of mental phenomena sensible and explainable. Personality, which for John Stuart Mill was a factor to be cultivated on moral grounds, in the approach proposed by Stern became an integrating factor of an *all-inclusive human science.* This approach had its followers later on: Most notably, Gordon Allport (1968) emphasized specifically the influence of Stern in shaping his person-centered view of psychology. And as the reviews by Lamiell (2003) and the theoretical papers in Lamiell and Deutsch (2000) indicate, the influence of these person- and activity-centered (constructivist) ideas is starting to be felt again.

Even though very personalistic, Stern never became an oversimplifying critic of psychology as a possible science. For him, psychology was the study "of the person having experience or capable of having experience" (Stern, 1938, p. vii). Though in accordance with his German idealism, he was very value- and culture-oriented, the Dilthey (1894) and Spranger (1926) type of division into two psychologies, one causal, the other "understanding," did not appeal to him. He remained a monist in a strange sense. If we look at the "substrate" of the soul, he claimed, one has to conclude, "The substratum of mind must be something *that has existence going beyond or prior to the differentiation into the mental and the physical,* thereby validating personalism: it is the study of the whole human person. Psychology is a part of this study of the original unity of the individual" (Stern, 1938, p. 69).

Karl Bühler and Early Ethology

A third intellectual ancestor of present-day positive psychology comes from the very beginnings of the field that later become ethology. Early ethologists, such as Heinroth, Uexkühl, and Konrad Lorenz, clearly described three factors while unraveling animal behavior (see Lorenz, 1965, for a review). The first is the postulation of species-specific behavioral patterns. The development of these patterns is determined and characteristic to the species, in evolutionary terms, but it also requires environment-dependent critical experiences. In addition, precisely because of the existence of innate/internal programs, the animal can never be described merely as a passive, reactive creature: Its entire behavioral range is an expression of internal behavior program patterns.

In the 1920s and 1930s, Karl Bühler (Bühler, 1922, 1927, 1934/1990, 1936) tried to unify psychology by using these early ethological principles. The key element in this unification was the idea that all behavior—from the simplest animal behavior to human culture creating—is assumed to be meaningful. Contrary to the postulation of a split or schism between natural science and human science psychology (Spranger, 1926), proposed by the followers of Dilthey (1894), rationality is a characteristic of all behavior. Moreover, according to Bühler, behavior is always a self-initiated activity. Not even animals—and certainly not humans—can be regarded as merely reactive creatures, or mere automata. They always attempt to construct a model of their environment. In this modeling activity, the role of Darwinian selection and its broader interpretation is pivotal for Bühler (1922, 1936). He was the first to formulate those two principles, which control today's philosophy of the mind (Dennett, 1996) and philosophy of neural processes (Changeux, 1983; Edelman, 1987): All behavioral organization is characterized by an early stage, where a rich and redundant inventory of behaviors is formed with an excessive number of elements and associations, and a later, selective stage, where certain patterns are chosen on the basis of environmental feedback. This two-phase formulation has three forms: According to Bühler, the first is represented by instincts, the second by habits, and the third by rationality. The main point about the relationships among the three levels—as expressed very definitely by Karl Popper, a disciple of Bühler's (Popper, 1972)—is that instead of risking survival, like in Darwinian evolution, in intellectual selection, we are only risking our ideas. These three levels differ in their flexibility, but the organizing principle is the same with all of them. First, there is an attempt to develop a variety of behaviors, which are later reduced based on feedback from the environment. With more flexibility, with more internal selection, as Campbell (1974) put it, the same process becomes more flexible and thereby produces more unique and enjoyable experiences.

All three of these prominent figures are predecessors of positive psychology in the sense that they emphasize the delight of knowledge. For them, knowledge typically appears as its own reward. But, because of their integrative and sign-based knowledge interpretation, they have been included in later 20th-century theories that emphasize the significance of cognitive motivation. Their concept of development is original as well: From Stern and Bühler on, development is considered to be the formation and formulation of internal knowledge and knowledge-handling procedures. For all of these authors, the value of knowledge, the cultivation of personality, and a stress on initiative and independence are crucial. For them, development is a formation of knowledge for its own sake, i.e., guided by intrinsic principles. As for the motivational component, for all of these authors, it was clear that there is a seeming paradox: Even seemingly useless mental activities are useful, since they assure the avoidance of boredom and promote mental life.

References

Allport, G. (1968). *The person in psychology.* Boston: Beacon.

Bentham, J. (1789/1948). *An introduction to the principles of morals and legislation.* New York: Haffner.

Blumenthal, A. L. (1970). *Psychology and language: Historical aspects of psycholinguistics.* New York: Wiley.

Bühler, K. (1922). *Die geistige Entwicklung des Kindes* (3rd ed.). Jena: Fischer.

Bühler, K. (1927). *Die Krise der Psychologie.* Jena: Fischer.

Bühler, K. (1934/1990). *Theory of language: The representational function of language* (D. F. Goodwin, Trans.). Amsterdam: J. Benjamins. (Original work published 1934)

Bühler, K. (1936). *Die Zukunft der Psychologie und die Schule.* Vienna & Leipzig.

Campbell, D. T. (1974). Evolutionary epistemology. In Paul A. Schlipp (Ed.), *The philosophy of Karl Popper* (pp. 413–463). La Salle, IL: Open Court.

Changeux, J. P. (1983). *L'homme neuronal.* Paris: Fayard.

Chomsky, N. (1968). *Language and mind.* New York: Harcourt.

Dennett, D. (1996). *Darwin's dangerous idea.* New York: Simon and Schuster.

Dilthey, W. (1894). Ideen über eine beschreibdende und zerglierdendre Psychologie. *Sitzungberichte der Akademie der Wissenschaften zu Berlin, 2,* 1309–1407.

Edelman, G. M. (1987). *Neural Darwinism: The theory of neural group selection.* New York: Basic.

Humboldt, W. von. (1827). *Ideen zu einem Versuch die Grenzen der Wirksamkeit des Staats zu bestimmen.* Berlin: Deuticke.

Karmiloff-Smith, A. (1998). Development itself is a key to understanding developmental disorders. *Trends in Cognitive Sciences, 2,* 389–398.

Krech, D., Rosenzweig, M. R., & Bennett, E. L. (1960). Effects of environmental complexity and training on brain chemistry. *Journal of Comparative and Physiological Psychology, 53*, 509–519.

Lamiell, J. T. (2002). William Stern: More than "the IQ guy." In G. A. Kimble, C. A. Boneau, and M. Wertheimer (Eds.), *Portraits of pioneers in psychology* (Vol. 2, pp. 77–85). Washington, DC: American Psychological Association and Erlbaum.

Lamiell, J. T. (2003). *Beyond individual and group differences: Human individuality, scientific psychology, and William Stern's critical personalism.* Thousand Oaks, CA: Sage.

Lamiell, J. T., & Deutsch, W. (2000). In the light of a star: An introduction to William Stern's critical personalism. *Theory and Psychology, 10*(6), 715–730.

Lorenz, K. (1965). *Evolution and modification of behavior.* Chicago: University of Chicago Press.

Mill, J. (1829/1967). *Analysis of the phenomena of the human mind.* New York: A.M. Kelley.

Mill, J. S. (1859). *On liberty.* London: Trübner.

Mill, J. S. (1873/1969). *Autobiography, and other writings.* Boston: Houghton Mifflin.

Mill, J. S. (1962). *Essays on politics and culture* (G. Himmelfarb, Ed.). Garden City, NY: Doubleday.

Oyama, S. (2000). *The ontogeny of information.* Durham, NC: Duke University Press.

Pinker, S. (1997). *How the mind works.* New York: Norton.

Popper, K. R. (1972). *Objective knowledge: An evolutionary approach.* Oxford: Clarendon.

Smith, R. (1997). *The Fontana history of the human sciences.* London: Fontana.

Spranger, E. (1926). Die Frage nach der Einheit der Psychologie. *Sitzungsberichte der Preussischen Akademie der Wissenschaften. Philosophisch-Historische Klasse, 1926:* 172–199.

Stern, W. (1905). *Helen Keller.* Berlin: Reuther.

Stern, W. (1911). *Die differenzielle Psychologie in ihren methodischen Grundlagen.* Jena: Fischer.

Stern, W. (1936). Autobiography. In C. A. Murchison & E. G. Boring (Eds.), *A history of psychology in autobiography* (Vol. 3). Worcester, MA: Clark University Press.

Stern, W. (1938). *General psychology from a personalistic standpoint.* New York: Philosophical Library.

Stern, W., & Stern, C. (1907). *Die Kindersprache.* Jena: Fischer.

2

The Values in Action (VIA)
Classification of Strengths

CHRISTOPHER PETERSON

The un*DSM* and the Real *DSM*

The fledgling field of positive psychology calls for as much focus on strength as on weakness, as much interest in building the best things in life as in repairing the worst, and as much concern with fulfilling the lives of healthy people as healing the wounds of the distressed (Seligman, 2002; Seligman & Csikszentmihalyi, 2000). The past concern of psychology with human problems is of course understandable and will not be abandoned any time in the foreseeable future, but psychologists interested in promoting human potential need to pose different questions from their predecessors who assumed a disease model.

The most critical tools for positive psychologists are a vocabulary for speaking about the good life and assessment strategies for investigating its components. For the past several years, we have focused our attention on positive traits—strengths of character, such as curiosity, kindness, and hope. What are the most important of these, and how can they be measured as individual differences? So long as we fail to identify the specifics, different groups—despite common concern for human goodness—will simply talk past one another when attempting to address the issue of character.

For instance, is character defined by what someone does *not* do, or is there a more active meaning? Is character a singular characteristic of an individual, or is it composed of different aspects? Is character socially constructed and laden with idiosyncratic values, or are there universals suggesting a more enduring basis? Does character—however we define it—exist in degrees, or is it just something that one happens to have or not? How does character develop? Can it be learned? Can it be taught, and who might be the most effective teacher?

The VIA Classification of Strengths

We have laid the groundwork that will allow these questions to be answered. Our project—the VIA (Values in Action) Classification of Strengths—means to complement the *Diagnostic and Statistical Manual* (*DSM*) of the American Psychiatric Association (1994) by focusing on what is right about people and specifically about the strengths of character that make the good life possible (Peterson & Seligman, 2004). We followed the example of the *DSM* and its collateral creations by proposing a classification scheme and devising ways of assessing its entries. The VIA Classification is the first major project deliberately developed from the perspective of positive psychology, and we hope that it will be instructive as the field develops.

We recognize the components of good character as existing at different levels of abstraction. *Virtues* are the core characteristics valued by moral philosophers and religious thinkers: wisdom, courage, love, justice, temperance, and transcendence. These six broad categories of virtue emerge consistently from historical surveys. We speculate that these are universal, perhaps grounded in biology through an evolutionary process that selected for these predispositions toward moral excellence as means of solving the important tasks necessary for survival of the species.

Character strengths are the psychological ingredients—processes or mechanisms—that define the virtues. Said another way, they are distinguishable routes to displaying one or another of the virtues. For example, the virtue of wisdom can be achieved through such strengths as curiosity, love of learning, judgment, creativity, and what we call *perspective*—having a "big picture" on life. These strengths are similar in that they all involve the acquisition and use of knowledge, but they are also distinct. Again, we regard these strengths as ubiquitously recognized and valued, although a given individual will rarely, if ever, display all of them (Walker & Pitts, 1998). We approach character strengths as dimensional traits—individual differences—that exist in degrees.

We generated the entries for the VIA Classification by reviewing pertinent literatures that addressed good character—from psychiatry, youth development, character education, religion, philosophy, organizational studies, and of course psychology. From the many candidate strengths identified, we winnowed the list by combining redundancies and applying the following criteria:

1. *A strength needs to be manifest in the range of an individual's behavior— thoughts, feelings, and/or actions—in such a way that it can be assessed.* In other words, a character strength should be traitlike in the sense of having a degree of generality across situations and stability across time.
2. *A strength contributes to various fulfillments that comprise the good life for the self and for others.* Although strengths and virtues no doubt determine how an individual copes with adversity, our focus is on how they fulfill

an individual. In keeping with the broad premise of positive psychology, strengths allow the individual to achieve more than the absence of distress and disorder. They "break through the zero point" of psychology's traditional concern with disease, disorder, and failure to address quality-of-life outcomes (Peterson, 2000).

3. *Although strengths can and do produce desirable outcomes, each strength is morally valued in its own right, even in the absence of obvious beneficial outcomes.* To say that a strength is morally valued is an important qualification, because there exist individual differences that are widely valued and contribute to fulfillment but still fall outside of our classification. Consider intelligence or athletic prowess. These talents and abilities are cut from a different cloth than character strengths like bravery or kindness. Talents are valued more for their tangible consequences (acclaim, wealth) than are character strengths. Someone who "does nothing" with a talent like a high IQ or physical dexterity risks eventual disdain. In contrast, we never hear the criticism that a person did nothing with his or her hope or authenticity. Talents and abilities can be squandered, but strengths and virtues cannot.

4. *The display of a strength by one person does not diminish other people in the vicinity but rather elevates them.* Onlookers are impressed, inspired, and encouraged by their observation of virtuous action. Admiration is created but not jealousy, because character strengths are the sorts of characteristics to which all can—and do—aspire. The more people surrounding us who are kind, or curious, or humorous, the greater our own likelihood of acting in these ways.

5. *As suggested by Erikson's (1963) discussion of psychosocial stages and the virtues that result from their satisfactory resolutions, the larger society provides institutions and associated rituals for cultivating strengths and virtues.* These can be thought of as simulations, trial runs that allow children and adolescents to display and develop a valued characteristic in a safe (as-if) context in which guidance is explicit.

6. *Yet another criterion for a character strength is the existence of consensually recognized paragons of virtue.* Paragons of character display what Allport (1961) called a "cardinal trait," and the ease with which we can think of paragons in our own social circles gives the lie to the claim that virtuous people are either phony or boring (Wolf, 1982). Certainly, the virtuous people we each know are neither. In one of our preliminary attempts at validating assessment strategies, we asked our research assistants to nominate people of their acquaintance who are paragons of virtue and prevail upon them to complete our measures. No one had any difficulty thinking of appropriate respondents.

7. *A final criterion is that the strength is arguably unidimensional and not able to be decomposed into other strengths in the classification.* For example, the character strength of "tolerance" meets most of the other criteria enumerated but is a complex blend of critical thinking, kindness, and fairness. The character strength of "responsibility" seems to result from persistence and teamwork. And so on.

When we applied these criteria to the candidate strengths we identified through literature searches, what resulted were 24 positive traits organized under six broad virtues (see Table 2.1). We hasten to add that there are other positive traits that a positive psychology practitioner might wish to encourage among clients—for example, ambition, autonomy, and patience, to name but a few—and their absence in our classification reflects only our judgment that these are not as universally valued as the included entries.

It is worth noting that the entries in our classification overlap considerably with those in two other contemporary classifications arrived at in very different

Table 2.1. VIA Classification of Character Strengths

1. *Wisdom and Knowledge: Cognitive Strengths That Entail the Acquisition and Use of Knowledge*
   - Creativity: thinking of novel and productive ways to do things; includes artistic achievement but is not limited to it
   - Curiosity and Interest in the World: taking an interest in all of ongoing experience; finding all subjects and topics fascinating; exploring and discovering
   - Judgment and Critical Thinking: thinking things through and examining them from all sides; not jumping to conclusions; being able to change one's mind in light of evidence; weighing all evidence fairly
   - Love of Learning: mastering new skills, topics, and bodies of knowledge, whether on one's own or formally; obviously related to the strength of curiosity but goes beyond it to describe the tendency to add systematically to what one knows
   - Perspective: being able to provide wise counsel to others; having ways of looking at the world that make sense to self and to other people

2. *Courage: Emotional Strengths That Involve the Exercise of Will to Accomplish Goals in the Face of Opposition, External or Internal*
   - Bravery: not shrinking from threat, challenge, difficulty, or pain; speaking up for what is right even if there is opposition; acting on convictions even if unpopular; includes physical bravery but is not limited to it
   - Persistence: finishing what one starts; persisting in a course of action in spite of obstacles; "getting it out the door"; taking pleasure in completing tasks
   - Authenticity/Honesty: speaking the truth but more broadly presenting oneself in a genuine way; being without pretense; taking responsibility for one's feelings and actions
   - Vitality: approaching life with excitement and energy; not doing things halfway or halfheartedly; living life as an adventure; feeling alive and activated

3. *Love: Interpersonal Strengths That Involve "Tending" and "Befriending" Others (Taylor et al., 2000)*
   - Intimacy: valuing close relations with others, in particular those with whom sharing and caring are reciprocated; being close to people
   - Kindness: doing favors and good deeds for others; helping them; taking care of them
   - Social Intelligence: being aware of the motives and feelings of other people and oneself; knowing what to do to fit in to different social situations; knowing what makes other people tick

ways from the strategy that produced the VIA list. First, French philosopher André Comte-Sponville (2001) surveyed classical and contemporary Western philosophical traditions for mention of the "qualities that constitute the excellence and essence of humankind" (book dustjacket). He included politeness and gentleness (which we did not because they seem prerequisites for more substantive strengths) and excluded several of the VIA strengths (e.g., appreciation of beauty, curiosity, and vitality), but otherwise the agreement is substantial.

Second, Marcus Buckingham and Donald Clifton (2001) of the Gallup organization described "work-place themes" that emerged from focus groups with thousands of individuals about the traits that contribute to excellent performance

Table 2.1. *(continued)*

4. *Justice: Civic Strengths That Underlie Healthy Community Life*

- Citizenship: working well as member of a group or team; being loyal to the group; doing one's share
- Fairness: treating all people the same according to notions of fairness and justice; not letting personal feelings bias decisions about others; giving everyone a fair chance
- Leadership: encouraging a group of which one is a member to get things done and at the same time facilitating good relations within the group; organizing group activities and seeing that they happen

5. *Temperance: Strengths That Protect Against Excess*

- Forgiveness/Mercy: forgiving those who have done wrong; giving people a second chance; not being vengeful
- Humility/Modesty: letting one's accomplishments speak for themselves; not seeking the spotlight; not regarding oneself as more special than one is
- Prudence: being careful about one's choices; not taking undue risks; not saying or doing things that might later be regretted
- Self-Regulation: regulating what one feels and does; being disciplined; controlling one's appetites and emotions

6. *Transcendence: Strengths That Forge Connections to the Larger Universe and Provide Meaning*

- Appreciation of Beauty and Excellence: noticing and appreciating beauty, excellence, and/or skilled performance in all domains of life, from nature to art to mathematics to science to everyday experience
- Gratitude: being aware of and thankful for the good things that happen; taking time to express thanks
- Hope: expecting the best in the future and working to achieve it; believing that a good future is something that can be brought about
- Humor: liking to laugh and tease; bringing smiles to other people; seeing the light side; making (not necessarily telling) jokes
- Spirituality: having coherent beliefs about the higher purpose and meaning of the universe; knowing where one fits within the larger scheme; having beliefs about the meaning of life that shape conduct and provide comfort

at work. They included strengths that are culture-bound (e.g., competition) as well as strengths that strike us as complex blends of more basic strengths (e.g., communication), but the agreement is again substantial. We are encouraged that the VIA Classification is a good list.

Assessment of the VIA Strengths

What distinguishes the VIA Classification from previous attempts to articulate good character is its simultaneous concern with assessment, and we will now describe our work to date on measurement. Sophisticated social scientists sometimes respond with suspicion when they hear our goal, reminding us of the pitfalls of self-reporting and the validity threat posed by "social desirability" (Crowne & Marlowe, 1964). We do not dismiss these considerations out of hand, but their premise is worth examining from the vantage of positive psychology. We seem to be quite willing, as researchers and practitioners, to trust what individuals say about their problems. With notable exceptions, like substance abuse and eating disorders, in which denial is part and parcel of the problem, the preferred way to measure psychological disorder relies on self-reporting. So why not ascertain wellness in the same way? Perhaps we accept self-reports about the negative but not the positive because we do not believe that the positive really exists. That is the pervasive assumption that positive psychology urges us to reject.

Suppose that people really do possess moral virtues. Most philosophers emphasize that virtuous activity involves choosing virtue in light of a justifiable life plan (Yearley, 1990). In more psychological language, this characterization means that people can reflect on their own virtues and talk about them to others. They may of course be misled and/or misleading, but virtues are not the sort of entities that are in principle outside the realm of self-commentary (cf. Nisbett & Wilson, 1977). Furthermore, character strengths are not "contaminated" by a response set of social desirability; they are socially desirable, especially when reported with fidelity.

We can point to previous research that measured character strengths with self-report questionnaire batteries (e.g., Cawley, Martin, & Johnson, 2000; Greenberger, Josselson, Knerr, & Knerr, 1975; Ryff & Singer, 1996). In no case did a single methods factor order the data. Rather, different clusters of strengths always emerged. External correlates were sensible. These conclusions converge with what we have learned to date from our own attempts to measure the VIA strengths with self-report questionnaires. We acknowledge the possibility that some strengths of character lend themselves less readily to self-reporting than do others, but it is easy to understand why. Almost by definition, strengths like authenticity and bravery are not the sorts of traits usually attributed to oneself. But this consideration does not preclude the use of self-reporting to assess other strengths of character.

As part of the VIA Classification, we set about creating measures that allow the character strengths in the VIA Classification to be assessed among English speakers in the contemporary Western world. We were wary of becoming so fixated on issues of reliability—which of course are important—that we might neglect the even more important issues of validity. We have devised separate self-report inventories for adults and for young people (ages 10–17). We have also developed a structured interview and are beginning to devise measures of character strengths that rely on informants; this strategy may allow us to extended the assessment of character to the young, the quick, the famous, the dead, and the otherwise unwilling. Reliability and validity evidence is accumulating; progress reports can be found in Park and Peterson (2005); Peterson and Park (2004); Peterson, Park, and Seligman (2005); and Peterson and Seligman (2004).

The VIA Strengths and the "Real" Psychopathologies

When positive psychology first took form in the late 1990s, those who christened it were careful to distance the field from business-as-usual psychology and its underlying disease model. As Seligman (2002) phrased the goal of positive psychology, it was to move people not from -3 to 0 but from +2 to +5. Accordingly, positive psychology would seem to have little to say about distress and disorder. The clinic—unlike schools, businesses, sports, and the arts—is apparently not a "natural home" for positive psychology (cf. Seligman & Peterson, 2003).

I think it fair to say that the thinking of most positive psychologists has since changed on these matters. For starters, the terrorist attacks of September 11, 2001, and their aftermath showed us that what is best in life often is shown when people rise mightily to an occasion (Peterson & Seligman, 2003). Crisis may not be the prerequisite for all strengths of character, but it certainly is for those strengths that philosophers deem corrective (Yearley, 1990). In some of our work with the Values in Action Inventory of Strengths (VIA-IS), we have found that people may come out of a crisis better off than those who never had the crisis. To be sure, we would not want to program crises for our children in the hope that they will surmount them to become better people. But neither should we eschew all risk (cf. Romer, 2003). Positive psychology should recognize that there are lessons to be learned from failure and disappointment, even from crisis and stress: "'Tis an ill wind that blows no good."

Accordingly, I want to propose here that positive psychology in general and the VIA Classification in particular have something to say about psychological disorder. Indeed, this should have been a positive psychology goal all along. If positive psychology is to complement business-as-usual psychology, which uses the lens of abnormality to view normality, then why not use the lens of normality or even supernormality to view abnormality?

When the VIA Classification project began, we fell into the casual habit of referring to our classification as the un*DSM*. Although we have never used this flip label in anything we have published (until now), some clarification is needed because it seems to have caught on (e.g., Peterson, 2003). In calling our project the un*DSM*, we are not touting it as a replacement, an improvement, or even as an alternative to the diagnostic manual of the American Psychiatric Association. Rather, just as 7-Up was once marketed as the uncola (if you remember the advertisements from some years ago) to mean that it was something different than cola, we merely wanted to emphasize that the VIA Classification is something different than the *DSM*. The world needs both, just as the world needs— or at least wants—different carbonated beverages.

In his introductory comments to a conference a few years ago, Martin Seligman (2003) said something provocative. I forget exactly how he phrased it, but what many heard him say is that clinical psychology is dead. I do not think he really meant that except to wake people up after a rich meal, but I know that many conference participants were indeed provoked because they have since been talking about this comment.

Regardless, I have a different point of view. Clinical psychology is not remotely dead. People have problems. People's problems deserve good solutions that are informed by science, especially the science of clinical psychology. But clinical psychology might profitably reinvent itself, to move from a pale psychiatry without prescription "privileges" (what a strange word in this context), to a science that does what psychology does best: use rigorous research to investigate processes and mechanisms suggested by theory (Persons, 1986).

If the VIA Classification has done a good job of telling us what the important strengths of character might be and by implication what optimal functioning means (i.e., the presence of some or many of the character strengths), then why not use the absence of these strengths as the hallmark of "real" psychological disorder? To my view, the real disorders of concern to psychology should not be schizophrenia or bipolar disorder. These arguably are illnesses and fit well into psychiatry's disease model. They are not myths, and they have a clear biological basis. But are they the sorts of problems that psychology should be studying?

Consider the possibility that mean-spiritedness, social estrangement, or pessimism are the real disorders that should be of concern to psychology. There are legitimate objections to this assumption, and I have thought of many of them myself. Viewing disorders as character defects or deficiencies is explicitly value-laden, and have we not been taught that values should not intrude into science? The rejoinder is that business-as-usual clinical psychology and psychiatry are already value-laden, but the values are clumsily draped in the language of neurotransmitters. We might be better served by making our value assumptions about psychological disorders explicit and then see where we are taken. So, in the remainder of this chapter, I take seriously the hypothesis that the absence of character strengths constitutes the real psychological disorder. Doing so does not put clinical psychology out of business nor drive a nail into its coffin. Rather, it might expand what clinical psychologists best do.

To repeat, I have no quarrel with psychiatrists. Bless them for trying to help people with illnesses like schizophrenia. But most people who embark on therapy are not driven there by illness. Rather, they have trouble getting along with their spouses, or they do not quite like their jobs, or they feel bored and empty. These are not real illnesses and in many cases probably not symptoms of real illnesses. To use the phrase of Thomas Szasz (1961), these are problems in living, in some cases occasioned by terrible circumstances but in other cases manifestations of problems with character. The *DSM* handles such problems with NOS diagnoses—not otherwise specified. Consider 309.90: Adjustment Disorder NOS. What can this possibly mean?

Adjustment disorder is a label applied to people who show impairment in reaction to a stressor, but when we cannot specify the predominant symptoms (anxiety, depression, physical complaints, withdrawal, and so on), we deem it NOS. I suspect this is a very common diagnosis, and I make the confident prediction that neuroimaging will never find a specific part of the brain responsible for disorder 309.90, nor will geneticists locate chromosomes responsible for it.

The VIA Classification arguably provides a more useful vantage on such NOS diagnoses. If it does, we have the makings of a psychological *DSM.* Ever since 1952, psychologists have been complaining about the American Psychiatric Association's catalog of disorders, but complaining has not resulted in a classification with which psychologists might feel comfortable. The VIA Classification identifies ways of doing well, and by implication, it also identifies ways of doing poorly. We know that many character strengths are associated with life satisfaction and well-being (Park, Peterson, & Seligman, 2004). A potentially important study would be to use the VIA-IS to screen people entering therapy. I assume that, in most cases, one or another character strength will be conspicuously depressed if not altogether absent. If we ask people why they have come to therapy and what their goals and wishes might be, I further assume that what they say will be phrased in terms of the VIA strengths. They are not kind enough, or they are not a team player, or they are not curious about the world in which they live.

We can expand this implied classification by subdividing strength deficiencies into states and traits that reflect their mere absence versus those that reflect their psychological opposite. So, there would seem to be a difference between someone who lacks a sense of humor and someone who is the wettest of blankets. This distinction does not work well with respect to all strengths, but for the sake of completeness, it is worth attempting for each of the 24 VIA entries.

Finally, we can expand even further this implied classification by remembering Aristotle's (2000) doctrine of the mean: All virtues (strengths of character) reside between deficiency and excess. So, another set of disorders can be generated by considering exaggerations of the 24 VIA strengths. I hasten to say that, in our research, we have never found anybody who was across-the-board too kind or too humorous or too optimistic.[1] But we have found that almost all people with a signature strength experience an occasional downside when they use it in the wrong circumstances (Peterson & Seligman, 2004).

The Real *DSM*

Let me be more systematic. As implied by what I have so far said, one can generate a coherent set of disorders by considering in turn each of the 24 VIA strengths in Table 2.1 and asking (i) what psychological state or trait reflects its absence; (ii) what state or trait signifies its opposite; and (iii) what state or trait displays its exaggeration. What results from this brainstorming is a set of 24 classes of disorders, shown in Table 2.2. I will discuss some of these in detail, but first these caveats.

To begin, unlike the *DSM* and its underlying medical model, I think these disorders (and the corresponding strengths) exist in degrees. With respect to each, people's behavior can be placed along a continuum:

opposite → absence → strength → exaggeration

As a working yet testable assumption, we can regard this as a single dimension, but note that it would not be enough to determine that someone lacks a strength in order to say just what sort of disorder characterizes the individual. Not having a strength may mean simply its absence, but it may also take more extreme forms: showing its opposite or its exaggerated version.

Second, the labels I have chosen for the various disorders are a mixed lot. In some cases, they refer to well-recognized individual differences already extensively studied by psychologists. In other cases, I used an ordinary language term that has apparently not been the topic of psychological inquiry, as shown by the failure of my PsycINFO keyword searches. And in still other cases, I coined a term that seems to capture the meaning of the disorder in question. I resorted to this last option only when the first two were unsuccessful, but the fact that I was forced to create neologisms is evidence for the potential utility of the endeavor. Unanticipated entries in my classification of the real psychological disorders have substantive meanings and imply that the scheme is not just post hoc.

Third, although I describe the disorders with nouns, as if they were properties of the individual, this is just shorthand. These disorders—like the strengths from which they were deduced—are evident in an individual's behavior: thoughts, feelings, and actions. They are traitlike individual differences. The more frequently someone behaves in a disordered way and the more settings in

Table 2.2. Classification of Psychological Disorders

Strength	Absence	Opposite	Exaggeration
Disorders of Wisdom and Knowledge			
Creativity	Conformity	Triteness	Eccentricity
Curiosity/Interest	Disinterest	Boredom	Morbid curiosity/ Nosiness
Judgment/Critical thinking	Unreflectiveness	Gullibility	Cynicism
Love of learning	Complacency	Orthodoxy	Know-it-all-ism
Perspective	Shallowness	Foolishness	None*
Disorders of Courage			
Bravery	Fright/Chicken Little-ism	Cowardice	Foolhardiness
Persistence	Laziness	Helplessness	Obsessiveness
Authenticity/Honesty	Phoniness	Deceipt	Righteousness
Vitality	Restraint	Lifelessness	Hyperactivity
Disorders of Love			
Intimacy	Isolation/Autism	Loneliness/Avoidance of commitment	Emotional promiscuity
Kindness	Indifference	Cruelty/Mean- spiritedness	Intrusiveness
Social intelligence	Obtuseness/ Cluelessness	Self-deception	Psychobabble
Disorders of Justice			
Citizenship	Selfishness	Narcissism	Chauvinism
Fairness	Partisanship	Prejudice	Detachment
Leadership	Compliance	Disruptiveness/ Sabotage	Despotism
Disorders of Temperance			
Forgiveness/Mercy	Mercilessness	Vengefulness	Permissiveness
Humility/Modesty	Footless Self-esteem	Arrogance	Self-deprecation
Prudence	Sensation seeking	Recklessness	Prudishness/ Stuffiness
Self-regulation	Self-indulgence	Impulsivity	Inhibition
Disorders of Transcendence			
Appreciation of beauty/Excellence	Oblivion	*Schadenfreude*-ism	Snobbery
Gratitude	Rugged individualism	Entitlement	Ingratiation
Hope	Present orientation	Pessimism/Despair	Pollyannaism
Humor	Humorlessness	Dourness	Buffoonery
Spirituality	Anomie	Alienation	Fanaticism

*I am willing to be convinced otherwise, but I think it is impossible to have too much perspective.

which these behaviors occur, the more willing we should be to "diagnose" the given disorder (cf. Buss & Craik, 1983). At present, I intend no further meaning. These disorders may or may not have a deeper existence. They may or may not be the manifestation of some latent entity, e.g., brain anomalies, disordered biochemistry, DNA from the shallow end of the gene pool, bad habits, dysfunctional cognitive styles, or demonic possession. These are empirical questions.

Fourth, the labels I have chosen are unambiguously moral in flavor, yet as noted, this is only an apparent shortcoming of my classification. After all, people with psychological disorders are annoying, alarming, or offensive. Essentially every linguistic analysis of "abnormality" arrives at this conclusion (e.g., Peterson, 1996). Rather than arguing in vain that my classification is value-neutral, I prefer to say that it is value-informed and to suggest that more productive lines of inquiry would ask who is annoyed, alarmed, or offended by these ways of behaving and why.

Once I generated my list of disorders, I was struck by the conceptual overlap between many of them and what the *DSM* tries to do with its Axis II, that is, personality disorders, defined as long-standing patterns of dysfunctional behavior (American Psychiatric Association, 1994). I realize that reliable diagnosis of most of the *DSM* personality disorders has not been achieved, but perhaps this is the result of trying to define these patterns of behaving in terms of a symptom menu, as if they were chicken pox or strep throat rather than problematic ways of relating to others (cf. Mellsop, Varghese, Joshua, & Hicks, 1982).

Fifth, along these lines, "my" disorders provide some insight into why the *DSM* includes the disorders that it does. It can be difficult to say why depression per se is a disorder, especially in light of discussions about its occasional utility and its basis in the evolutionary history of our species (cf. Alloy & Abramson, 1979; Nesse, 1990). But if we examine depression further in terms of its association with such difficulties as disinterest, indifference, helplessness, isolation and loneliness, pessimism, and alienation, then we can readily understand when and why depression is a psychological problem. At least in principle, a person who is "depressed" only in the sense of being sad and subdued does not have a problem. This person might simply be solemn and cautious, and Prozac should not be prescribed to counteract what may really be strengths of character.

Finally, my classification is not exhaustive. Remember that the starting point was ubiquitous virtues and the strengths that contribute to them. There is no shortage of problematic ways of behaving that lack universality, and the existence of more culture-bound disorders does not detract from the utility of this classification as a broadly applicable scheme. A more refined classification, tailored for example to the contemporary United States, would include such psychological disorders as rampant materialism, shameless self-aggrandizement, 15-minute celebrity, and the "male" disorder of excessive gadgets attached to one's belt.

Some Illustrative Disorders

Space does not permit discussion of all the classes of disorders proposed in Table 2.2, so let me just illustrate a few of them. I start by drawing on what we know about the character strength (Peterson & Seligman, 2004) and then give rein to some speculation about what its absence, opposite, and exaggeration might entail. There are few data in support of what I say, so take my statements with a grain of salt. Nonetheless, there may be some fruitful hypotheses for exploration lurking amid my assertions.

Disorders of Creativity

Faced with a desired goal, does the individual engage in novel yet appropriate behavior to reach that goal? If so, he or she is displaying the strength of *creativity*. This strength family includes what psychologists refer to as Big C creativity, but it is not limited to traditional endeavors within the fine arts. Rather, it seems to be captured by what Sternberg et al. (2000) referred to as practical intelligence or, more bluntly, street smarts. Original and ingenious people find appropriate shortcuts in the journey of life. They know how to arrange bulky furniture in small apartments, how to find bargains in stores, and when to check their luggage at the airport (and when not to).

The absence of originality, almost by definition, is quite common, and perhaps I go too far in labeling this a disorder. Let me simply label it as *conformity* and refer the reader to the decades of thoughtful discussion by social psychologists regarding its pro's and con's (e.g., Asch, 1956). Another way to think about conformity as a disorder is at the group level. The absence of originality and ingenuity is probably not a problem for any given individual. But when an entire group or society lacks originality, then that group is apt to stagnate.

I do not hesitate to say that the opposite of originality and ingenuity—*triteness*—is a psychological disorder. It is also an aesthetic offense. Think of all the interviews you have heard with professional athletes, 99% of whom give the most scripted answers imaginable. I have no insight into their true motives in using trite phrases, but I cringe when I hear, "The victory has not sunk in" or "this is a must-win game" or "there is no 'I' in team." There of course is triteness in all venues of life, and I suspect that in some societies—like the contemporary United States—it creates a cultural contradiction. We the people value originality yet love to follow fads, whether watching "American Idol" and "Survivor" on television or buying the latest Christmas present or evaluating political candidates only with respect to a small number of hot-button issues or getting tattooed and pierced—tastefully, of course.

The exaggeration of originality and ingenuity is *eccentricity*, novelty for its own sake, sort of the psychological equivalent of a Rube Goldberg machine. Not all tasks in life require a brand-new solution, and someone who always devises new solutions that create more problems than they solve has a disorder. We call them weird or creepy; their novelty makes us uncomfortable. There is an interesting psychological literature on eccentrics (Weeks, 1988). In some cases, it seems as if exhibitionism is at the root of it all, and in other cases, the eccentric person is simply out of touch with the reactions of others.

Disorders of Curiosity and Interest in the World

Curiosity and *interest in the world* entail openness to experience and flexibility vis-à-vis matters that do not fit preconceptions. Curious people do not simply tolerate ambiguity but are intrigued by it. There is often a degree of domain specificity here, but we can imagine as well people who are catholic in their curiosity. Curiosity and interest are active cognitive orientations and are not shown by those who passively assimilate information, e.g., couch potatoes clicking their remotes. Some writers dub this strength *investigativeness*, which underscores its active nature (Vagi & Lefcourt, 1988). There exists a well-defined psychological field of curiosity, which provides various curiosity scales, many of which conceptualize curiosity as a broad trait, shown by question asking and by exploration (Loewenstein, 1994).

The absence of curiosity and interest is simply that: disinterest. *Disinterest* is a problematic way of behaving because it imposes a limit on what the person can know about the world and his or her place within it. Such an individual is likely to stagnate at school or work. Relationships will suffer as someone fails to grow along with a friend or lover.

The opposite of curiosity and interest is *boredom*, and there is a large research literature on boredom and boredom susceptibility, including a host of individual difference measures (Smith, 1981). Boredom on the face of it is problematic, but if one needs further convincing, researchers have explicitly linked boredom to anxiety and depression.

Exaggerated curiosity and interest are dubbed *morbid* when they focus on sex and violence (Zuckerman & Litle, 1986). Critics of the entertainment media assume that television, movies, and the Internet create morbid curiosity, whereas apologists argue that Jerry Springer and colleagues are merely satisfying an already-existing societal need. Regardless, morbid curiosity deadens one's sensitivity to suffering and blunts moral outrage. Consider reality TV casts, which often feature a bunch of good-looking people with borderline personality disorders. These shows are the psychological equivalent of a freak show, with a focus on character deformity. We as a culture have evolved enough so that we no longer find physically disabled people amusing. I hope that the day will come soon when we stop finding character impairment amusing.

A less dramatic exaggeration of curiosity and interest is *nosiness:* prying into the private business of other people. I do not mean gossip per se, which has useful social purposes when done between consenting adults. Rather, I mean aggressive television news reporters who stick a microphone in the face of victims, college students who read the e-mail of their roommates, and neighbors who sort through one another's garbage. Or how about the annoying stranger who sits next to you on a plane and peppers you with inappropriate questions: "Have you always been this fat?" And just yesterday, someone sat down at one of my computers and, without asking, started to click on my Netscape bookmarks. I can only hope that he found www.areyouannoyingornot.com.

Nosiness is a psychological disorder because it exhausts its targets, making them vigilant and ultimately defensive. Furthermore, I suspect that nosiness shows no adaptation; it only escalates as the person seeks ever more titillating items of information. Any activity that consumes a large amount of time means that other activities will be neglected. I call this the "24 hours in a day principle," and it provides a rationale for pathologizing all of the exaggerated states and traits discussed in my scheme.

Disorders of Judgment and Critical Thinking

People with the strength of *judgment* and *critical thinking* reason matters through and examine them from all sides and angles before choosing what they believe and how to act. They do not jump to conclusions, and they rely on solid evidence to make decisions. In an earlier version of this classification, we identified this strength as *rationality.* We still like this label for its denotations, but we found that few individuals wanted to claim rationality for their own because of its connotations. Rationality conjures up visions of cold calculation juxtaposed to empathy and emotion. These connotations are misleading because all we mean by this strength is the sifting of information in an objective fashion. We think that empathy and feeling are well served by this strength, not precluded by it. Regardless, we jettisoned the label in favor of judgment and critical thinking. This strength embodies what Jahoda (1958) and others have dubbed *reality-orientation* and is captured as well by Ellis's (1962) discussion of *mental health,* e.g., not confusing wants and needs, downplaying oughts and shoulds, and so on.

The absence of critical thinking is *unreflectiveness:* accepting information simply as given without recognizing the possibility that it may be incorrect or that different spins on it are possible. The social psychological literature on rumor documents the situational influences on unreflectiveness under the rubric of *groupthink* (Janis, 1982), and the dispositional risk factors include authoritarianism, dogmatism, and the lack of cognitive complexity. Again, I regard the problematic nature of this suggested disorder as self-evident. Think of all the times that someone says regretfully, "If only I had known." Often, what this means is "If only I had thought critically about the matter."

Critical thinking has become a buzzword among educators, for good reason. With the explosion of information on the World Wide Web and 24-hour news shows, students (and citizens in general) need to be shaken from an unreflective mode. What information is worth taking seriously, and how is the decision to be made? The same lack of reflection can also characterize someone's everyday life. We did a study some years ago that yielded sobering results (Cook & Peterson, 1986). We asked college students to offer causal explanations for events in their life, and once we heard their answers, we asked them to provide relevant evidence for their causal beliefs. A very small number of students used Kelley's (1973) normative attribution "principles" (a social cognitive rendering of Humean causality) to justify their attributions, but a much larger number of students failed to provide a remotely appropriate form of evidence. Either they cited the event in question as evidence for their provided cause ("I fight with my family because they are rigid, and I know they are rigid because we fight"), or they stared at us blankly ("I have no evidence, but that is the cause").

Unreflectiveness slides into the opposite of critical thinking: *gullibility*, the active embracing of unsubstantiated, incorrect, or incoherent information. Remember the point that "rationality" seems to have earned a bad rap, and perhaps this is why some people seem to flaunt their lack of critical thinking, calling it intuition or faith or open-mindedness. To be sure, all of these labels sound desirable, but when they are used to justify stupidity, then we have an insidious celebration of psychological disorder. More people in the United States believe in the existence of UFOs than in the efficacy of psychotherapy. More people read their horoscopes daily than watch the evening news. Do not misunderstand what I am saying: Mysticism can be a coherent worldview, and there are important matters that can only be accepted on faith. But critical thinking does not need to be tossed out the door; if anything, a person is well served by thinking through the differences between the tenets of his or her religion and the scientific principles of gravity.

The exaggeration of judgment and critical thinking is *cynicism:* knowing the price of everything and the value of nothing. The cynical individual criticizes everything, often in articulate fashion, but offers no solutions. This sort of criticism dampens group activities. No project is worth doing. No restaurant is worth visiting. No movie is worth seeing. No leader is worth following. Voting is pointless.

Disorders of Love of Learning

Does the individual have domains in which he or she is expert? Is this expertise valued by people in the person's immediate social circle and/or by the larger world? And does the person show a love of learning about these domains, even in the absence of external incentives to do so? For example, postal workers all have zip code expertise, but this accumulated knowledge may or may not reflect a strength. Designation depends on the person's motivation for acquiring this expertise and his or her success in "giving it away" to willing others.

Most psychological research in this area has looked at a student's love of academic learning and subject matter appreciation, usually emphasizing intrinsic motivation, but I intend a broader meaning that includes a love of learning about current events, art, literature, cooking, nature, or sports. To understand love of learning, it is productive to turn to the research literature on competence, mastery, and effectance because these constructs speak to the fulfillments that result from exercise of this strength (White, 1959).

Someone with no love of learning shows *complacency*, and there is likely overlap with disinterest, as already discussed. A complacent person is a bump on a log at school or work or home. Newspapers, magazines, and books are for show only. Libraries are unexplored. The person has no hobbies or passionate interests. Complacent people create boredom in others. The opposite of this strength family is *orthodoxy*, by which I mean not only a disinclination to acquire new information but an active stand against so doing. "Orthodox" is an adjective usually used to describe a religious preference, but I do not limit its meaning to intransigent spiritual beliefs. Indeed, I can easily imagine someone within an orthodox congregation who displays a great love of learning about religion and other aspects of the world. Critical to orthodoxy as a psychological disorder is resistance to learning new information or skills. Think of your Luddite colleagues who refuse to use e-mail. Orthodox individuals know just a few things but most crucial is that they do not need to know anything else. Like Archie Bunker, they long for the good old days and believe that nothing new has happened in the world worth learning since the Hoover administration. The research literature on authoritarianism and especially dogmatism seems relevant to orthodoxy as we have defined it.

Exaggerated love of learning shows itself as *know-it-all-ism* or—to be pedantic—being *pedantic*. Here we have someone who has (perhaps) mastered the details of a given domain and talks endlessly about it to unwilling people. The problem is not with the knowledge or even the enthusiasm for it, but with the way the expertise is used: to assault others and put them down for their presumed ignorance. Maybe it is just me, but it seems as if computer experts have an above-average prevalence of this disorder. A simple question—"How can I open this file?"—leads to an endless discourse on operating systems, RAM, ROM, the pro's and con's of the Microsoft monopoly, and new products that one must buy in order to stay current. College professors are also in a high-risk category, and the reader can provide appropriate examples, I am sure.

Conclusion

If my classification is viable, it means that we can identify real psychological disorders from the vantage of positive psychology and specifically from the vantage of the VIA Classification. In its few years of existence, positive psychology has matured to the point where it can take seriously the possibility of moving people from −3 to +5. As the attention of positive psychology turns to interventions intended to cultivate the good life, let us not overlook the troubled among us. They too deserve a better existence. I predict that positive psychology will some-day generate a host of strategies for the treatment and prevention of the "real" disorders. Positive psychology is important enough to pervade all of psychology, including clinical psychology, and in so doing, it will give new life to a discipline that is already quite alive.

Note

1. There is a thriving self-help genre for women who "love too much," but its premise may be a mawkish fiction. The real problem is probably loving the wrong person too much, which is to say not at all, because mature love needs to be recip-rocated. In our studies with literally thousands of respondents, we have examined life satisfaction as a function of each of the character strengths (Park, Peterson, & Seligman, 2004). Our sample sizes allow a fine-grained examination of this func-tion, e.g., comparing the top 1% or the top 5% to those who score just lower, for example, with respect to kindness or humor. No matter how the samples are split, the relationship between life satisfaction and character is relentlessly monotonic. The top of the top are higher in life satisfaction than those in the mere top. Said another way, the place where life satisfaction is notably absent is at the lower end of a strength—the bottom 5% or 10%. Aristotle notwithstanding, the typical prob-lem with a virtue lies in its deficiency and not its excess.

References

Alloy, L. B., & Abramson, L. Y. (1979). Judgment of contingency in depressed and non-depressed students: Sadder but wiser? *Journal of Experimental Psychology, 108*, 441–485.

Allport, G. W. (1961). *Pattern and growth in personality.* New York: Holt, Rinehart, & Winston.

American Psychiatric Association. (1994). *Diagnostic and statistical manual of men-tal disorders* (4th ed.). Washington, DC: Author.

Aristotle. (2000). *Nicomachean ethics* (R. Crisp, Trans.). Cambridge: Cambridge University Press.

Asch, S. E. (1956). Studies of independence and conformity: A minority of one against a unanimous majority. *Psychological Monographs, 70*(9), 416.

Buckingham, M., & Clifton, D. O. (2001). *Now, discover your strengths.* New York: Free Press.

Buss, D. M., & Craik, K. H. (1983). The act frequency approach to personality. *Psy-chological Review, 90*, 105–126.

Cawley, M. J., Martin, J. E., & Johnson, J. A. (2000). A virtues approach to person-ality. *Personality and Individual Differences, 28*, 997–1013.

Comte-Sponville, A. (2001). *A small treatise on the great virtues* (C. Temerson, Trans.). New York: Metropolitan.

Cook, M. L., & Peterson, C. (1986). Depressive irrationality. *Cognitive Therapy and Research, 10,* 293–298.

Crowne, D. P., & Marlowe, D. (1964). *The approval motive: Studies in evaluative dependence.* New York: Wiley.

Ellis, A. (1962). *Reason and emotion in psychotherapy.* New York: Stuart.

Erikson, E. (1963). *Childhood and society* (2nd ed.). New York: Norton.

Greenberger, E., Josselson, R., Knerr, C., & Knerr, B. (1975). The measurement and structure of psychosocial maturity. *Journal of Youth and Adolescence, 4,* 127–143.

Jahoda, M. (1958). *Current concepts of positive mental health.* New York: Basic.

Janis, I. L. (1982). *Victims of groupthink.* Boston: Houghton Mifflin.

Kelley, H. H. (1973). The process of causal attribution. *American Psychologist, 28,* 107–128.

Loewenstein, G. (1994). The psychology of curiosity: A review and reinterpretation. *Psychological Bulletin, 116,* 75–98.

Mellsop, G., Varghese, F., Joshua, S., & Hicks, A. (1982). The reliability of Axis II of DSM-III. *American Journal of Psychiatry, 139,* 1360–1361.

Nesse, R. M. (1990). Evolutionary explanations of emotions. *Human Nature, 1,* 261–289.

Nisbett, R. E., & Wilson, T. D. (1977). Telling more than we can know: Verbal reports on mental processes. *Psychological Review, 84,* 231–259.

Park, N., & Peterson, C. (in press). Assessment of character strengths among youth: The Values in Action Inventory of Character Strengths Among Youth. In K. Moore & L. Lippman (Eds.), *What do children need to flourish? Conceptualizing and measuring indicators of positive development.* New York: Kluwer Academic/Plenum.

Park, N., Peterson, C., & Seligman, M. E. P. (2004). Strengths of character and well-being. *Journal of Social and Clinical Psychology, 23,* 603–619

Persons, J. B. (1986). The advantage of studying psychological phenomena rather than psychiatric diagnoses. *American Psychologist, 41,* 1252–1260.

Peterson, C. (1996). *The psychology of abnormality.* Fort Worth, TX: Harcourt Brace.

Peterson, C. (2000). The future of optimism. *American Psychologist, 55,* 44–55.

Peterson, C. (2003, August 9). *The unDSM-1: Positive psychology and the classification of strengths and virtues: The Values in Action (VIA) Classification.* Invited address at the 111th Annual Meeting of the American Psychological Association (Toronto).

Peterson, C., & Park, N. (2004). Classification and measurement of character strengths: Implications for practice. In P. A. Linley & S. Joseph (Eds.), *Positive psychology in practice* (pp. 433–446). New York: Wiley.

Peterson, C., Park, N., & Seligman, M. E. P. (2005). Assessment of character strengths. In G. P. Koocher, J. C. Norcross, & S. S. Hill III (Eds.), *Psychologists' desk reference* (2nd ed., pp. 93–98). New York: Oxford University Press.

Peterson, C., & Seligman, M. E. P. (2003). Character strengths before and after September 11. *Psychological Science, 14,* 381–384.

Peterson, C., & Seligman, M. E. P. (2004). Character strengths and virtues: A handbook and classification. New York: Oxford University Press; Washington, DC: American Psychological Association.

Romer, D. (Ed.). (2003). *Reducing adolescent risk: Toward an integrated approach.* Thousand Oaks, CA: Sage.

Ryff, C. D., & Singer, B. (1996). Psychological well-being: Meaning, measurement, and implications for psychotherapy research. *Psychotherapy and Psychosomatics, 65,* 14–23.

Seligman, M. E. P. (2002). *Authentic happiness.* New York: Free Press.

Seligman, M. E. P. (2003, October 3). *Introductory comments.* Invited address at the First Positive Psychology International Summit (Gallup Organization, Washington, DC).

Seligman, M. E. P., & Csikszentmihalyi, M. (2000). Positive psychology: An introduction. *American Psychologist, 55,* 5–14.

Seligman, M. E. P., & Peterson, C. (2003). Positive clinical psychology. In L. G. Aspinwall & U. M. Staudinger (Eds.), *A psychology of human strengths: Fundamental questions and future directions for a positive psychology* (pp. 305–317). Washington, DC: American Psychological Association.

Smith, R. P. (1981). Boredom: A review. *Human Factors, 23,* 329–340.

Sternberg, R. J., Forsythe, G. B., Hedlund, J., Horvath, J. A., Wagner, R. K., Williams, W. M., Snook, S. A., & Grigorenko, E. L. (2000). *Practical intelligence in everyday life.* New York: Cambridge University Press.

Szasz, T. S. (1961). *The myth of mental illness.* New York: Hoeber.

Taylor, S. E., Klein, L. C., Lewis, B. P., Gruenewald, T. L., Gurung, R. A. R., & Updegraff, J. A. (2000). Biobehavioral responses to stress in females: Tend-and-befriend, not fight-or-flight. *Psychological Review, 107,* 422–429.

Vagi, A. B., & Lefcourt, H. M. (1988). Investigativeness as a moderator of stress. *Canadian Journal of Behavioural Science, 20,* 93–108.

Walker, L. J., & Pitts, R. C. (1998). Naturalistic conceptions of moral maturity. *Developmental Psychology, 34,* 403–419.

Weeks, D. J. (1988). *Eccentrics: The scientific investigation.* London: Stirling University Press.

White, R. W. (1959). Motivation reconsidered: The concept of competence. *Psychological Review, 66,* 297–333.

Wolf, S. (1982). Moral saints. *Journal of Philosophy, 79,* 419–439.

Yearley, L. H. (1990). *Mencius and Aquinas: Theories of virtue and conceptions of courage.* Albany: State University of New York Press.

Zuckerman, M., & Litle, P. (1986). Personality and curiosity about morbid and sexual events. *Personality and Individual Differences, 7,* 49–56.

3

Positive Personality Development

Approaching Personal Autonomy

DMITRY LEONTIEV

P ositive development has not yet found its place among the "pillars of positive psychology" (Seligman, 2002a, 2002b). However, it appears no less important than positive emotions, positive traits, and positive institutions. Unlike positive emotions, it is always synergetic: It brings benefits not only to the developing person, but also to other persons surrounding him or her. Unlike positive traits, it is something a person cannot reach, but rather must cultivate all the time with incessant efforts. Unlike positive institutions, it is something for which a person can take full responsibility. What Seligman calls the *Nikki principle*—"by identifying, amplifying, and concentrating on these strengths in people at risk we will do effective prevention" (Seligman, 2002b, p. 5)—is not so much about the strengths themselves, but rather about the process of their actualization. This process belongs, to be sure, to the domain of the professional responsibility of psychologists, but healthy mature adults also apply these sort of positive self-regulation strategies to themselves, thus doing the effective-prevention job. When this occurs systematically, we may speak of a self-sustaining positive personality development pattern.

It is more difficult to study processes and regulation mechanisms than traits and emotional states. The emphasis on processes, however, helps us to become aware of some of the problems and challenges that positive psychology is facing today. Taking them seriously would help positive psychology to become a unified explanatory paradigm in general psychology, rather than remain a special interest area.

Challenges for Positive Psychology

It is no surprise that the idea of positive psychology has become popular so quickly—not only because it is extremely important, but also because it answers the most important question of our profession, the question about its meaning. Why are we psychologists? What's good in it? Why do we work at all? Answers in terms of adjustment, resolving conflicts and tensions, and fulfilling needs are not so convincing. The goal of helping humans to be happy is something far better as a justification of our profession. If we manage to solve the task of fire prevention as well as the task of fire extinguishing (Seligman, 2002a), it may lift the whole profession of psychology to a new level, to a new place in society.

There are, however, several risks and several challenges in our present-day situation. Positive psychology today is an ideology rather than a theory. It cannot help being an ideology, in an unbiased meaning of the word, for it embraces a number of quite different theoretical approaches. There is no unified theoretical explanatory model behind them at this moment, and we must find a way to integrate the efforts of scholars with rather different theoretical orientations. This situation is similar to the earlier project of humanistic psychology; in both cases there were no unified theoretical models. Humanistic psychology failed to elaborate such a model; positive psychology has a chance to do this. We must learn some lessons from the history of humanistic psychology to avoid the mistakes that have been made in the course of fulfilling the humanistic project.

The first challenge is the necessity to embrace not only the positive, but also the negative in the unified explanatory framework. Remember the old saying: The only condition necessary and sufficient for evil to win is that the good-willed people don't pay attention to it. There is no good apart from evil; maturation makes a person not only more capable of doing good, but also more capable of doing evil, and more sensitive to both—in the world and in one's own soul (May, 1972). All of the negative has some roots in us and in the structure of our lives, as does the positive. We cannot solve the task of preventing negative outcomes if we fail to treat both aspects simultaneously in a unified explanatory framework, focusing on the points where the developmental paths may bifurcate. "Life demands that we know the worst and make the best of it" (Allport, 1961, p. 556).

The second challenge is the necessity to move toward essential explanation. Newly elaborated metaphysical foundations are something very important today for positive psychology to develop. I would remind the reader here of two important dichotomies. The first one was proposed in the 1930s, independently from each other but at approximately the same time, by two great positively oriented thinkers, Lev Vygotsky (1982) and Victor Frankl (1987). They both said that psychology must be height psychology, as opposed both to depth psychology and to surface psychology. We should not keep at the surface. We must move to some essential mechanisms in order to explain the phenomena and tendencies we find at the surface. But this is not movement into the depth, when we are speaking of the positive human attributes, of human strengths and virtues; it should be height psychology rather than depth psychology.

The second dichotomy that is rather important is the opposite of the Galilean and Aristotelian mode of thinking, which was put forward by Kurt Lewin (1935).

Ancient science from Aristotle to our times used to ascribe some observable properties and traits to objects themselves. So the weight of a body was treated as an attribute of the body. A new stage of the development of science started when Galileo found that weight is not a property of things inherent in them. It's the result of some interplay of forces: The weight of an object is not an inalienable property of that object, but rather a result of its gravitational interaction with the earth.

In psychology, despite Lewin's efforts, Aristotelian thinking still exerts a strong influence. Trying to compose lists of positive traits, virtues, and strengths is quite a helpful thing, but we should not stop there. A very important task is to move toward explanatory models in order to understand what lies behind what we call optimism, happiness, gratitude, etc. The problem is to find how these come about and what interplay of forces lies behind such observable manifestations.

The third challenge is the necessity to consider the variety of types and levels of human life strategies or regulation mechanisms. There are different sorts of happiness, flow, well-being, and so on. Some people experience highly positive emotions through violence, while their victims experience quite the opposite. Not only creativity, but many criminal activities require extraordinary craftsmanship and talent; they challenge one's skills and competence. Not only in spiritual leaders and philosophers, but also in fanatic terrorists, we find a comprehensive and stable personal meaning. Hence, the experience of happiness, flow, and meaning does not say much about how good a person is. Subjective criteria fail to make distinctions between the completely different processes lying behind them. We must move beyond subjectivity to the wider objective context. We cannot do without it, just as we cannot do without the subjective.

Moral norms and values cannot provide the necessary criteria, because they are linked to a historically defined society. Societies differ and change; so do norms and values. Nowadays, one of the prevailing processes is the differentiation of societies into groups and subcultures with norms and values of their own, which often do not have much in common with the values of society as a whole. It seems important to include a cultural framework for positive psychology (see, e.g., Massimini & Delle Fave, 2000), while staying aware of the relativity of every special culture. What we need is a transcultural vision that frees us from the symbolic ties of our original cultures and allows us to see them as a possibility, rather than as a necessity (see Berry & Epstein, 1999).

The theory we need should consider the variety of regulatory processes underlying positive traits and emotions. My belief is that there is no single principle of behavior regulation, but rather a set of principles and different mechanisms that develop and change in our lives. We switch from one level to another, from one regulating principle to another, and this explains much of the variety of human manifestations, especially why developmental processes lead to a pleasing, good, and meaningful life in one condition and to an unpleasant, bad, and

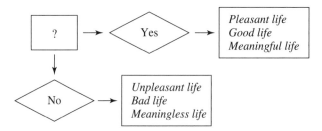

Figure 3.1.   Unified Context for Positive and Negative Psychologies

meaningless life in another condition (see Figure 3.1). I have the feeling that understanding the ways of managing our own lives must be the most important research and applied task for positive psychology.

The Variety of Human Regulations

The 20th century, more than previous periods of history, was full of very different examples of what a human being can be—a godlike creature or a beast. The variety of human behavior ranged from unbelievable heights of the human spirit to the complete betrayal of humanity. As a philosophical metaphor for this phenomenon, I propose the concept of a *sporadic human being*. Although there are not much experimental data that could directly support it, it is enough to look at the world around us to see the evidence. The idea of sporadic human functioning means that the trajectories of our lives are not always at the same level. We sink to lower, subhuman levels and then we ascend to human levels again. The *human level* comprises the level of behavior regulation that is inherent only in human beings, as distinct from the animal world. *Subhuman levels* are those mechanisms of regulation that are common to other animal species.

Some thinkers have suggested similar ideas. For instance, Rollo May (1967) noticed that our consciousness shifts along a continuum between the states of being an active subject and being a passive object: In some cases we let ourselves be driven by something; in other cases we take the initiative into our own hands, but we are able to switch voluntarily from one state to another. This is another form of the idea that we may function at different levels. There are human potentialities inherent in every person, but not in every person are they actualized at any given point of time.

The psychological model that follows from this idea of sporadic human functioning answers a key question, the favorite question of Edward Deci (Deci & Flaste, 1995) and of the present author: Why do people do what they do? I call it the *multiregulation personality model* (Leontiev, 1999, in press). As we will not be satisfied with a single universal answer, we shall find a variety of answers to this question, which reflect different principles of behavior regulation or different logics of human behavior.

A. The logic of *drive gratification* produces the answer: "Because I want (need, strive to) something." This is the simplest explanatory principle and is common for human and animal behavior.

B. The logic of *responding to stimuli* produces the answer: "Because something or someone provoked or teased me." This is also an explanation that is valid both for human and animal behavior; it plays an important role in the personal strategy of denying responsibility for one's actions.

C. The logic of *learned habits and dispositions* produces the answer: "Because I always behave this way." Quite a number of psychological problems fit this logic, including skills acquisition, attitude formation and change, character and individual style, and so forth.

D. The logic of *social norms and expectations* produces the answer: "Because this is the way one should behave and the way most people behave in this situation." This logic is determined by the distinctively human phenomenon of society, mediated by collective culture. The manifestations of this social logic, though distinctively human, characterize an impersonal yet socialized individual.

E. The logic of *life world* or the logic of *life necessity* produces the answer: "Because this is necessary (important) for me." This logic is also only inherent in humans. All of the animal behaviors (logics A, B, and C) are tied to the immediate environmental and internal impulses, to the situation "here and now"; all of the sources of its determination lie within the (external + internal) situation. Unlike animals, however, humans are able to put their activities into the context of their life-world, rather than just into the actual situation; they are determined by the world at large rather than by the environment. This means that in a human action following this logic, reasons and incentives located far beyond the immediate situation, including distant consequences and complicated connections, are taken into account. It is not a purely rational logic and a purely cognitive capacity, though cognitive schemes play an important role in the regulation processes based on this logic. It is the product of meaning-related regulation of human behavior. This kind of regulation serves to subsume individual activities to one's life world at large, rather than to the demands of the current situation, to the logic of life necessity rather than to the logic of actual need satisfaction, responding to external stimuli, applying stereotyped operations, or conforming to social "oughts."

F. The logic of *possibilities* produces the answer: "Why not?" This logic transcends the logic of life necessity; it represents the next developmental stage of personal maturity, which is not common for all human adults. The limitations of the logic of life necessity (E) are the continuation of its benefits. Even though they enable a person to transcend any given situation and to adjust to his or her life world at large, they tie one down to the facticity of this life-world and its anticipated development. A radically new future cannot develop from this facticity. The ability to transcend the determination of behavior by one's life-world, which is inherent in the mature personality, requires the logic of human freedom.

G. The logic of *ultimate understanding* produces the answer: "Because this corresponds to the way that things are." Ordinarily, the person feels that he or she has no choice because the world is organized so that there is only one way to do things. But this logic has a special purpose: to understand some kind of ultimate truth. Very few ever reach it. Of course, subjective certainty cannot be a good criterion, for among the insane, it is very deep. There is, however, a good criterion to tell a spiritual leader from a self-confident maniac: Two genuine sages will come to an agreement despite inevitable differences in their teachings, and two maniacs never will. At this level, one feels extremely free, though aware of having no choice to be otherwise.

Presumably there are special mechanisms and regulatory systems underlying each of these described logics of human behavior; however, in actuality they don't function separately, but rather are combined in multilevel systems. These seven principles may be treated as seven dimensions of our behavior. Every action can be split into seven vectors, each of the vectors representing a projection of the whole action in terms of each logic. These logics, however, are rarely present in pure forms; as a rule, they are combined and intertwined even in relatively simple behavioral acts and sequences of actions; taken together, they make human behavior multicontrolled and provide the basis for individual differences in regulation.

Keeping this model in mind, we may, first, see considerable individual differences in the development of each logic. Second, there are developmental trends and successions with respect to the seven principles. One of the issues pressing toward the elaboration of this model was the question: Where does personality start? By what age may we state that personality is already formed? It's not something inborn, but when does it start? This model suggests that the seven logics develop in a parallel way, though not at the same time. For example, manifestations of the fifth logic characteristic of personality can be seen at a rather early age, during the first year, but this logic becomes the defining one at a much later stage. Third, clinical psychology provides enough examples of separate types of distortions of these regulatory systems. The task of psychotherapy may be articulated as restoring the balance between these regulatory systems.

The ability of self-control, characteristic of a psychologically sound person, presupposes the balanced development of all seven (or, at least, the first five) regulatory systems; the dominant role should belong to the highest, distinctively human ones. The relationship between these higher laws of behavior regulation and the lower ones has been brilliantly expressed by Hegel: "Circumstances or urges dominate a person only to the extent to which he allows them to do it" (1927, p. 45). The dominance of E level or higher levels over subordinate ones is the constituent characteristic and the basis of personality as a distinctively human way of being (Leontiev, 1999). Personality is viewed as a system of self-regulation based on a structured subjective representation of one's relations to the world and the subjugation of one's life activities to the stable structure of such relations rather than to external stimuli, momentary urges, learned readiness, or social pressures.

Emancipation as the Vector of Personality Development

Can there be personality development other than biological maturation and socialization? Textbooks in the psychology of personality usually describe everything but the core of personality. Can we conceive of personality development that could not be reduced to biological or social development, to socialization processes or physical maturation? This question cannot be answered without first considering the nature of personhood. Contemporary views stress the complexity of personhood based on functions of identity, self-understanding, and agency (Martin, 2003). Erich Fromm (1956a) paid attention to the inherent duality of human nature. Human beings belong to two different sets of regulations: to the world of natural causality and to the special human world. Human beings find themselves thrown into the world and separated from their natural roots. One faces the choice between two different strategies of living: either stick to the natural ground and merge with companions, with the tribe, with the family, with the blood and soil links or find one's own independent, autonomous way in the world and find new organizing principles of being-in-the-world that cannot be derived from the world of natural causation. Personhood consists in the capacity to stand alone, keeping the whole human world within oneself.

This capacity of separate functioning is not inborn. In the process of human development, both in philogenesis and ontogenesis, we start becoming humans as a part of a symbiotic unit and gradually pass through a succession of stages of emancipation. Fromm (1956b) used the concept of psychological symbiosis to characterize the relations between a human infant and its mother. What happens in the course of development is the overcoming of this symbiosis, the emancipation from this initial, original connectedness. As Nobel Prize–winner Joseph Brodsky put it, "A human being is an autonomous creature, and throughout life, your autonomy keeps growing. This can be likened to a space ship: at first gravity acts upon it to some extent—attraction to your home, to your base. . . . But as [a] human being moves off [in]to space, (s)he starts obeying other, outer laws of gravity" (Brodsky, 2000, p. 472)

There are different stages of emancipation (see Figure 3.2). Birth is a physical disconnection of two organisms, the infant and the mother. First, they had a shared bodiness, they were in the same body, and then they become two different bodies. This is the physical emancipation. But in fact, we are not yet completely born;

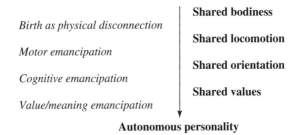

Birth as physical disconnection	**Shared bodiness**
Motor emancipation	**Shared locomotion**
Cognitive emancipation	**Shared orientation**
Value/meaning emancipation	**Shared values**

Autonomous personality

Figure 3.2   Personhood Development as Progressive Emancipation

we stay in many respects closely connected to the mother. A. N. Leont'ev (1978) spoke of two births of personality: "the first time when there appear[s] in a child in clear forms [the] polymotivation and subordination of his actions . . . , and a second time when his conscious personality appears" (p. 128). Step by step, the child learns movements and develops autonomous locomotion. Motor emancipation is the second stage after physical disconnection. Then comes cognitive emancipation, when the child elaborates a picture of the world that is his or her own. And the last stage is value or meaning emancipation, which corresponds to the adolescent crisis. This kind of emancipation marks the possibility of autonomous functioning. Before this critical point in development, the main factors determining the shaping of personality are environmental influences. But after this point, the activity of the person him- or herself becomes the main factor. An autonomous person is the end point of this progressive emancipation process. The person has his or her own law and acts in accordance with it. As in the original Greek sense of the word *autonomy,* autonomous persons impose their own regulatory principles to the way they manage their lives.

Autonomy is born from the fires of the adolescent crisis when infantile forms of activity and autoregulation merge into the mature self-determination pattern. Kaliteyevskaya and Leontiev (2004) in their existential model of autodetermination treat freedom and responsibility as psychological mechanisms having different natural and genetic roots, but converging into one in the mature adult personality. Freedom is a special form of human activity; its distinctive property is personal causation, that is, the controllability of activity by the subject at every point. Responsibility is a special form of internal value-mediated autoregulation presuming recognition and conscious management of one's ability in order to cause changes both in oneself and in the environment. Both merge, making two sides of a coin, in their mature forms; however, in the history of individual personality development, they emerge from different roots. The development of freedom comes from the awareness of one's rights and resources for activity and the elaboration of value criteria for making choices. The development of responsibility comes from the internalization of activity regulation, the transformation of overt regulation by the other person (adult) into internal self-regulation. The integration of both trends on the basis of personal values is the core of the adolescent crisis; it marks the person's ascendance to a new level of relating to the world, the level of autodetermination. The failure of this integration produces quasi freedom, which lacks responsibility, and quasi responsibility, which lacks freedom; the former appears as impulsive rebelling ("freedom from" rather than "freedom to"), the latter as the hard labor of implementing the introjected values of others, rather than those of one's own. Two empirical studies with 140 adolescents based on the factor and cluster analysis of several relevant multiscale inventories revealed four patterns of personality development that correspond to the four options of crossing freedom and responsibility (Figure 3.3): autonomous (integrated freedom and responsibility), impulsive (quasi freedom), symbiotic (quasi responsibility), and conformist (lacking both freedom and responsibility). The resulting developmental model accounts for the nature of mental health, personality development, and the goals of psychotherapy.

Causation and Mediation

The last question is: What gives us autonomy? How do we manage to escape the overriding fate of natural causation? In fact, natural causation is not all-encompassing. Nobel Prize winner in chemistry Ilya Prigogine (Prigogine &

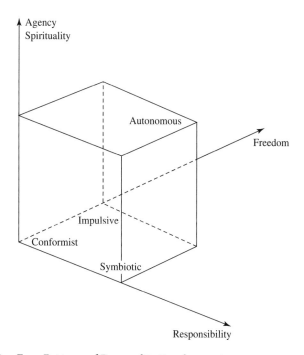

Figure 3.3.   Four Patterns of Personality Development

Stengers, 1984) found that processes in inorganic matter have breaks in determination, which he called *bifurcation points.* At these bifurcation points, the chemical processes may take either of two possible directions, and there are no factors that predetermine which of the two directions the process will take. If this is possible in inorganic processes, why can it not be possible in human activity? So even if we stay at the level of causation in natural processes, we see that there is some space for freedom and self-determination. And what we do here is mediate our activity. We cannot eliminate the natural forces that act upon us, but we can mediate them. According to Lev Vygotsky, all human action has a mediated structure. A stimulus does not automatically produce a response; the response is mediated through the introduction of some instrument, material or mental, that helps in mastering one's own response. For instance, Vygotsky (1983) showed that a way of mastering the situation of choice is to cast lots. We may use some additional instrument to make a decision when the natural interplay of forces cannot bring us to some definite decision. We may introduce some new elements to the situation to help us decide. And this is the way we become free from the external and internal influences in terms of drives and influences. Rollo May (1981) stated that freedom is located in the pause between stimulus and response. When we pause, we become free; we are no longer a part of the endless chain of natural causation. When we are not aware of this choice, we cannot pause, and we are not free. In line with this, the great Russian and Georgian philosopher Merab Mamardashvili explained the puzzle of Hamlet. Why does Hamlet hesitate all the time? Mamardashvili (1996) explains this through the ancient idea of the wheel of fortune—everything is linked to everything else; everything has consequences for everything else. But the human way of dealing with our lives, is to try to break these chains. Hamlet is well aware of all of these chains. The situation objectively requires some action from him. But he does not want to take it. He is aware of this; he is pausing; and he is looking for some exit out of the situation. He fails to find a real exit, but the whole story of Hamlet is the story of a man of dignity with a highly developed conscious awareness, who understands the structure, faces the challenge of the wheel of fortune, and tries to find a way out. That's what Hamlet does during the entire story: He fails to go beyond his predetermined tragedy, but the struggle for it is his glory.

Mediation is the key word for Vygotsky's cultural historical paradigm with its focus on mastering behavior. There may be different forms of mediation, and in all of these we escape natural processes and have the possibility to become the masters of our lives.

1. *Cognitive mediation.* Activity is mediated by cognitive processes and schemes. Salvatore Maddi (1971) in his theory of human needs states that at the human level we meet some needs that we never meet at the animal level, namely, those used in imagination, symbolization, and judgment. Maddi shows that when these needs dominate over biological and social needs, we

no longer perceive ourselves as ruled by social roles and biological needs. We try to build our own inner world, and this is the most important thing in all human functioning. We may escape from natural causation just because this world of our own gives us a very important degree of freedom.

2. *Ontological mediation.* In the famous experiments by Bruner and Goodman (1947), children who were asked to compare the size of coins and the size of paper circles judged the coins to be larger than the paper circles; this distortion was much more prevalent in children from poor families than in children from rich families. The ultimate cause that influences these results is the objective structure of a life-world where money matters. In another classic experiment (Solley & Haigh, 1957), children had to draw Santa Claus in September, November, and December, including just before Christmas and right after it. Santa Claus was initially quite small, but then he grew, and, in particular, his bag of gifts became larger and larger. But on the day after Christmas, the Santa Clauses were very small again. No special cognitive processes can explain this, but objectively Santa Claus takes a larger and larger place in the children's lives as Christmas approaches and they reflect this dynamic of their life-world in their drawings.

3. *Cultural, or semiotic, mediation.* This type of mediation has been extensively studied in a number of research traditions. Signs and symbols, from language and gestures to religious concepts, mediate our activity, giving it a new quality (see Valsiner, 2001). In fact, the idea of God is for us a symbol of overcoming natural causation. It's something above nature. We refer to God when we are going to do something against natural causation, against natural laws. The core of all moral rules is also this type of mediation.

4. *Structural mediation.* Motives and values are hierarchically arranged. We may not follow some motive because it contradicts some more important, superordinate one. This is why we don't do some things that would bring us immediate gratification: We know that other people might spit on our graves if we did them—and we consider this an important motive. So the influence of a motive is mediated by the influence of superordinate motives.

The main characteristic of a meaningful life is that it is a life mediated by mental contents, by the world we build. Activity mediation is the heart of personal autonomy and agency, in fact, neither would be possible without it. At least half of the positive psychology core virtues (Seligman, 2002a, p. 11) are associated with the strong capacity to mediate one's actions. It takes a special kind of strength to approach this level of human functioning, the building of a meaningful world.

Conclusion

The concept of positive personality development refers to both the direction of developmental processes and to their qualitative contents. An objective criterion of development is the degree to which we approach and use specifically human capacities and potentialities rather than subhuman ones. We may speak of progressive emancipation as the general direction of this process and personal autonomy as its goal. The two theoretical models described above explain why human development so often deviates from a positive direction. The multiregulation personality model (D. Leontiev, in press) accounts for the variety of behavior regulation mechanisms in humans, and the developmental autodetermination model (E. Kaliteyevskaya, D. Leontiev, 2004), explains both successes and failures in becoming the master of one's own life. Positive personality development leads to personal autonomy, meaning, and happiness; however, it also presupposes effort, responsibility, and risk taking—both on the part of the psychologists and on the part of their clients and research participants.

References

Allport, G. (1961). *Pattern and growth in personality.* New York: Holt, Rinehart & Winston.

Berry, E., & Epstein, M. (1999). *Transcultural experiments: Russian and American models of creative communication.* New York: St. Martin's.

Brodsky, J. (2000). *Bolshaya Kniga Intervyu* (Big book of interviews). Moscow: Zakharov.

Bruner, J., & Goodman, C. (1947). Value and need as organizing factors in perception. *Journal of Abnormal and Social Psychology, 47,* 33–44.

Deci, E., & Flaste, R. (1995). *Why we do what we do: Understanding self-motivation.* New York: Penguin.

Frankl, V. (1987). Zur Geistigen Problematik der Psychotherapie (1938). In V. Frankl, *Logotherapie und Existenzanalyse* (pp. 15–30). Muenchen: Piper.

Fromm, E. (1956a). *The sane society.* London: Routledge & Kegan Paul.

Fromm, E. (1956b). *The art of loving.* New York: Harper & Row.

Hegel, G. W. F. (1927). Philosophische Propadeutik. In *Sämtliche Werke* (Vol. 3). Stuttgart: Frommann.

Kaliteyevskaya, E., & Leontiev, D. (2004). When freedom meets responsibility: Adolescence as the critical point of positive personality development. In A. Delle Fave (Ed.), *Positive psychology* [Special issue of *Ricerche di Psicologia, 27*(1), 103–115].

Leont'ev, A. N. (1978). *Activity, consciousness, and personality.* Englewood Cliffs, NJ: Prentice-Hall.

Leontiev, D. (1999). *Psikhologiya Smysla* (The psychology of personal meaning). Moscow: Smysl.

Leontiev, D. (in press). The variety of human regulations. In D. Leontiev (Ed.), *Motivation, consciousness, and self-regulation.*

Lewin, K. (1935). *The dynamic theory of personality.* New York: McGraw-Hill.

Maddi, S. (1971). The search for meaning. In W. J. Arnold & M. M. Page (Eds.), *Nebraska symposium on motivation 1970* (pp. 137–186). Lincoln: University of Nebraska Press.

Mamardashvili, M. (1996). *Neobkhodimost Sebya* (The necessity of oneself). Moscow: Labirint.

Martin, J. (2003). Emergent persons. *New Ideas in Psychology, 21,* 85–99.

Massimini, F., & Delle Fave, A. (2000). Individual development in a bio-cultural perspective. *American Psychologist, 55*(1), 24–33.

May, R. (1967). *Psychology and the human dilemma.* Princeton, NJ: Van Nostrand.

May, R. (1972). *Power and innocence.* New York: Norton.

May, R. (1981). *Freedom and destiny.* New York: Norton.

Prigogine, I., & Stengers, I. (1984). *Order out of chaos: Man's new dialogue with nature.* Toronto: Bantam.

Seligman, M. E. P. (2002a). *Authentic happiness.* New York: Free Press.

Seligman, M. E. P. (2002b). Positive psychology, positive prevention, and positive therapy. In C. R. Snyder & S. J. Lopez (Eds.), *The handbook of positive psychology* (pp. 3–12). New York: Oxford University Press.

Solley, C. M., & Haigh, G. (1957). A note to Santa Claus. *Topeka Research Papers, The Menninger Foundation, 18*(3), 4–5.

Valsiner, J. (2001). Process structure of semiotic mediation in human development. *Human Development, 44,* 84–97.

Vygotsky, L. (1982). Problema Soznaniya (The problem of consciousness). In L. Vygotsky, *Sobranie Sochinenii* (Collected works) (Vol. 1, pp. 156–167). Moscow: Pedagogika.

Vygotsky, L. (1983). Istoriya Razvitiya Vysshikh Psikhicheskikh Funktsii (Developmental history of the higher mental functions). In L. Vygotsky, *Sobranie Sochinenii* (Collected works) (Vol. 3, pp. 6–328). Moscow: Pedagogika.

4

Spirituality

Recent Progress

ROBERT A. EMMONS

The primary purpose of this chapter is to present the most recent developments in the scientific study of spirituality. At the outset, I must confess the near impossibility of this task. Recent research on religion and spirituality as human phenomena is almost as vast and diverse as religious and spiritual life itself. A literature search using the PsycINFO database for the 10-year period 1994–2003 returned nearly 1,800 citations for the terms "spirituality" and "spiritual" and nearly 1,300 for "religion" and "religiosity." This review, therefore, must of necessity be quite selective. A substantial majority of the studies on religion and spirituality have occurred within the applied areas of clinical, counseling, and health psychology and have examined links between religion and mental health and psychological, physical, and interpersonal well-being (for reviews, see Ferriss, 2002; Hackney & Sanders, 2003; Kim, 2003; Koenig, McCullough, & Larson, 2001; Smith, McCullough, & Poll, 2003). I will not attempt to summarize this voluminous literature here. The interested reader is advised to consult the above sources. My overriding concern, rather, will be to sketch the newest lines of research that are emerging that show promise of contributing significantly to the psychology of religion and spirituality and that might impact the broader field of positive psychology. The field of positive psychology has distinguished itself from earlier historical movements that have shared some of the same conceptual turf by emphasizing definitional clarity and methodological rigor. This being the case, I will highlight progress in defining and measuring spiritual constructs and discuss the implications of these constructs (and, by extension, the spiritual dimension of human life) for the science of positive psychology.

Researchers in the field of the psychology of religion (where the research on spirituality is anchored) have approached the scientific study of spirituality at roughly three levels of analysis: spirituality as a general trait, spirituality as reflected in personal goals and intentions, and spirituality as reflected in specific emotions and emotional processes, such as gratitude, awe, reverence, wonder, and forgiveness. This multilevel approach assumes that spirituality is multidimensional and is reflected in people's subjective experience in distinct, though related ways. At the trait level, spirituality is seen as a capacity or ability on which individuals differ. At the level of goals or concerns, spirituality is seen as a motivating force that drives and directs personalized goals that one strives to obtain. The presence of the trait of spirituality and goals centered around spiritual concerns increases the likelihood that the person will experience spiritual feeling states, which include awe, gratitude, humility, love, and hope (level three). A representative sampling of work in each of these three domains will be presented.

Progress in Defining Spirituality

What is spirituality? Until recently, vagueness was perhaps the most appropriate adjective to apply to this construct. Historically, the topic has been marginalized within the scientific study of psychology. Because of its unbounded and seemingly infinite nature, serious scientists tended to approach the topic cautiously, if at all. This is understandable. In order for progress to occur in a scientific discipline, there must be some consensus concerning the meaning of core constructs and their measurement. A lack of precision does hamper progress in the field. However, agreement on the meaning of spirituality and religion has been hard to come by as the religious landscape in the broader culture and in psychology is changing with a new breed of spirituality that is often distinct from traditional conceptions of religion (Hill, 1999). Adding to the confusion, religious and spiritual variables are increasingly being included in experimental and epidemiological studies, but spirituality is conceived of and measured differently from study to study.

Yet recent efforts are beginning to demonstrate that the concept may be scientifically tractable after all. Several definitions have been offered, and these have opened the door for the scientific study of spirituality. Since the 1990s, there has been arguably more print devoted to conceptualizing religion and spirituality than to any other topic in the psychology of religion. It has become fashionable, both culturally and in the scientific literature, to differentiate between the spiritual and the religious. Psychologists have exerted as much effort as anyone in debating the meaning of these terms. The noun *spirit* and the adjective *spiritual* are being used to refer to an ever-increasing range of experiences rather than being reserved for those occasions of use that specifically imply the existence of nonmaterial forces or persons. *Spirituality* comes from the Latin *spiritus,* meaning breath, or "the animating or vital principle of a person" (Oxford English Dictionary). The concept of spirituality stems from Christian theology. Here, spirituality may most naturally be defined as the result of the work of the Holy Spirit in humans—more specifically, in human beings' souls and activities (Řičan, 2003). Because psychology must deal with natural rather than supernatural levels of description and explanation, however, *spirit* has come to be defined in solely human terms. *Spirituality* has been defined as "a deep sense of belonging, of wholeness, of connectedness, and of openness to the infinite" (Kelly, 1995, pp. 4–5); as that which "involves ultimate and personal truths" (Wong, 1998, p. 364); and as "a way of being and experiencing that which comes about through awareness of a transcendent dimension and that is characterized by certain identifiable values in regard to self, others, nature, life and whatever one considers to be the Ultimate" (Elkins, 1988, p. 10). Spirituality has been said to refer to how an individual "lives meaningfully with ultimacy, his or her response to the deepest truths of the universe as he or she apprehends these" (Bregman & Thierman, 1995, p. 149). Spirituality—in contrast to religion—means something spontaneous, informal, creative, universal; it means authentic inner experience and freedom of individual expression, of seeking, even of religious experimenting.

Although historically spirituality was not distinguished from religion, the two concepts have become untethered in contemporary parlance. Dollahite (1998) defined *religion* as "a covenant faith community with teachings and narratives that enhance the search for the sacred and encourage morality" (p. 5). Religions are rooted in authoritative spiritual traditions that transcend the person and point to larger realities within which the person is embedded. Spiritualities *may* be contextualized within faith communities though they need not be. Religions are sets of beliefs, symbols, and practices about the "reality of superempirical orders that make claims to organize and guide human life" (Smith, 2003, p. 98).

In contrast to religion, conceptions of spirituality do not always have a transcendent reference point, a fact that has led to much confusion over its meaning in research contexts. Most contemporary meanings of *spirituality* distinguish among religious spirituality, natural spirituality, and humanistic spirituality. Elkins (2001), a vocal proponent of humanistic-oriented spirituality, offers six qualities of spirituality that seem to represent a blending of Spilka's (Spilka et al., 2003) three types: Spirituality is universal; it is a human phenomenon; its common core is phenomenological; it is our capacity to respond to the numinous; it is characterized by a "mysterious energy"; and its ultimate aim is compassion. Other authors have emphasized the relational, moral, or ethical character of spirituality (Carlson, Erikson, & Seewald-Marquardt, 2003). While some have argued that the movement toward spirituality represents a movement away from traditional religion (Elkins, 2001), others contend that the increased emphasis on spirituality indicates an increased respect for the inner, contemplative practices of traditional religious systems (Hill et al., 2000; Wuthnow, 1998).

A number of contemporary psychologists using the term *spirituality* go one step further. Instead of remaining at the most general level of theorizing, they describe in detail, rather pragmatically, what spiritual people may experience, what they say, how they act. In this usage, the spirit being referred to in spirituality is not the Holy Spirit, but rather the human spirit, representing the highest of human potential. For example, according to Beck (1986), a spiritual person is one who displays 13 characteristics, including (1) insight and understanding; (2) a sense of context and perspective; (3) awareness of the interconnectedness of things, of unity within diversity, and of patterns within the whole; optimism; (4) acceptance of the inevitable; (5) gratitude, gladness, humility; and (6) love, "the characteristic par excellence of the spiritual person" (cited in Wulff, 1997, p. 7).

Zinnbauer, Pargament, and Scott (1999) and Hill et al. (2000) systematically reviewed the evolving meanings of the terms *religion* and *spirituality*. Achieving some degree of definitional clarity is desirable, though not necessarily essential for scientific progress and the establishment of a cumulative knowledge base. After all, many disciplines have failed to provide a core consensual definition and still flourished. For example, the field of personality psychology lacks a single, consensual definition of what personality is. On the basis of both historical considerations and a growing empirical literature, the authors caution against viewing spirituality and religiousness as incompatible and suggest that the common tendency to polarize the terms simply as individual versus institutional or "good" versus "bad" is not fruitful for future research. Also cautioning against the use of restrictive, narrow definitions or overly broad definitions that can rob either construct of its distinctive characteristics, the authors propose a set of criteria that recognizes the constructs' conceptual similarities and dissimilarities. Both religion and spirituality include the subjective feelings, thoughts, experiences, and behaviors that arise from a search for the sacred. The term *search* refers to attempts to identify, articulate, maintain, or transform. The term *sacred* refers to a "divine being, divine object, ultimate reality, or Ultimate Truth as perceived by the individual" (Hill et al., 2000, p. 68). The concept of the sacred as the single, key defining feature of religion and of spirituality has its historical precedence in the influential writings of Otto (1917/1958) and Eliade (1959). People are *spiritual* to the degree to which they are trying to know, find, experience, or relate to what they perceive as sacred. For extremely spiritual people whose lives are totally devoted to the search for the sacred, i.e., for those who find the whole of life sacred, there is little difference between religion and spirituality. Religion may or may not also include the search for nonsacred goals, such as social identity or health in the context of the search for the sacred, as well as prescribing rituals that facilitate a search for the sacred, which are validated and supported by a faith community. These authors suggest that a dynamic view of spirituality and religion centered on a search process offers considerable potential for understanding the influence of the spiritual and religious realm in everyday life.

Building upon this definition, Pargament (1999) has argued that conceiving of spirituality in terms of an ability to imbue everyday experience, goals, roles, and responsibilities with sacredness opens new avenues for empirical exploration. For example, Mahoney et al. (1999) found that when marital partners viewed their relationship as imbued with divine qualities, they reported greater levels of marital satisfaction, more constructive problem-solving behaviors, decreased marital conflict, and greater commitment to the relationship, compared to couples who did not see their marriage in a sacred light. Similarly, Tarakeshwar, Swank, Pargament, and Mahoney (2002) found that a strong belief that nature is sacred was associated with greater pro-environmental beliefs and a greater willingness to protect the environment.

Behavioral scientists make distinctions between spirituality and religion, but what about the general public? Marler and Hadaway (2002) explored the relationship between perceptions of "being religious" and "being spiritual" in a national sample of American Protestants. When people are given the option, do they tend to describe themselves as religious, as spiritual, as both, or as neither? According to their data, the vast majority of Americans surveyed identified themselves as both religious and spiritual. Across several different studies using a variety of samples, the percentage of individuals describing themselves as both religious and spiritual ranged from 59% to 74%. This was compared to the 14–20% who described themselves as spiritual only; the religious-only group accounted for between 4 and 14% of those surveyed; and those who selected the "neither" option constituted the smallest group (3–12%). Other research has revealed that spirituality and religion are seen as considerably overlapping concepts, with spirituality tending to be viewed as a broader concept, encompassing religion (Zinnbauer et al., 1997). A similar pattern has been reported in research in European nations (Řičan, 2003; Stifoss-Hanssen, 1999).

Level I: Measuring Spirituality as Traits

Measurement is fundamental to scientific progress, as the Gallup organization readily knows. Major advances in scientific disciplines are typically preceded by major breakthroughs in measurement methods. The 1980s and 1990s saw an explosion of new inventories in the psychology of religion. One authoritative reference volume (Hill & Hood, 1999) provides detailed information on more than 100 standardized measures of religiousness and spirituality. These are grouped into 17 major clusters, including religious beliefs and practices, religious attitudes, religious values, religious development, religious orientation, religious commitment and involvement, spirituality and mysticism, forgiveness, religious coping, and religious fundamentalism. In contrast to measures of religiousness, the authors lamented that relatively few measures of spirituality were available at the time they began their review. Two new measures, however, have recently appeared and seem to have considerable promise. Importantly, they each appear to be transportable across cultures and spiritual traditions.

Spiritual Transcendence Index

The Spiritual Transcendence Index (Seidlitz & Abernethy, 2002) is an eight-item measure based upon the authors' definition *of spiritual transcendence* as "a subjective experience of the sacred that affects one's self-perception, feelings, goals, and ability to transcend difficulties" (Seidlitz & Abernethy, 2002, p. 441). Sample items from the STI include "I maintain an inner awareness of God's presence in my life"; "I try to strengthen my relationship with God"; and "Maintaining my spirituality is a top priority for me." In keeping with the definition of spirituality offered earlier in this chapter, the scale was designed to reflect various conceptualizations of spirituality while emphasizing its sacred core. Half of the items include a theistic referent (God), while the other half refer to a person's spirituality. No mention is made of organized religion. Several studies document the scale's criterion validity and discriminant validity, including positive correlations with intrinsic religiousness and a lack of correlation with the personality trait of openness to experience.

Spiritual Transcendence Scale

Piedmont (1999) developed the Spiritual Transcendence Scale (STS), a 20-item measure designed to measure spirituality as a facet of personality. According to Piedmont, *spiritual transcendence* is "the capacity of individuals to stand outside of their immediate sense of time and place and to view life from a larger, more objective perspective. This transcendent perspective is one in which a person sees a fundamental unity underlying the diverse strivings of nature" (Piedmont, 1999, p. 988). In developing the STS, a consortium of theological experts from diverse faith traditions, including Buddhism, Hinduism, Quakerism, Lutheranism, Catholicism, and Judaism was assembled. This focus group identified aspects of spirituality that were common to all of these faiths. The resulting items were analyzed within the context of the Five Factor Model (FFM) and were shown to constitute an independent individual-differences dimension. The STS manifested a single overall factor composed of three "facet" scales: *prayer fulfillment*, a feeling of joy and contentment that results from personal encounters with a transcendent reality (e.g., "I find inner strength and/or peace from my prayers or meditations"); *universality*, a belief in the unitary nature of life (e.g., "I feel that on a higher level all of us share a common bond"); and *connectedness*, a belief that one is part of a larger human reality that cuts across generations and across groups (e.g., "I am concerned about those who will come after me in life"). The STS displayed incremental validity by significantly predicting a number of relevant psychological outcomes (e.g., stress experience, social support, interpersonal style) even after the predictive effects of personality were removed (Piedmont, 1999). For the STS to be shown to capture a universal aspect of spirituality, it would be necessary to show that the instrument remains reliable and valid in culturally diverse, religiously heterogeneous samples. Piedmont and Leach (2003) have documented the utility of the STS in a sample of Indian Hindus, Muslims, and Christians. Support was found for two of the facet scales and the overall domain (connectedness was not found to be reliable) in this sample. The STS was presented in English, a second language for these participants. This may have created difficulties in understanding the terminology, or the exemplars used as items might have lacked relevance in this culture. Nonetheless, these data highlight the value of cross-cultural research on spirituality and show the STS to reflect spiritual qualities relevant across very different religious traditions.

Cultural and Cross-Cultural Investigations

The study by Piedmont and Leach is notable in that it demonstrates the generalizability of a measure of spirituality across cultures and spiritual traditions. The cross-cultural study of spirituality and religion is still in its infancy, yet studies are beginning to appear in the literature. Additionally, the developers of new measures of spirituality and religiousness are aware of the necessity to validate their instruments outside of their own cultures and faith traditions. For example, Worthington (2003) validated the Religious Commitment Inventory (an instrument assessing the degree to which a person adheres to his or her religious values and beliefs in daily life) in separate samples of Christians, Buddhists, Muslims, and Hindus, and Tarakeshwar, Pargament, and Stanton (2003) developed and validated a measure of spiritual coping in Hindus. Thus, we are seeing an increasing interest in the development of measures of various aspects of spirituality that are valid for use in diverse religious traditions. Tarakeshwar, Stanton, and Pargament (2003) have recently argued that religion is an overlooked factor in cross-cultural psychological research, and they provide recommendations for integrating religious and spiritual variables into cross-cultural and cultural research studies. What is especially revealing from some initial cross-cultural studies is that when it comes to comparing spiritual processes and well-being indices across traditions, the differences among faiths are considerably less than their similarities (Jianbin & Mehta, 2003; Tarakeshwar, Pargament, & Stanton, 2003).

An example of a cultural research study is the recent examination of spirituality and well-being in Korea (Kim, 2003). Kim documents how spiritual resources (prayer, participation, religious and spiritual values) and religious organizations have contributed to societal indicators of well-being in Korea, such as educational attainment, income level, and overall quality of life. For example, welfare institutions, hospitals, orphanages, and philanthropic organizations are much more likely to be operated by religious organizations than by governmental or nongovernmental institutions thus demonstrating "the centrality of religion in enhancing societal quality of life" (Kim, 2003, p. 161).

Level II: Personal Goals

A second level of analysis for conceptualizing spirituality is in terms of personalized goals or strivings, or what Emmons and colleagues have called "ultimate concerns" (Emmons, 1999; Emmons, Cheung, & Tehrani, 1998). A rapidly expanding database now exists that demonstrates that personal goals are a valid representation of how people structure and experience their lives: They are critical constructs for understanding the ups and downs of everyday life, and they are key elements for understanding both the positive life as well as psychological dysfunction (Karoly, 1999). People's priorities, goals, and concerns are key determinants of their overall quality of life. The possession of and progression toward important life goals are essential for long-term well-being. Several investigators have found that individuals who are involved in the pursuit of personally meaningful goals possess greater emotional well-being and better physical health than do persons who lack goal direction (see Emmons, 1999, for a review).

At this level of analysis, spirituality is the centering of individual and collective life around dynamic patterns of goals that make life meaningful, valuable, and worth living (Jernigan, 2001). I (Emmons, 1999) proposed that both religion and spirituality deal with the ultimate concerns of people and that a spiritual perspective can illuminate the origins of some of the most profound human strivings. One of the functions of a religious belief system and a spiritual world view is to provide "an ultimate vision of what people should be striving for in their lives" (Pargament & Park, 1995, p. 15) and the strategies to reach those ends. Given the prevalence of religion in society, it would be surprising, then, if spiritual and religious concerns did not find expression in one form or another through personal goals. At first glance, it might seem odd to speak of religious or spiritual goals, the way one talks about achievement goals, health goals, or financial goals. After all, religions are beliefs systems, full of doctrines, practices, rituals, and symbols. Yet we speak quite openly of a "spiritual quest," of a searching for the sacred. In form, there is nothing inherently different about religious and spiritual goals in comparison to any other type of goal. Religious and spiritual goals, like other goals, are internal mental representations of desired states toward which a person has committed to working. Religions recommend the ultimate goal of binding with the sacred and prescribe rituals for its realization. By identifying and committing themselves to spiritual goals, people strive to develop and maintain a relationship to the sacred. Participants report typically trying to "be aware of the spiritual meaningfulness of my life," "discern and follow God's will for my life," "bring my life in line with my beliefs," and "communicate my faith to other people."

Personal goals are assessed by asking people to reflect on, and then list, the various objectives toward which they are striving. Not all of these strivings may be consciously accessible or articulated, however, as many are assumed to operate at the preconscious, schematic level. In our research, we have found that people differ in their tendency to attribute spiritual significance to their strivings, with percentages of spiritual strivings ranging from 0 to nearly 50%, depending upon the nature of the sample studied. College males have the lowest level of avowed spiritual strivings, whereas elderly, church-going females tend to have the highest levels. In both community-based and college-student samples, we have found that the presence of intimacy strivings, generativity strivings, and spiritual strivings within a person's goal hierarchy predict greater subjective well-being (SWB), particularly higher positive affect. In each case, we examined the proportion of striving in that category relative to the total number of strivings generated. This provides a rough index of the centrality of each motivational theme within the person's overall goal hierarchy. Spiritual strivings are related to higher levels of SWB, especially to greater positive affect and to both marital and overall life satisfaction (Emmons, Cheung, & Tehrani, 1998). In the Emmons et al. (1998) study, these relations were stronger for women than for men, in accord with the literature on gender differences in religion and SWB. Spiritual strivings were also rated as more important, requiring more effort, and engaged in for more intrinsic reasons than were nonspiritual strivings. Investing goals with a sense of sacredness confers upon them a power to organize experience and to promote well-being that is absent in nonsacred strivings (Mahoney & Pargament, in press). In their sample of 150 community adults, Mahoney and Pargament found that people tended to place a high priority on strivings that they viewed as sacred. They devoted more time and energy to spiritual strivings and derived greater satisfaction and sense of meaning from them relative to strivings that were more self-focused and materially oriented.

What accounts for the unique ability of spiritual strivings to predict well-being outcomes? As Pargament (2002) has convincingly argued, identifying that which is sacred and striving to protect and preserve the sacred lends deep significance to human existence, a significance that is difficult to explain through more basic psychological or social levels of description. Spiritual strivings may have a unique empowering function; people are more likely to persevere in these strivings, even under difficult circumstances. This empowering function may be stronger in groups that have limited access to other resources, such as racial minorities, the elderly, and the chronically ill (Pargament, 1997). People are more likely to take measures to protect and preserve strivings that focus on the sacred and to devote time and effort toward their realization. People admit that in today's secular culture, whether their spiritual strivings are socially accepted or socially sanctioned, they derive tremendous meaning and purpose from them. Spiritual strivings are also likely to provide stability and support in times of crisis by reorienting people to what is ultimately important in life (Emmons, Colby, & Kaiser, 1998).

Motivational constructs such as goals have been ignored by researchers attempting to develop measures of spirituality. Yet people often define themselves and their lives by what they are trying to do and by who they are trying to be. Spiritual and religious goals, above all others, appear to provide people with significant meaning and purpose. Well-validated assessment instruments have been developed for measuring personal goals, and these offer a second level of analysis for assessing individual differences in spirituality. An analysis of spirituality as a goal-based meaning system facilitates an understanding of the dynamic, process-oriented function of spirituality and could provide a unifying framework for its psychological study.

Level III: Spiritual Emotions

The third and final level at which spirituality might be conceptualized and measured is at the level of emotion, or affect. The connection between spirituality and emotion is a long and intimate one. Emotion or affect has always been seen as a central component in spiritual and religious experiences. What does it mean to say that emotions are spiritual? First, spiritual emotions are those emotions that are more likely to occur in sacred (e.g., churches, synagogues, mosques) settings than in nonsacred settings. However, this does not mean that sacred emotions cannot be experienced in nonsacred settings. Second, sacred emotions are those that are more likely to be elicited through spiritual or religious practices (e.g., worship, prayer, meditation) than by nonspiritual activities. However, this does not mean that they cannot be activated through nonspiritual channels (e.g., contemplating nature) as well. Third, sacred emotions are more likely to be experienced by people who self-identify as religious or spiritual (or both) than by people who do not think of themselves as either spiritual or religious. However, sacred emotions can be felt (on occasion) by people who do not think of themselves as religious or spiritual. Fourth, sacred emotions are those emotions that religious and spiritual systems around the world have traditionally sought to cultivate in their adherents. Fifth, sacred emotions are those emotions experienced when individuals imbue seemingly secular aspects of their lives (e.g., family, career, events) with a spiritual significance (Mahoney et al., 1999; Pargament, 2002). Among those emotions most likely to be thought of as sacred, gratitude, awe, reverence, and wonder are the top contenders. These emotions are beginning to be taken seriously by research psychologists.

Gratitude

Gratitude is an emotional response to a gift. It is the appreciation felt after one has been the beneficiary of an altruistic act. Some of the most profound reported experiences of gratitude can be religiously based or associated with reverent wonder toward an acknowledgment of the universe (Goodenough, 1998), including the perception that life itself is a gift. In the great monotheistic religions of the world, the concept of gratitude permeates texts, prayers, and teachings. Worship with gratitude toward God for the many gifts and mercies are common themes, and believers are urged to develop this quality. A spiritual framework thus provides the backdrop for experiences and expressions of gratitude. The spiritual quality of gratitude is aptly conveyed by Streng (1989): "[I]n this attitude people recognize that they are connected to each other in a mysterious and miraculous way that is not fully determined by physical forces, but is part of a wider, or transcendent context" (p. 5).

McCullough and colleagues (McCullough, Kilpatrick, Emmons, & Larson, 2001) recently reviewed the classical moral writings on gratitude and synthesized them with contemporary empirical findings. They suggested that the positive emotion of gratitude has three moral functions: It serves as a moral barometer (an affective readout that is sensitive to a particular type of change in one's social relationships, the provision of a benefit by another moral agent that enhances one's well-being), a moral motivator (prompting grateful people to behave prosocially themselves), and a moral reinforcer (that increases the likelihood of future benevolent actions). McCullough, Emmons, and Tsang (2002) found that measures of gratitude as a disposition were positively correlated with nearly all of the measures of spirituality and religiousness, including spiritual transcendence, self-transcendence, and the single-item religious variables. The grateful disposition was also related to measures of spiritual and religious tendencies. Although these correlations were not large (i.e., few of them exceeded $r = .30$), they suggest that spiritually or religiously inclined people have a stronger disposition to experience gratitude than do their less spiritual/religious counterparts. Thus, spiritual and religious inclinations may facilitate gratitude, but it is also conceivable that gratitude facilitates the development of religious and spiritual interests (Allport et al., 1948) or that the association of gratitude and spirituality/religiousness is caused by extraneous variables yet to be identified. The fact that the correlations of gratitude with these affective, prosocial, and spiritual variables were obtained using both self-reports and peer reports of the grateful disposition suggests that these associations are substantive and not simply the product of monomethod biases in measurement. This study may also be useful for explaining why religiously involved people are at a lower risk for depressive symptoms or other mental health difficulties.

McCullough, Emmons, and Tsang (2002) found that people who reported high levels of spirituality reported more gratitude in their daily moods, as did people higher in religious interest, general religiousness, and intrinsic religious orientation. Interestingly, however, the extrinsic, utilitarian religious orientation and quest-seeking religious orientation were not significantly correlated with the amount of gratitude in daily mood. These findings suggest that people high in conventional forms of religiousness, especially people for whom religion is a fundamental organizing principle (i.e., people high in intrinsic religiousness), and people who report high levels of spiritual transcendence experience more gratitude in their daily moods than do their less religious/spiritual counterparts. Watkins, Woodward, Stone, and Kolts (2003) found that the trait of gratitude correlated positively with intrinsic religiousness and negatively with extrinsic religiousness. The authors suggest that the presence of gratitude may be a *positive* affective hallmark of religiously and spiritually engaged people, just as an absence of depressive symptoms is a *negative* affective hallmark of spiritually and religiously engaged people. They likely see benefits as gifts from God, "the first cause of all benefits" (Watkins et al., 2003, p. 437).

Awe and Reverence

Few would disagree that the emotions of awe and reverence are central to spiritual experience. Awe was the cornerstone of Otto's (1917/1958) classic analysis of religious experience. The essence of religious worship, for Otto, was the overpowering feeling of majesty and mystery in the presence of the holy that is at the same time fascinating and dreadful. This juxtaposition of fear and fascination is a hallmark of religious awe (Wettstein, 1997).

Several philosophers of emotion have offered conceptual analyses of awe in which they define awe and distinguish it from reverence and related states. Roberts (2003) describes *awe* as a "sensitivity to greatness," accompanied by a sense of being overwhelmed by the object of greatness and reverence as "an acknowledging subjective response to something excellent in a personal (moral or spiritual) way, but qualitatively above oneself" (2003, p. 268). The major distinction between awe and reverence, for Roberts, is that awe could equally be experienced in response to something perceived as vastly evil as to something vastly good, but reverence is typically reserved for those things or persons esteemed worthy of it, in a positive or moral sense. Similarly, Woodruff (2001) states, "Reverence is the well-developed capacity to have the feelings of awe, respect and shame when these are the right feelings to have" (p. 8). Solomon (2002) argues that awe is passive whereas reverence is active: To be awestruck implies paralysis, while reverence leads to active engagement and responsibility toward that which a person reveres.

In contrast to these substantial theological and philosophical writings, little research in the psychology of religion has focused on either awe or reverence as a religious emotion. Many psychologists mention awe in their studies of religious experiences, but few have attempted to study it systematically. Maslow (1964) included the experience of awe under the broad umbrella of "peak experiences" (1964, p. 65), an umbrella that included "practically everything that, for example, Rudolf Otto defines as characteristic of religious experience" (Maslow, 1964, p. 54). Several other studies have included awe under the slightly less broad category of "mystical experiences," but since awe is not the purpose of these studies, their research and conclusions are difficult to utilize with respect to awe. For example, though Hardy (1979) lists "[a]we, reverence, wonder" as a category of religious experience recorded in his database, his examples merely include a description of the "it" of a particular mystical experience as "beneficent, but aweful" or mention awe as an aftereffect of the experience. Interestingly, Hardy (1979) found that awe was not a particularly frequently reported experience: Awe, reverence, and wonder occurred in 7% of reported religious experiences that he collected, compared to 21% for joy and happiness and 25% for peace and security. Likewise, when Hood (1975) included awe as an item on his mysticism scale, he was not interested in the experience of awe per se, but in the mystical experience that might (or might not) produce awe.

Keltner and Haidt (2003) have recently offered a prototypical approach to awe that represents an important new contribution. According to their definition, an awe experience includes both a *perceived vastness* (whether of power or magnitude) and a *need for accommodation,* which is an "inability to assimilate an experience into current mental structures" (p. 304). Variation in the valence of an awe experience is due to whether the stimulus is appraised in terms of beauty, exceptional ability, virtue, perceived threat, or supernatural origin. In contrast, those experiences that do not include both perceived vastness and a need for accommodation are not occurrences of awe, but are simply members of the awe family. For example, "surprise" involves accommodation without vastness. Feelings of deference involve vastness without accommodation. Keltner and Haidt (2003) conceive of awe as a virtue or human strength, the "ability to find, recognize and take pleasure in the existence of goodness in the physical and social worlds. . . . A person low on this strength goes about daily life as if wearing blinders to that which is beautiful and moving." This strength is labeled "Awe/Responsiveness to Beauty and Excellence" (Awe/RBE) in the VIA taxonomy of human strengths (Peterson & Seligman, 2004). Awe/RBE is not marked by clearly observable action tendencies, but it may be associated with expressions similar to those for surprise, with physiological symptoms, such as goosebumps, and with motivation for the improvement of self and society. Unfortunately, there is little empirical research on human response to beauty, and until this changes anything we say about Awe/RBE remains largely speculative.

As the study of awe is still in its early stages, future research should begin with the prototype approach to awe offered by Keltner and Haidt (2003) and the definition of reverence offered by philosophers and theologians (Roberts, 2003; Woodruff, 2001) and develop tests to measure individual differences in these experiences. Once a reliable measure of awe and reverence exists, individual differences in these experiences can be explored, as well as their relation to religion and spirituality, their developmental antecedents, and their relationship to emotional and physical well-being.

Wonder

Wonder is another emotion with a significant spiritual thrust that has received scant empirical attention by psychologists. Bulkeley (2002) defined *wonder* as "the emotion excited by an encounter with something novel and unexpected, something that strikes a person as intensely powerful, real, true, and/or beautiful" (p. 6). Experiences of wonder are a significant feature of many of the world's religious, spiritual, and philosophical traditions (Bulkeley, 2002). Brand (2001) provided a phenomenological account of "wonder-joy": profound and deeply moving experiences of positive emotions where there is a co-occurrence of feelings of wonder, joy, gratitude, awe, yearning, poignancy, intensity, love, and compassion. Wonder is an opening up of the heart to the persons or profound circumstances being witnessed and is triggered by a variety of circumstances (Brand, 2001). Bulkeley (2002) proposed that the experience of wonder involves a twofold process of (1) a sudden decentering of the self when faced with something novel and unexpectedly powerful, followed by (2) an ultimate recentering of the self in response to new knowledge and understanding. It is evident that the wonder that Bulkeley describes and the sense of awe described by Haidt and Keltner have much in common; it will be up to future research to establish the unique properties of these overlapping states.

Forgiveness

Forgiveness is not an emotion per se, but can be thought of as a spiritual process that has emotion-regulating properties. Forgiveness, when successfully executed, can reduce negative emotions, such as anger, resentment, and grief (Coyle & Enright, 1997).

There have been a handful of studies that have been explicitly designed to examine the impact of forgiveness on the remediation of negative emotions. Witvliet and her colleagues (Witvliet, Ludwig, & Bauer, 2002; Witvliet, Ludwig, & Vander Laan, 2001) have examined subjective emotions and emotional physiology during forgiving and unforgiving imagery. In their initial study, Witvliet et al. (2001) found that when participants visualized forgiving responses toward people who had offended them, they experienced significantly less anger, sadness, and overall negative arousal compared to when they rehearsed the offense or maintained a grudge. Paralleling the self-reports were greater sympathetic nervous system (SNS) arousal (skin conductance and blood pressure increases) and facial tension during unforgiving imagery. A follow-up study examined the emotions of transgressors (Witvliet et al., 2002). When transgressors imagined seeking forgiveness from their victims, the transgressors reported lower levels of sadness, anger, and guilt and higher levels of hope and gratitude if they imagined the victim genuinely forgiving them. Imagining reconciliation rather than forgiveness led to a similar reduction in negative (anger, sadness, guilt) emotions and increases in positive (gratitude, hope, empathy) emotions.

Forgiveness interventions have also been shown to be successful in alleviating depression, anxiety, and grief in post-abortion men (Coyle & Enright, 1997) and depression and anxiety in incest survivors (Freedman, 1999). In the latter study, the intervention group also showed significant gains in overall levels of hopefulness, suggesting, as did the work of Witvliet and colleagues, that forgiveness is involved in facilitating positive emotions as well as in reducing negative emotions. The ability of forgiveness interventions to increase certain positive emotions is one of the more surprising findings in the research literature on forgiveness to date.

In one of the few cultural studies on forgiveness, Huang and Enright (2000) examined forgiveness and anger in a Taiwanese sample. Adults recalled an incident of deep, interpersonal hurt, and their affective state was recorded both during and after recall. The researchers found that when participants granted forgiveness unconditionally out of a sense of compassion, self-reported levels of anger were lower than when they forgave out of a sense of duty or obligation. Thus, the effectiveness *of* forgiveness to reduce negative emotions is contingent upon the motivation *for* forgiveness.

Mindfulness

In addition to forgiveness, another spiritually based emotional-management strategy is mindfulness meditation. A number of philosophical, psychological, and spiritual traditions, both Eastern and Western, highlight the importance of mindfulness. *Mindfulness* is an enhanced attention to and awareness of the present and is currently the subject of innumerable books, seminars, and workshops designed to facilitate this quality of consciousness as a means to helping people live more authentic, happier lives.

Brown and Ryan (2003) developed a self-report instrument called the Mindful Attention Awareness Scale (MAAS) to measure mindfulness and administered it to subjects ranging from college students to working adults to Zen meditators to cancer patients. In mindfulness, which Brown and Ryan (2003) showed is a unique quality of consciousness, two experiences work in tandem: attending to present, ongoing events and experiences while allowing new events and experiences to come into awareness. In their research, Brown and colleagues have found that more mindful individuals, as measured by the MAAS, have a greater self-regulatory capacity and higher levels of well-being. Those who are more mindful are more attuned to their emotions, as reflected in a higher concordance between their explicit, or self-attributed, emotional states and implicit, or nonconscious, emotions. Because implicit measures are not susceptible to conscious control and manipulation, this suggests that more mindful individuals are more attuned to their implicit emotions and reflect that knowledge in their explicit, affective self-descriptions. This is consistent with the theory that posits that present-centered awareness and attention facilitates self-knowledge, a crucial element of integrated functioning.

A number of studies have shown that mindfulness has direct relations to well-being outcomes as well. For example, Brown and Ryan (2003; Study 1) reported that, like other personal qualities, mindfulness can be cultivated and enhanced or neglected and allowed to diminish. Brown and Ryan (2003; Study 2) showed that people who actively cultivated a heightened attention to and awareness of what's taking place in the present moment through meditative practices had higher levels of mindfulness. And in a clinical study with early-stage cancer patients who received training in mindfulness as the central element of an 8-week stress-reduction program (Brown & Ryan, 2003; Study 5), those individuals who showed greater increases in mindfulness, as assessed by the MAAS, showed greater declines in mood disturbance and stress.

Conclusion

A distinguished clinical psychologist wrote, "If we omit spiritual realities from our account of human behavior, it won't matter much what we keep in, because we will have omitted the most fundamental aspect of human behavior" (Bergin, 1997, p. xi). Understanding people requires taking their spiritual lives seriously. Taking spirituality seriously means that we develop ways to measure and research it in its diverse manifestations and contexts. Great strides have been made in the scientific study of spirituality, and I have tried to convey some of this progress in this chapter. Yet much work remains to be done before spirituality will be fully integrated into our models of positive human functioning.

References and Suggested Readings

Allport, G. W., Gillespie, J. M., & Young, J. (1948). The religion of the post-war college student. *Journal of Psychology, 25,* 3–33.

Andresen, J. (Ed.). (2001). *Religion in mind: Cognitive perspectives on religious belief, ritual, and experience.* Cambridge: Cambridge University Press.

Baer, R. A. (2003). Mindfulness training as a clinical intervention: A conceptual and empirical review. *Clinical Psychology: Science and Practice, 10,* 125–143.

Beck, C. (1986). Educating for spirituality. *Interchange, 17,* 148–156.

Bergin, A. E. (1997). Preface. In P. S. Richards and A. E. Bergin (Eds.), *A spiritual strategy for counseling and psychotherapy.* Washington, DC: American Psychological Association.

Berry, J. W., & Worthington, E. L., Jr. (2001). Forgivingness, relationship quality, stress while imagining relationship events, and physical and mental health. *Journal of Counseling Psychology, 48,* 447–455.

Berry, J. W., Worthington, E. L., Jr., Parrott, L., III, O'Connor, L. E., & Wade, N. G. (2001). Dispositional forgivingness: Development and construct validity of the Transgression Narrative Test of Forgivingness (TNTF). *Personality & Social Psychology Bulletin, 27,* 1277–1290.

Brand, W. (2001). Experiencing tears of wonder-joy: Seeing with the heart's eye. *Journal of Transpersonal Psychology, 33,* 99–111.

Bregman, L., & Thierman, S. (1995). *First person mortal: Personal narratives of ill-ness, dying, and grief.* New York: Paragon.

Brown, K. W., & Ryan, R. M. (2003). The benefits of being present: Mindfulness and its role in psychological well-being. *Journal of Personality and Social Psychology, 84,* 822–848.

Bulkeley, K. (2002, November). *The evolution of wonder: Religious and neuroscientific perspectives.* Paper presented at the annual meeting of the American Academy of Religion, Toronto, Canada.

Carlson, D., Erikson, M. J., & Seewald-Marquardt, A. (2003). The spiritualities of therapists' lives: Using therapists' spiritual beliefs as a resource for relational ethics. *Journal of Family Psychotherapy, 13,* 215–236.

Coyle, C. T., & Enright, R. D. (1997). Forgiveness intervention with post-abortion men. *Journal of Consulting & Clinical Psychology, 65,* 1042–1046.

Dollahite, D. C. (1998). Fathering, faith, and spirituality. *Journal of Men's Studies, 7,* 3–15.

Eliade, M. (1959). *The sacred and the profane: The nature of religion.* New York: Harper & Row.

Elkins, D. N. (1988). Towards a humanistic-phenomenological spirituality: Defini-tion, description, and measurement. *Journal of Humanistic Psychology, 28,* 5–18.

Elkins, D. N. (2001). Beyond religion: Toward a humanistic spirituality. In K. J. Schneider, J. T. Bugental, & J. F. Pierson (Eds.), *The handbook of humanistic psy-chology: Leading edges in theory, research,and practice* (pp. 201–212). Thousand Oaks, CA: Sage.

Emmons, R. A. (1999). *The psychology of ultimate concerns.* New York: Guilford.

Emmons, R. A., Cheung, C., & Tehrani, K. (1998). Assessing spirituality through personal goals: Implications for research on religion and subjective well-being. *Social Indicators Research, 45,* 391–422.

Emmons, R. A., Colby, P. M., & Kaiser, H. A. (1998). When losses lead to gains: Personal goals and the recovery of meaning. In P. T. P. Wong & P. S. Fry (Eds.), *The human quest for meaning* (pp. 163–178). Mahwah, NJ: Erlbaum.

Ferriss, A. L. (2002). Religion and the quality of life. *Journal of Happiness Studies, 3,* 199–215.

Freedman, S. (1999). A voice of forgiveness: One incest survivor's experience for-giving her father. *Journal of Family Psychotherapy, 10,* 37–60.

Gillani, N. B., & Smith, J. C. (2001). Zen meditation and ABC relaxation theory: An exploration of relaxation states, beliefs, dispositions, and motivations. *Journal of Clinical Psychology, 57,* 839–846.

Goodenough, U. (1998). *The sacred depths of nature.* New York: Oxford University Press.

Hackney, C. H., & Sanders, G. S. (2003). Religiosity and mental health: A meta-analysis of recent studies. *Journal for the Scientific Study of Religion, 42,* 43–55.

Hardy, A. (1979). *The spiritual nature of man: A study of contemporary religious expe-rience.* Oxford: Clarendon.

Hill, P. C. (1999). Giving religion away: What the study of religion offers psychol-ogy. *International Journal for the Psychology of Religion, 9,* 229–249.

Hill, P.C., & Hood, R. W., Jr. (1999). *Measures of religiosity.* Birmingham, AL: Religious Education Press.

Hill, P. C., Pargament, K. I., Wood, R. W., Jr., McCullough, M. E., Swyers, J. P., Larson, D. B., & Zinnbauer, B. J. (2000). Conceptualizing religion and spirituality: Points of commonality, points of departure. *Journal for the Theory of Social Behavior, 30,* 51–77.

Hood, R., Jr. (1975). The construction and preliminary validation of a measure of mystical experience. *Journal for the Scientific Study of Religion, 14,* 29–41.

Huang, S., & Enright, R. D. (2000). Forgiveness and anger-related emotions in Taiwan: Implications for therapy. *Psychotherapy: Theory, Research, Practice, Training, 37,* 71–79.

Jernigan, H. L. (2001). Spirituality in older adults: A cross-cultural and interfaith perspective. *Pastoral Psychology, 49,* 413–437.

Jianbin, X., & Mehta, K. K. (2003). The effects of religion on subjective aging in Singapore: An interreligious comparison. *Journal of Aging Studies, 17,* 485–502.

Karoly, P. (1999). A goal systems perspective on personality, psychopathology, and change. *Review of General Psychology, 3,* 264–291

Kelly, E. W., Jr. (1995). *Spirituality and religion in counseling and psychotherapy.* Alexandria, VA: American Counseling Association.

Keltner, D., & Haidt, J. (2003). Approaching awe: A moral, spiritual, and aesthetic emotion. *Cognition and Emotion, 17,* 297–314.

Kim, A. E. (2003). Religious influences on personal and societal well-being. *Social Indicators Research, 63,* 149–170.

Koenig, H. K., McCullough, M. E., & Larson, D., (Eds.). (2001). *Handbook of religion and health.* New York: Oxford University Press.

Mahoney, A., & Pargament, K. I. (in press). A higher purpose: The sanctification of personal strivings. *International Journal for the Psychology of Religion.*

Mahoney, A., Pargament, K. I., Jewell, T., Swank, A. B., Scott, E., Emery, E., & Rye, M. (1999). Marriage and the spiritual realm: The role of proximal and distal religious constructs in marital functioning. *Journal of Family Psychology, 13,* 321–338.

Marler, P. L., & Hadaway, C. K. (2002). "Being religious" or "being spiritual" in America: A zero-sum proposition? *Journal for the Scientific Study of Religion, 41,* 289–300.

Maslow, A. H. (1964). *Religions, values, and peak experiences.* New York: Penguin.

Mattis, J. S., Hearn, K. D., & Jagers, R. J. (2002). A relational framework for the study of religiosity and spirituality in the lives of African Americans. *Journal of Black Psychology, 28,* 197–214.

McCullough, M. E. (2001). Forgiveness: Who does it and how do they do it? *American Psychological Society, 10,* 194–197.

McCullough, M. E., Emmons, R. A., & Tsang, J. (2002). The grateful disposition: A conceptual and empirical topography. *Journal of Personality & Social Psychology, 82,* 112–127.

McCullough, M. E., Kilpatrick, S. D., Emmons, R. A., & Larson, D. B. (2001). Is gratitude a moral affect? *Psychological Bulletin, 127,* 249–266.

McCullough, M. E., Pargament, K. I., & Thoresen, C. E. (Eds.). (2000). *Forgiveness: Theory, practice and research.* New York: Guilford.

McCullough, M. E., & Worthington, E. L., Jr. (1999). Religion and the forgiving personality. *Journal of Personality, 67,* 1141–1164.

McCullough, M. E., Worthington, E. L., Jr., & Rachal, K. C. (1997). Interpersonal forgiving in close relationships. *Journal of Personality & Social Psychology, 73,* 321–336.

Miller, W. R. (Ed.). (1999). *Integrating spirituality into treatment: Resources for practitioners.* Washington, DC: American Psychological Association.

Otto, R. (1958). *The idea of the holy* (J. W. Harvey, Trans.). Oxford: Oxford University Press. (Original work published 1917)

Oxford English Dictionary. (1989). New York: Oxford University Press.

Pargament, K. I. (1997). *The psychology of religion and coping.* New York: Guilford.

Pargament, K. I. (1999). The psychology of religion *and* spirituality? Yes and no. *International Journal for the Psychology of Religion, 9,* 3–16.

Pargament, K. I. (2002). The bitter and the sweet: An evaluation of the costs and benefits of religiousness. *Psychological Inquiry, 13,* 168–181.

Pargament, K. I., & Park, C. L. (1995). Merely a defense? The variety of religious means and ends. *Journal of Social Issues, 51,* 13–32.

Park, Y. O., & Enright, R. D. (1997). The development of forgiveness in the context of adolescent friendship conflict in Korea. *Journal of Adolescence, 20,* 393–402.

Peterson, C. M., & Seligman, M. E. P. (Eds.) (2004). *Character strengths and virtues: A handbook and classification.* New York: Oxford University Press.

Piedmont, R. L. (1999). Does spirituality represent the sixth factor of personality? Spiritual transcendence and the five-factor model. *Journal of Personality, 67,* 985–1014.

Piedmont, R. L., & Leach, M. M. (2003). Cross-cultural generalizability of the spiritual transcendence scale in India: Spirituality as a universal aspect of human experience. *American Behavioral Scientist, 45,* 1888–1901.

Řičan, P. (2003). Spirituality in psychology: The concept and its context. *Studia Psychologica, 45,* 249–257.

Richards, P. S., & Bergin, A. E. (1997). *A spiritual strategy for counseling and psychotherapy.* Washington, DC: American Psychological Association.

Roberts, R. C. (2003). *Emotions: An essay in aid of moral psychology.* New York: Cambridge University Press.

Seidlitz, L., & Abernethy, A. D. (2002). Development of the spiritual transcendence index. *Journal for the Scientific Study of Religion, 41,* 439–453.

Seligman, M. E. P., & Csikszentmihalyi, M. (2000). Positive psychology: An introduction. *American Psychologist, 55,* 5–14.

Smith, C. (2003). *Moral, believing animals: Human personhood and culture.* New York: Oxford University Press.

Smith, T. B., McCullough, M. E., & Poll, J. (2003). Religiousness and depression: Evidence for a main effect and the moderating influence of stressful life events. *Psychological Bulletin, 129,* 614–636.

Solomon, R. D. (2002). *Spirituality for the skeptic.* New York: Oxford University Press.

Spilka, B., Hunsberger, B., Gorsuch, R., Jr., & Hood, R. W. (2003). *The psychology of religion: A empirical approach* (3rd ed.). New York: Guilford.

Stifoss-Hanssen, H. (1999). Religion and spirituality: What a European ear hears. *International Journal for the Psychology of Religion, 9,* 25–33.

Streng, F. J. (1989). Introduction: Thanksgiving as a worldwide response to life. In J. B. Carman & F. J. Streng (Eds.), *Spoken and unspoken thanks: Some comparative soundings* (pp. 1–9). Dallas, TX: Center for World Thanksgiving.

Tarakeshwar, N., Pargament, K. I., & Stanton, J. (2003). Initial development of a measure of religious coping among Hindus. *Journal of Community Psychology, 31,* 607–628.

Tarakeshwar, N., Stanton, J., & Pargament, K. I. (2003). Religion: An overlooked dimension in cross-cultural psychology. *Journal of Cross-Cultural Psychology, 34,* 377–394.

Tarakeshwar, N., Swank, A. B., Pargament, K. I., & Mahoney, A. (2002). Theological conservatism and the sanctification of nature: A study of opposing religious correlates of environmentalism. *Review of Religious Research 42,* 387–404.

Watkins, P. C., Woodward, K., Stone, T., & Kolts, R. L. (2003). Gratitude and happiness: Development of a measure of gratitude and relationships with subjective well-being. *Social Behavior & Personality, 31*(5), 431–452.

Wettstein, H. (1997). Awe and the religious life. *Judaism: A Quarterly Journal of Jewish Life and Thought, 46,* 387–407.

Witvliet, C. V., Ludwig, T. E., & Bauer, D. J. (2002). Please forgive me: Transgressors' emotions and physiology during imagery of seeking forgiveness and victim responses. *Journal of Psychology and Christianity, 21,* 219–233.

Witvliet, C. V., Ludwig, T. E., & Vander Laan, K. L. (2001). Granting forgiveness or harboring grudges: Implications for emotion, physiology, and health. *Psychological Science, 12,* 117–123.

Wong, P. T. P. (1998). Meaning-centered counseling. In P. T. P. Wong & P. S. Fry (Eds.), *The human quest for meaning* (pp. 395–435). Mahwah, NJ: Erlbaum.

Woodruff, P. (2001). *Reverence: Renewing a forgotten virtue.* New York: Oxford University Press.

Worthington, E. L., Jr. (2003). The Religious Commitment Inventory: 10: Development, refinement, and validation of a brief scale for research and counseling. *Journal of Counseling Psychology, 50*(1), 84–96.

Wulff, D. (1997). *Psychology of religion: Classical and contemporary* (2nd ed.). New York: Wiley.

Wuthnow, R. (1998). *After heaven: Spirituality in America since the 1950's.* Berkeley: University of California Press.

Zinnbauer, B. J., Pargament, K. I., Cole, B., & Rye, M. S. (1997). Religion and spirituality: Unfuzzying the fuzzy. *Journal for the Scientific Study of Religion, 36,* 549–564.

Zinnbauer, B. J., Pargament, K. I., & Scott, A. B. (1999). The emerging meanings of religiousness and spirituality: Problems and prospects. *Journal of Personality, 67,* 889–920.

PART II

POSITIVE EXPERIENCES

The three chapters that comprise this section focus on the momentary aspects of positive experiences. This is only a relative distinction, however, because practically all of the authors represented in this book are aware that transient emotions and long-term effects are organically related: It is unlikely that a person who has felt happy throughout life is going to be dissatisfied or depressed at its end. This organic relationship between the immediate and the lasting is well illustrated in the work of Barbara Fredrickson, whose broaden-and-build theory of positive emotions has become one of the central conceptual achievements from the first years of positive psychology.

Fredrickson started with a simple but fundamental question: Why do positive emotions exist? It is clear why we should experience negative emotions: Fear, anger, and even envy help an organism survive in competitive and dangerous environments, and thus one would expect them to be selected through evolution as useful behavioral tools. But what's the good of positive emotions like joy or satisfaction?

Based on previous work, especially that of A. M. Isen, and on her own extensive line of experiments, Fredrickson concluded that feeling joy or contentment broadens a person's mindset, making novel responses more likely; at the same time, positive emotions build resilience for confronting challenges in the future. Particularly impressive in this respect is the "undo" effect that positive experiences appear to have, promoting cardiovascular recovery after stressful stimulation. The previous understanding assumed that positive emotions were simply signals about the positive state of the organism. If this is all there was to it, positive emotions would make at best a small contribution to well-being. The broaden-and-build theory claims that positive emotions are not just reflections of optimal functioning, but that they actively *produce* it—thus establishing a strong rationale for the importance of studying positive emotions.

Another well-known construct that has important implications for positive psychology is that of emotional intelligence, or EI. In their chapter, Daisy Grewal and Peter Salovey describe how the concept originated and how it is measured, and then they give a brief survey of the research dealing with EI, namely, the ability to understand one's own feelings and that of others. The benefits reported are mainly of three kinds: EI facilitates thought (as Antony Damasio and other neurologists are beginning to demonstrate, emotion often helps reason, rather than conflicting with it); second, it improves the quality of experience; and third, it leads to more positive actions. Youth with high EI are not only less anxious or depressed, but they engage in less risky behaviors, have more friends, and enjoy greater social support.

From the very beginning, positive psychology was as concerned with building a *domain,* or body of knowledge, as it was with building a *field,* or a body of practitioners who could make a decent living from the applications of the new knowledge. The chapter by Jane Henry points to the potential contributions of positive psychology to new forms of therapy and to the formation of new cadres of therapists. The growth of clinical psychology has had the unfortunate consequence of extending the pathological perspective to cover "normal" behavior: Job performance, family interactions, and life stages, such as adolescence and old age, tend to be described with vocabulary and with concepts borrowed from the study of mental illness. After reviewing the hundreds of extant therapies in terms of five main types, Henry concludes that most of them are variations on the "talking cure" ushered in by Freud.

Positive psychology suggests a different approach, based not on introspection and dialogue, but on *constructive action.* Helping patients to change the quality of their experiences by changing activities and life patterns; by modeling positive behaviors and successful outcomes—these are the directions that Henry sees therapy taking in the future. Instead of asking the patient to focus inward on the sources of conflict and pain, therapy should help to redirect attention toward challenging tasks that might ignite the patient's autonomous strivings. Such a sea change in the practice of therapy is not only indicated on theoretical grounds, but as Henry suggests, it seems to be preferred by the population served by clinicians.

It is instructive to compare the four more-theoretical chapters of part I with the more research-based chapters in the present section. Although the terms and the concepts often do not map on each other, there is a great deal of agreement about what are the important phenomena with which positive psychology deals and on how they connect with human well-being. For instance, both the broaden-and-build and EI theories could be recast in terms of the grander theories concerning the emancipation of consciousness common to the first four chapters. In all of these perspectives, what counts is people's ability to take charge of their psychic energy, instead of letting it be ruled by instincts or conventions. Personal autonomy while connected to a meaningful social context is the common subtext of these chapters—and Jane Henry builds on this consensus to derive her therapeutic implications.

5

The Broaden-and-Build Theory
of Positive Emotions

BARBARA L. FREDRICKSON

At first blush, it might appear that positive emotions are important to positive psychology simply because positive emotions are markers of optimal well-being. Certainly, moments in people's lives characterized by experiences of positive emotions—such as joy, interest, contentment, love, and the like—are moments in which they are not plagued by negative emotions, such as anxiety, sadness, anger, and the like. Consistent with this intuition, the overall balance of people's positive to negative emotions has been shown to contribute to their subjective well-being (Diener, Sandvik, & Pavot, 1991). In this sense, positive emotions signal optimal functioning. But this is far from their whole story. I argue that positive emotions also produce optimal functioning, not just within the present, pleasant moment, but over the long term as well. The bottom-line message is that people should cultivate positive emotions in themselves and in those around them not just as end-states in themselves, but also as means to achieving psychological growth and improved psychological and physical well-being over time.

History of Positive Emotions Research

This view of positive emotions represents a significant departure from traditional approaches to the study of positive emotions. In this section, I provide a brief, selective review of the history of research on positive emotions.

Neglected Relative to Negative Emotions

Relative to the negative emotions, positive emotions have received little empirical attention. There are several, interrelated reasons for this. One reason, which has plagued psychology more generally (Seligman & Csikszentmihalyi, 2000), is the traditional focus on psychological problems alongside remedies for those problems. Negative emotions—when extreme, prolonged, or contextually inappropriate—produce many grave problems for individuals and society, ranging from phobias and anxiety disorders, aggression and violence, depression and suicide, eating disorders and sexual dysfunctions, to a host of stress-related physical disorders. Although positive emotions do at times pose problems (e.g., mania, drug addiction), these problems have often assumed lower priority among psychologists and emotion researchers. So, due in part to their association with problems and dangers, negative emotions have captured the majority of research attention.

Another reason that positive emotions have been sidelined is the habit among emotion theorists of creating models of emotions in general. Such models are typically built to the specifications of those attention-grabbing negative emotions (e.g., fear and anger), with positive emotions squeezed in later, often seemingly as an afterthought. For instance, key to many theorists' models of emotion is the idea that emotions are, by definition, associated with specific action tendencies (Frijda, 1986; Frijda, Kuipers, & Schure, 1989; Lazarus, 1991; Levenson, 1994; Oatley & Jenkins, 1996; Tooby & Cosmides, 1990). Fear, for example, is linked with the urge to escape, anger with the urge to attack, disgust with the urge to expel, and so on. No theorist argues that people invariably act out these urges when feeling particular emotions. But rather, people's ideas about possible courses of action narrow in on a specific set of behavioral options. A key idea in these models is that having a specific action tendency come to mind is what made an emotion evolutionarily adaptive: These were among the actions that worked best in getting our ancestors out of life-or-death situations. Another key idea is that specific action tendencies and physiological changes go hand in hand. So, for example, when you have an urge to escape when feeling fear, your body reacts by mobilizing the appropriate autonomic support for the possibility of running by redirecting blood flow to large muscle groups.

Although specific action tendencies have been invoked to describe the form and function of positive emotions as well, the action tendencies identified for positive emotions are notably vague and underspecified (Fredrickson & Levenson, 1998). Joy, for instance, is linked with aimless activation, interest with attending, and contentment with inactivity (Frijda, 1986). These tendencies are far too general to be called specific (Fredrickson, 1998). Although a few theorists earlier noted that fitting positive emotions into emotion-general models posed problems (Ekman, 1992; Lazarus, 1991), this acknowledgment was not accompanied by any new or revised models to better accommodate the positive emotions. Instead, the difficulties inherent in "shoehorning" the positive emotions into emotion-general models merely tended to marginalize them further. Many theorists, for instance, minimized challenges to their models by maintaining their focus on negative emotions, paying little or no attention to positive emotions.

Confused With Related Affective States

Perhaps because they have received less direct scrutiny, the distinctions among positive emotions and other, closely related affective states, such as sensory pleasure and positive mood, have often been blurred, instead of sharpened. Although working definitions of emotions vary somewhat across researchers, consensus is emerging that emotions (both positive and negative) are best conceptualized as multicomponent response tendencies that unfold over relatively short time spans. Typically, emotions begin with an individual's assessment of the personal meaning of some antecedent event—what Lazarus (1991) called the *person-environment relationship*, or *adaptational encounter*. Either conscious or unconscious, this appraisal process triggers a cascade of response tendencies that manifest across loosely coupled component systems, such as subjective experience, facial expressions, and physiological changes.

Sometimes, various forms of sensory pleasure (e.g., sexual gratification, satiation of hunger or thirst) are taken to be positive emotions because they share with positive emotions a pleasant subjective feel and include physiological changes and because sensory pleasure and positive emotions often co-occur (e.g., sexual gratification within a loving relationship). Yet emotions differ from physical sensations in that emotions typically require cognitive appraisals or meaning assessments to be initiated. In contrast to positive emotions, pleasure can be caused simply by changing the immediate physical environment (e.g., eating or otherwise stimulating the body). Moreover, whereas pleasure depends heavily on bodily stimulation, positive emotions more often occur in the absence of external physical sensation (e.g., joy at receiving good news or interest in a new idea). Pleasurable sensations, then, are best considered automatic responses to fulfilling bodily needs. In fact, Cabanac (1971) suggested that people experience sensory pleasure with any external stimulus that "corrects an internal trouble." A cool bath, for instance, is only pleasant to someone who is overheated (who thus needs to be cooled). Likewise, food is pleasant to the hungry person, but becomes less pleasant—even unpleasant—as that person becomes satiated.

Positive emotions are also often confused with positive moods. Yet emotions differ from moods in that emotions are about some personally meaningful circumstance (i.e., they have an object), are typically short-lived, and occupy the foreground of consciousness. In contrast, moods are typically free-floating or objectless, more long-lasting, and occupy the background of consciousness (Oatley & Jenkins, 1996; Rosenberg, 1998). These distinctions between emotions and moods, however, are guarded more at theoretical than empirical levels. In research practice, virtually identical techniques are used for inducing positive moods and positive emotions (e.g., giving gifts, viewing comedies).

Functions Linked to Urges
to Approach or Continue

Most commonly, the function of all positive emotions has been identified as facilitating approach behavior (Cacioppo, Priester, & Berntson, 1993; Davidson, 1993; Frijda, 1994) or continued action (Carver & Scheier, 1990; Clore, 1994). From this perspective, experiences of positive emotions prompt individuals to engage with their environments and partake in activities, many of which were evolutionarily adaptive for the individual, its species, or both. This link between positive emotions and activity engagement provides an explanation for the often-documented positivity offset, or the tendency for individuals to experience mild positive affect frequently, even in neutral contexts (Cacioppo, Gardner, & Berntson, 1999; Diener & Diener, 1996). Without such an offset, individuals would most often be unmotivated to engage with their environments. Yet, with such an offset, individuals exhibit the adaptive bias to approach and explore novel objects, people, or situations.

Although positive emotions do often appear to function as internal signals to approach or continue, they share this function with other positive affective states as well. Sensory pleasure, for instance, motivates people to approach and continue consuming whatever stimulus is biologically useful for them at the moment (Cabanac, 1971). Likewise, free-floating positive moods motivate people to continue along any line of thinking or action that they have initiated (Clore, 1994). As such, functional accounts of positive emotions that emphasize tendencies to approach or continue may only capture the lowest common denominator across all affective states that share a pleasant subjective feel. This traditional approach leaves additional functions that are unique to positive emotions uncharted.

A New Theory for Positive Emotions

Traditional approaches to the study of emotions have tended to ignore positive emotions, squeeze them into purportedly emotion-general models, confuse them with closely related affective states, and describe their function in terms of generic tendencies to approach or continue. Sensing that these approaches did not do justice to positive emotions, I developed an alternative model for positive emotions that better captures their unique effects. I call this the broaden-and-build theory of positive emotions because positive emotions appear to broaden people's momentary thought-action repertoires and build their enduring personal resources (Fredrickson, 1998, 2001).

I contrast this new model to traditional models based on specific action tendencies. Specific action tendencies work well to describe the form and function of negative emotions and should be retained for models of this subset of emotions. Without loss of theoretical nuance, a specific action tendency can be redescribed as the outcome of a psychological process that narrows a person's momentary thought-action repertoire by calling to mind an urge to act in a particular way (e.g., escape, attack, expel). In a life-threatening situation, a narrowed thought-action repertoire promotes quick and decisive action that carries direct and immediate benefit: Specific action tendencies called forth by negative emotions represent the sort of actions that worked best to save our ancestors' lives and limbs in similar situations.

Yet positive emotions seldom occur in life-threatening situations. As such, a psychological process that narrows a person's momentary thought-action repertoire to promote quick and decisive action may not be needed. Instead, positive emotions have a complementary effect: Relative to neutral states and routine action, positive emotions broaden people's momentary thought-action repertoires, widening the array of the thoughts and actions that come to mind. Joy, for instance, creates the urge to play, push the limits, and be creative, urges evident not only in social and physical behavior, but also in intellectual and artistic behavior. Interest, a phenomenologically distinct positive emotion, creates the urge to explore, take in new information and experiences, and expand the self in the process. Contentment, a third distinct positive emotion, creates the urge to sit back and savor current life circumstances and to integrate these circumstances into new views of self and of the world. And love—viewed as an amalgam of distinct positive emotions (e.g., joy, interest, and contentment) experienced within contexts of safe, close relationships—creates recurring cycles of urges to play with, explore, and savor our loved ones. These various thought-action tendencies—to play, to explore, or to savor and integrate—each represent ways that positive emotions broaden habitual modes of thinking or acting. (For descriptions of pride and elevation from the perspective of the broaden-and-build theory, see Fredrickson & Branigan, 2001; for a description of gratitude, see Fredrickson, 2004.)

In contrast to negative emotions, which carry direct and immediate adaptive benefits in situations that threaten survival, the broadened thought-action repertoires triggered by positive emotions are beneficial in other ways. Specifically, broadened mindsets carry indirect and long-term adaptive benefits because broadening builds enduring personal resources.

Take play as an example. Specific forms of chasing play evident in juveniles of a species—like running up a flexible sapling or branch and catapulting in an unexpected direction—are reenacted in adults of that species exclusively during predator avoidance (Dolhinow, 1987). Such correspondences between juvenile play maneuvers and adult survival maneuvers suggest that juvenile play builds enduring physical resources (Boulton & Smith, 1992; Caro, 1988).

Play also builds enduring social resources: Social play, with its shared amusement and smiles, builds lasting social bonds and attachments (Aron, Norman, Aron, McKenna, & Heyman, 2000; Lee, 1983; Simons, McCluskey-Fawcett, & Papini, 1986), which can become the locus of subsequent social support. Childhood play also builds enduring intellectual resources by increasing creativity (Sherrod & Singer, 1989), creating theory of mind (Leslie, 1987), and fueling brain development (Panksepp, 1998). Similarly, the exploration prompted by the positive emotion of interest creates knowledge and intellectual complexity, and the savoring prompted by contentment produces self-insight and alters world views. So each of these phenomenologically distinct positive emotions shares the feature of augmenting an individual's personal resources, ranging from physical and social resources to intellectual and psychological resources (see Fredrickson, 1998, 2001; Fredrickson & Branigan, 2001, for more detailed reviews).

Importantly, the personal resources accrued during states of positive emotions are durable. They outlast the transient emotional states that led to their acquisition. By consequence, then, the often incidental effect of experiencing a positive emotion is an increase in one's personal resources. These resources can be drawn on in subsequent moments and in different emotional states. Through experiences of positive emotions, then, people transform themselves, becoming more creative, knowledgeable, resilient, socially integrated, and healthy individuals.

In short, the broaden-and-build theory describes the form of positive emotions in terms of broadened thought-action repertoires and describes their function in terms of building enduring personal resources. In doing so, the theory provides a new perspective on the evolved adaptive significance of positive emotions. Those of our ancestors who succumbed to the urges sparked by positive emotions—to play, explore, and so on—would have by consequence accrued more personal resources. When these same ancestors later faced inevitable threats to life and limb, their greater personal resources would have translated into greater odds of survival and, in turn, into greater odds of living long enough to reproduce. To the extent then, that the capacity to experience positive emotions is genetically encoded, this capacity, through the process of natural selection, would have become part of our universal human nature.

Summary of Current Research Findings

Empirical support for several key propositions of the broaden-and-build theory can be drawn from multiple subdisciplines within psychology, ranging from work on cognition and intrinsic motivation to attachment styles and animal behavior (for a review, see Fredrickson, 1998). This evidence suggests that positive emotions broaden the scopes of attention, cognition, and action and that they build physical, intellectual, and social resources. Yet, much of this evidence, because it pre-dated the broaden-and-build theory, provides only indirect support for the model. Here I will briefly describe recent direct tests of hypotheses drawn from the broaden-and-build theory.

Positive Emotions Broaden
Thought-Action Repertoires

Foundational evidence for the proposition that positive emotions broaden people's momentary thought-action repertoires comes from two decades of experiments conducted by Isen and colleagues (for a review, see Isen, 2000). They have documented that people experiencing positive affect show patterns of thought that are notably unusual (Isen, Johnson, Mertz, & Robinson, 1985), flexible (Isen & Daubman, 1984), creative (Isen, Daubman, & Nowicki, 1987), integrative (Isen, Rosenzweig, & Young, 1991), open to information (Estrada, Isen, & Young, 1997), and efficient (Isen & Means, 1983; Isen et al., 1991). They have also shown that those experiencing positive affect show increased preference for variety and accept a broader array of behavioral options (Kahn & Isen, 1993). In general terms, Isen has suggested that positive affect produces a "broad, flexible cognitive organization and ability to integrate diverse material" (Isen, 1990, p. 89), effects linked to increases in brain dopamine levels (Ashby, Isen, & Turken, 1999). So although Isen's work does not target specific positive emotions or thought-action tendencies per se, it provides the strongest evidence that positive affect broadens cognition. And whereas negative emotions have long been known to narrow people's attention, making them miss the forest for the trees (or the suspect's style of dress for the gun), more recent work suggests that positive affect also expands attention (Derryberry & Tucker, 1994). The evidence comes from studies that use global-local visual-processing paradigms to assess biases in attentional focus. Negative states, like anxiety, depression, and failure, predict local biases consistent with narrowed attention, whereas positive states, like subjective well-being, optimism, and success, predict global biases consistent with broadened attention (Basso, Schefft, Ris, & Dember, 1996; Derryberry & Tucker, 1994).

These findings provide initial empirical footing for the hypothesis, drawn from the broaden-and-build theory, that distinct types of positive emotions serve to broaden people's momentary thought-action repertoires, whereas distinct types of negative emotions serve to narrow these same repertoires. Together with Christine Branigan, I tested this broaden hypothesis by showing research participants short, emotionally evocative film clips to induce the specific emotions of joy, contentment, fear, and anger. We also used a non-emotional film clip as a neutral control condition. Immediately following each film clip, we measured the breadth of participants' thought-action repertoires. We asked them to step away from the specifics of the film and imagine being in a situation themselves in which similar feelings would arise. Given this feeling, we asked them to list what they would like to do right then. Participants recorded their responses on up to 20 blank lines that began with the phrase "I would like to . . ."

Tallying the things each participant listed, we found support for the broaden hypothesis. Participants in the two positive-emotion conditions (joy and contentment) identified more things that they would like to do right then relative to those in the two negative-emotion conditions (fear and anger) and, more important, relative to those in the neutral control condition. Those in the two negative-emotion conditions also named fewer things than those in the neutral control condition (Fredrickson & Branigan, 2005).

These data provide preliminary evidence that two distinct types of positive emotion—a high activation state of joy and a low activation state of contentment—each produce a broader thought-action repertoire than does a neutral state. Likewise, two distinct types of negative emotion—fear and anger—each produce a narrower thought-action repertoire than does a neutral state. This pattern of results supports a core proposition of the broaden-and-build theory: that distinct positive emotions widen the array of thoughts and actions that come to mind. By contrast, distinct negative emotions, as models based on specific action tendencies would suggest, shrink this same array. To date, seven different studies from our laboratory support the broaden hypothesis, using dependent measures of global-local visual processing (Fredrickson & Branigan, 2005; Johnson, Waugh, Wager, & Fredrickson, 2005), covert attentional orienting (Johnson et al., 2005), self-other confusion (Waugh, Hejmadi, Otake, & Fredrickson, 2005), and face recognition (Johnson & Fredrickson, in press). Supportive evidence from other laboratories is also emerging (Bolte, Goschke, & Kuhl, 2003; Gasper & Clore, 2002).

Positive Emotions Undo Lingering Negative Emotions

Evidence for the broaden hypothesis has clear implications for the strategies that people use to regulate their experiences of negative emotions. If negative emotions narrow the momentary thought-action repertoire, and positive emotions broaden this same repertoire, then positive emotions ought to function as efficient antidotes for the lingering effects of negative emotions. In other words, positive emotions might "correct" or "undo" the aftereffects of negative emotions; we call this the *undo hypothesis* (Fredrickson & Levenson, 1998; Fredrickson, Mancuso, Branigan, & Tugade, 2000). The basic observation that positive emotions (or key components of them) are somehow incompatible with negative emotions is not new and has been demonstrated in earlier work on anxiety disorders (e.g., systematic desensitization; Wolpe, 1958), motivation (e.g., opponent-process theory; Solomon & Corbit, 1974), and aggression (e.g., principle of incompatible responses; Baron, 1976). Even so, the precise mechanism ultimately responsible for this incompatibility has not been adequately identified. The broaden function of positive emotions may play a role. By broadening a person's momentary thought-action repertoire, a positive emotion may loosen the hold that a negative emotion has gained on that person's mind and body by dismantling or undoing preparation for specific action.

One marker of the specific action tendencies associated with negative emotions is increased cardiovascular activity, which redistributes blood flow to the relevant skeletal muscles. In the context of negative emotions, then, positive emotions should speed recovery from—or undo—this cardiovascular reactivity, returning the body to more midrange levels of activation. By accelerating cardiovascular recovery, positive emotions create the bodily context suitable for pursuing the broader array of thoughts and actions called forth.

My collaborators and I tested this undo hypothesis by first inducing a high-activation negative emotion in all participants (Fredrickson & Levenson, 1998; Fredrickson et al., 2000). In one study (Fredrickson et al., 2000), we used a time-pressured speech preparation task. In just 1 minute, participants prepared a speech on "Why you are a good friend," believing that their speech would be videotaped and evaluated by their peers. This speech task induced the subjective experience of anxiety along with increases in heart rate, peripheral vasoconstriction, and systolic and diastolic blood pressure. Into this context of anxiety-related sympathetic arousal, we randomly assigned participants to view one of four films. Two films elicited mild positive emotions (joy and contentment), and a third served as a neutral control condition. Notably, these three films, when viewed following a resting baseline, elicit virtually no cardiovascular reactivity (Fredrickson et al., 2000). So the two positive films used in this study are indistinguishable from neutrality with respect to cardiovascular changes. Our fourth film elicited sadness. We chose sadness as an additional comparison because, among the negative emotions, it has not been definitively linked to a high-energy action tendency and thus could be a contender for speeding cardiovascular recovery.

The undo hypothesis predicts that those who experience positive emotions on the heels of a high-activation negative emotion will show the fastest cardiovascular recovery. We tested this by measuring the time elapsed from the start of the randomly assigned film until the cardiovascular reactions induced by the negative emotion returned to baseline levels. In three independent samples, participants in the two positive emotion conditions (joy and contentment) exhibited faster cardiovascular recovery than those in the neutral control condition and faster than those in the sadness condition, which exhibited the most protracted recovery (Fredrickson & Levenson, 1998; Fredrickson et al., 2000).

Recalling that the two positive-emotion films and the neutral film did not differ in what they do to the cardiovascular system, these data suggest that they do differ in what they can undo within this system. Two distinct types of positive emotions—mild joy and contentment—share the ability to undo the lingering cardiovascular aftereffects of negative emotions. Although the precise cognitive and physiological mechanisms of this undo effect remain unknown, the broaden-and-build theory suggests that broadening at the cognitive level mediates undoing at the cardiovascular level. Phenomenologically, positive emotions may help people to place the events in their lives in broader context, lessening the resonance of any particular negative event.

Positive Emotions Fuel Psychological Resiliency

Evidence for the undo effect of positive emotions suggests that people might improve their psychological well-being, and perhaps also their physical health, by cultivating experiences of positive emotions at opportune moments to cope with negative emotions (Fredrickson, 2000). Folkman and colleagues have made similar claims that experiences of positive affect during chronic stress help people to cope (Folkman, 1997; Folkman & Moskowitz, 2000; Lazarus, Kanner, & Folkman, 1980). Evidence supporting this claim can be drawn from experiments showing that positive affect facilitates attention to negative, self-relevant information (Reed & Aspinwall, 1998; Trope & Neter, 1994; Trope & Pomerantz, 1998; for a review, see Aspinwall, 1998). Extrapolating from these findings, Aspinwall (2001) describes how positive affect and positive beliefs serve as resources for people coping with adversity (see also Aspinwall & Taylor, 1997; Taylor, Kemeny, Reed, Bower, & Gruenewald, 2000).

It seems plausible that some individuals, more than others, might intuitively understand and use the benefits of positive emotions to their advantage. One candidate for individual difference is psychological resilience. Resilient individuals are said to "bounce back" from stressful experiences quickly and efficiently, just as resilient metals bend, but do not break (Carver, 1998; Lazarus, 1993). This theoretical definition of resilience suggests that, relative to their less resilient peers, resilient individuals would exhibit faster cardiovascular recovery following a high-activation negative emotion. Additionally, the broaden-and-build theory suggests that this ability to bounce back to cardiovascular baseline may be fueled by experiences of positive emotion.

Michele Tugade and I tested these two hypotheses about resilient individuals by using the time-pressured speech preparation task described earlier to induce a high-activation negative emotion. We measured psychological resilience using Block and Kremen's (1996) self-report scale. Interestingly, resilience did not predict the levels of anxiety that participants reported experiencing during the speech task nor the magnitude of their cardiovascular reactions to the stressful task, both of which were considerable. Resilience did, however, predict participants' reports of positive emotions. Before the speech task was even introduced, more-resilient individuals reported higher levels of preexisting positive affect on an initial mood measure. And when later asked how they felt during the time-pressured speech preparation phase, more-resilient individuals reported that, alongside their high anxiety, they also experienced higher levels of happiness and interest.

As predicted by the theoretical definition of psychological resilience, more-resilient participants exhibited significantly faster returns to baseline levels of cardiovascular activation following the speech task. Moreover, as predicted by the broaden-and-build theory, this difference in time to achieve cardiovascular recovery was accounted for by differences in positive emotions (Tugade & Fredrickson, 2004).

These data suggest that positive emotions may fuel psychological resilience. In effect, then, resilient individuals may be—wittingly or unwittingly—expert users of the undo effect of positive emotions (Tugade & Fredrickson, 2002). A prospective field study of American college students before and after the terrorist attacks of September 11, 2001, provided consistent evidence. Relative to their less-resilient peers, resilient individuals were less likely to become depressed and more likely to experience postcrises growth following the attacks. More important, the greater positive emotions that resilient people experienced fully accounted for each of these beneficial effects (Fredrickson, Tugade, Waugh, & Larkin, 2003).

Positive Emotions Build Personal Resources

Evidence suggests, then, that positive emotions may fuel individual differences in resilience. Noting that psychological resilience is an enduring personal resource, the broaden-and-build theory makes the bolder prediction that experiences of positive emotions might also, over time, build psychological resilience, not just reflect it. That is, to the extent that positive emotions broaden the scopes of attention and cognition, enabling flexible and creative thinking, they should also augment people's enduring coping resources (Aspinwall, 1998, 2001; Fredrickson & Joiner, 2002; Isen, 1990).

Together with my students, I recently tested the build effect of positive emotions in a prospective study. Each evening for 1 month, college students logged on to a secure Website and reported the emotions they had experienced in the past 24 hours. Before and after the month of emotion reporting, participants completed measures of personal resources, including one of trait resilience. From these data we learned that participants who experienced the most positive emotions showed the greatest increases in trait resilience over the month (Fredrickson, Cohn, Brown, Mikels & Conway, 2005). These prospective data are consistent with the causal direction posited by the broaden-and-build theory: frequent experiences of positive emotions produce increments in personal resources. This finding is important because our past work has shown that resilience, as measured in this study, is a consequential trait that predicts both psychological well-being and growth, and physiological recovery (Fredrickson et al., 2003; Tugade & Fredrickson, 2004).

Positive Emotions Fuel Psychological and Physical Well-Being

By broadening people's mindsets and building their psychological resources, over time, positive emotions should also enhance people's emotional and physical well-being. Consistent with this view, studies have shown that people who experience positive emotions during bereavement are more likely to develop long-term plans and goals. Together with positive emotions, plans and goals predict greater psychological well-being 12 months post-bereavement (Stein, Folkman, Trabasso, & Richards, 1997; for related work, see Bonanno & Keltner, 1997; Keltner & Bonanno, 1997). One way that people experience positive emotions in the face of adversity is by finding positive meaning in ordinary events or within the adversity itself (Affleck & Tennen, 1996; Folkman & Moskowitz, 2000; Fredrickson, 2000). Importantly, the relation between positive meaning and positive emotions is considered reciprocal: Finding positive meaning not only triggers positive emotion, but also positive emotions—because they broaden thinking—should increase the likelihood of finding positive meaning in subsequent events (Fredrickson, 2000).

These suspected reciprocal relations among positive emotions, broadened thinking, and positive meaning suggest that, over time, the effects of positive emotions should accumulate and compound: The broadened attention and cognition triggered by earlier experiences of positive emotion should facilitate coping with adversity, and this improved coping should predict future experiences of positive emotion. As this cycle continues, people build their psychological resilience and enhance their emotional well-being.

The cognitive literature on depression had already documented a downward spiral in which depressed mood and the narrowed, pessimistic thinking it engenders influence one another reciprocally, over time leading to ever-worsening moods and even clinical levels of depression (Peterson & Seligman, 1984). The broaden-and-build theory suggests a complementary upward spiral in which positive emotions and the broadened thinking they engender also influence one another reciprocally, leading to appreciable increases in emotional well-being over time. Positive emotions may trigger these upward spirals, in part, by building resilience and influencing the ways that people cope with adversity. (For a complementary discussion of upward spirals, see Aspinwall, 1998, 2001.)

Together with Thomas Joiner, I conducted a prospective test of the hypothesis that, through cognitive broadening, positive emotions produce an upward spiral toward enhanced emotional well-being. We assessed positive and negative emotions, as well as a concept we call *broad-minded coping*, at two time points, 5 weeks apart. Broad-minded coping was tapped by items such as "think of different ways to deal with the problem" and "try to step back from the situation and be more objective."

Our data revealed evidence for at least a fragment of an upward spiral. Individuals who experienced more positive emotions than others, over time, became more resilient to adversity, as indexed by increases in broad-minded coping. These enhanced coping skills, in turn, predicted increased positive emotions over time (Fredrickson & Joiner, 2002). These findings suggest that positive emotions and broad-minded coping mutually build on one another: Positive emotions not only make people feel good in the present, but also—by broadening thinking and building resources—positive emotions increase the likelihood that people will feel good in the future.

What are the long-term consequences of such upward spirals? A recent longitudinal study that spanned 7 decades suggests that the payoff may be longer lives. The data come from a study of 180 Catholic nuns who pledged their lives not only to God but also to science. As part of a larger study of aging and Alzheimer's disease, these nuns agreed to give scientists access to their archived work and medical records (and to donate their brains at death). The work archives included autobiographies handwritten when the nuns were in their early 20s. Researchers scored these essays for emotional content, recording instances of positive emotions, like happiness, interest, love, and hope, and negative emotions, like sadness, fear, and disinterest. No association was found between negative emotional content and mortality, perhaps because it was rather rare in these essays. But a strong association was found between positive emotional content and mortality: Those nuns who expressed the most positive emotions lived on average 10 years longer than those who expressed the least positive emotions (Danner, Snowdon, & Friesen, 2001). This is not an isolated finding. Several other researchers have found the same solid link between feeling good and living longer, even when accounting for age, gender, health status, social class, and other possible confounds (Levy, Slade, Kunkel, & Kasl, 2002; Moskowitz, 2003; Ostir, Markides, Black, & Goodwin, 2000; Ostir, Markides, Peek, & Goodwin, 2001).

Concluding Remarks

The broaden-and-build theory underscores the ways in which positive emotions are essential elements within optimal functioning and therefore an essential topic within the emerging science of positive psychology. The theory, together with the research reviewed here, suggests that positive emotions (a) broaden people's attention and thinking, (b) undo lingering negative emotional arousal, (c) fuel psychological resilience, (d) build consequential personal resources, and (e) trigger upward spirals toward greater well-being in the future. Moreover, the broaden-and-build theory challenges existing paradigms because it casts positive emotions in a far more consequential role in the story of human welfare. Whereas traditional perspectives have suggested that positive emotions mark or signal health and well-being (Diener, 2000; Kahneman, 1999), the broaden-and-build theory suggests that positive emotions also produce health and well-being (Fredrickson, 2001). Put differently, to the extent that the broaden-and-build effects of positive emotions accumulate and compound over time, positive emotions carry the capacity to transform individuals for the better, making them healthier and more socially integrated, knowledgeable, effective, and resilient. As the evidence in support of the theory accumulates, the prescriptive message becomes clear: People should cultivate positive emotions in their own lives and in the lives of those around them not just because doing so makes them feel good in the moment, but also because doing so transforms people for the better and sets them on paths toward flourishing and healthy longevity.

The author would like to thank the University of Michigan, the National Institute of Mental Health (MH53971 and MH59615), and the John Templeton Foundation for supporting the research described in this chapter.

References

Affleck, G., & Tennen, H. (1996). Construing benefits from adversity: Adaptational significance and dispositional underpinnings. *Journal of Personality, 64,* 899–922.

Aron, A., Norman, C. C., Aron, E. N., McKenna, C., & Heyman, R. E. (2000). Couples shared participation in novel and arousing activities and experienced relationship quality. *Journal of Personality and Social Psychology, 78,* 273–284.

Ashby, F. G., Isen, A. M., & Turken, A. U. (1999). A neuropsychological theory of positive affect and its influence on cognition. *Psychological Review, 106,* 529–550.

Aspinwall, L. G. (1998). Rethinking the role of positive affect in self-regulation. *Motivation and Emotion, 22,* 1–32.

Aspinwall, L. G. (2001). Dealing with adversity: Self-regulation, coping, adaptation, and health. In A. Tesser & N. Schwarz (Eds.), *The Blackwell handbook of social psychology: Vol. 1. Intraindividual processes* (pp. 591–614). Malden, MA: Blackwell.

Aspinwall, L. G., & Taylor, S. E. (1997). A stitch in time: Self-regulation and proactive coping. *Psychological Bulletin, 121,* 417–436.

Baron, R. A. (1976). The reduction of human aggression: A field study of the influence of incompatible reactions. *Journal of Applied Social Psychology, 6,* 260–274.

Basso, M. R., Schefft, B. K., Ris, M. D., & Dember, W. N. (1996). Mood and global-local visual processing. *Journal of the International Neuropsychological Society, 2,* 249–255.

Block, J., & Kremen, A. M. (1996). IQ and ego-resilience: Conceptual and empirical connections and separateness. *Journal of Personality and Social Psychology, 70,* 349–361.

Bolte, A., Goschke, T., & Kuhl, J. (2003). Emotion and intuition: Effects of positive and negative mood on implicit judgments of semantic coherence. *Psychological Science, 14,* 416–421.

Bonanno, G. A., & Keltner, D. (1997). Facial expressions of emotion and the course of conjugal bereavement. *Journal of Abnormal Psychology, 106,* 126–137.

Boulton, M. J., & Smith, P. K. (1992). The social nature of play fighting and play chasing: Mechanisms and strategies underlying cooperation and compromise. In J. H. Barkow, L. Cosmides, & J. Tooby (Eds.), *The adapted mind: Evolutionary psychology and the generation of culture* (pp. 429–444). New York: Oxford University Press.

Cabanac, M. (1971). Physiological role of pleasure. *Science, 173,* 1103–1107.

Cacioppo, J. T., Gardner, W. L., & Berntson, G. G. (1999). The affect system has parallel and integrative processing components: Form follows function. *Journal of Personality and Social Psychology, 76,* 839–855.

Cacioppo, J. T., Priester, J. R., & Berntson, G. G. (1993). Rudimentary determinants of attitudes: II. Arm flexion and extension have differential effects on attitudes. *Journal of Personality and Social Psychology, 65,* 5–17.

Caro, T. M. (1988). Adaptive significance of play: Are we getting closer? *Tree, 3,* 50–54.

Carver, C. S. (1998). Resilience and thriving: Issues, models, and linkages. *Journal of Social Issues, 54,* 245–266.

Carver, C. S., & Scheier, M. F. (1990). Origins and functions of positive and negative affect: A control-process view. *Psychological Review, 97,* 19–35.

Clore, G. L. (1994). Why emotions are felt. In P. Ekman & R. Davidson (Eds.), *The nature of emotion: Fundamental questions* (pp. 103–111). New York: Oxford University Press.

Danner, D. D., Snowdon, D. A., & Friesen, W. V. (2001). Positive emotions in early life and longevity: Findings from the nun study. *Journal of Personality and Social Psychology, 80,* 804–813.

Davidson, R. J. (1993). The neuropsychology of emotion and affective style. In M. Lewis & J. M. Haviland (Eds.), *Handbook of emotion* (pp. 143–154). New York: Guilford.

Derryberry, D., & Tucker, D. M. (1994). Motivating the focus of attention. In P. M. Neidenthal & S. Kitayama (Eds.), *The heart's eye: Emotional influences in perception and attention* (pp. 167–196). San Diego, CA: Academic.

Diener, E. (2000). Subjective well-being: The science of happiness and a proposal for a national index. *American Psychologist, 55,* 34–43.

Diener, E., & Diener, C. (1996). Most people are happy. *Psychological Science, 7,* 181–185.

Diener, E., Sandvik, E., & Pavot, W. (1991). Happiness is the frequency, not the intensity, of positive versus negative affect. In F. Strack (Ed.), *Subjective well-being: An interdisciplinary perspective* (pp. 119–139). Oxford: Pergamon.

Dolhinow, P. J. (1987). At play in the fields. In H. Topoff (Ed.), *The natural history reader in animal behavior* (pp. 229–237). New York: Columbia University Press.

Ekman, P. (1992). An argument for basic emotions. *Cognition and Emotion, 6,* 169–200.

Estrada, C. A., Isen, A. M., & Young, M. J. (1997). Positive affect facilitates integration of information and decreases anchoring in reasoning among physicians. *Organizational Behavior and Human Decision Processes, 72*, 117–135.

Folkman, S. (1997). Positive psychological states and coping with severe stress. *Social Science Medicine, 45*, 1207–1221.

Folkman, S., & Moskowitz, J. T. (2000). Positive affect and the other side of coping. *American Psychologist, 55*, 647–654.

Fredrickson, B. L. (1998). What good are positive emotions? *Review of General Psychology, 2*, 300–319.

Fredrickson, B. L. (2000). Cultivating positive emotions to optimize health and well-being. *Prevention and Treatment, 3*. Retrieved September 17, 2003, from http://journals.apa.org/prevention/volume3/pre0030001a.html.

Fredrickson, B. L. (2001). The role of positive emotions in positive psychology: The broaden-and-build theory of positive emotions. *American Psychologist, 56*, 218–226.

Fredrickson, B. L. (2004). Gratitude, like other positive emotions, broadens and builds. In R. A. Emmons & M. E. McCullough (Eds.), *The psychology of gratitude* (pp. 145–166). New York: Oxford University Press.

Fredrickson, B. L., & Branigan, C. (2001). Positive emotions. In T. J. Mayne & G. A. Bonnano (Eds.), *Emotion: Current issues and future directions* (pp. 123–151). New York: Guilford.

Fredrickson, B. L., & Branigan, C. (2005). Positive emotions broaden the scope of attention and thought-action repertoires. *Cognition and Emotion, 19*, 313–332.

Fredrickson, B. L., Cohn, M. A., Brown, S. L., Mikels, J., & Conway, A. (2005). *Positive emotions: A pathway to human flourishing.* Manuscript in preparation.

Fredrickson, B. L., & Joiner, T. (2002). Positive emotions trigger upward spirals toward emotional well-being. *Psychological Science, 13*, 172–175.

Fredrickson, B. L., & Levenson, R. W. (1998). Positive emotions speed recovery from the cardiovascular sequelae of negative emotions. *Cognition and Emotion, 12*, 191–220.

Fredrickson, B. L., Mancuso, R. A., Branigan, C., & Tugade, M. (2000). The undoing effect of positive emotions. *Motivation and Emotion, 24*, 237–258.

Fredrickson, B. L., Tugade, M. M., Waugh, C. E., & Larkin, G. (2003). What good are positive emotions in crises?: A prospective study of resilience and emotions following the terrorist attacks on the United States on September 11th, 2001. *Journal of Personality and Social Psychology, 84*, 365–376.

Frijda, N. H. (1986). *The emotions.* Cambridge: Cambridge University Press.

Frijda, N. H. (1994). Emotions are functional, most of the time. In P. Ekman & R. Davidson (Eds.), *The nature of emotion: Fundamental questions* (pp. 112–122). New York: Oxford University Press.

Frijda, N. H., Kuipers, P., & Schure, E. (1989). Relations among emotion, appraisal, and emotional action readiness. *Journal of Personality and Social Psychology, 57*, 212–228.

Gasper, K., & Clore, G. L. (2002). Attending to the big picture: Mood and global versus local processing of visual information. *Psychological Science, 13*, 34–40.

Isen, A. M. (1990). The influence of positive and negative affect on cognitive organization: Some implications for development. In N. Stein, B. Leventhal, & T. Trabasso (Eds.), *Psychological and biological approaches to emotion* (pp. 75–94). Hillsdale, NJ: Erlbaum.

Isen, A. M. (2000). Positive affect and decision making. In M. Lewis & J. M. Haviland-Jones (Eds.), *Handbook of emotions* (2nd ed., pp. 417–435). New York: Guilford.

Isen, A. M., & Daubman, K. A. (1984). The influence of affect on categorization. *Journal of Personality and Social Psychology, 47,* 1206–1217.

Isen, A. M., Daubman, K. A., & Nowicki, G. P. (1987). Positive affect facilitates creative problem solving. *Journal of Personality and Social Psychology, 52,* 1122–1131.

Isen, A. M., Johnson, M. M. S., Mertz, E., & Robinson, G. F. (1985). The influence of positive affect on the unusualness of word associations. *Journal of Personality and Social Psychology, 48,* 1413–1426.

Isen, A. M., & Means, B. (1983). The influence of positive affect on decision-making strategy. *Social Cognition, 2,* 18–31.

Isen, A. M., Rosenzweig, A. S., & Young, M. J. (1991). The influence of positive affect on clinical problem solving. *Medical Decision Making, 11,* 221–227.

Johnson, K. J., & Fredrickson, B. L. (in press). "We all look the same to me": Positive emotions eliminate the own-race bias in face recognition. *Psychological Science.*

Johnson, K. J., Waugh, C. E., Wager, T., & Fredrickson, B. L. (2005). *Smile to see the forest: Expressed positive emotions broaden attentional scopes and increase attentional flexibility.* Manuscript under review.

Kahn, B. E., & Isen, A. M. (1993). The influence of positive affect on variety seeking among safe, enjoyable products. *Journal of Consumer Research, 20,* 257–270.

Kahneman, D. (1999). Objective happiness. In D. Kahneman, E. Diener, & N. Schwarz (Eds.), *Well-being: The foundations of hedonic psychology* (pp. 3–25). New York: Russell Sage.

Keltner, D., & Bonanno, G. A. (1997). A study of laughter and dissociation: Distinct correlates of laughter and smiling during bereavement. *Journal of Personality and Social Psychology, 73,* 687–702.

Lazarus, R. S. (1991). *Emotion and adaptation.* New York: Oxford University Press.

Lazarus, R. S. (1993). From psychological stress to the emotions: A history of changing outlooks. *Annual Review of Psychology, 44,* 1–22.

Lazarus, R. S., Kanner, A. D., & Folkman, S. (1980). Emotions: A cognitive-phenomenological analysis. In R. Plutchik & H. Kellerman (Eds.), *Theories of emotion* (pp. 189–217). New York: Academic.

Lee, P. C. (1983). Play as a means for developing relationships. In R. A. Hinde (Ed.), *Primate social relationships* (pp. 82–89). Oxford: Blackwell.

Leslie, A. M. (1987). Pretense and representation: The origins of "theory of mind." *Psychological Review, 94,* 412–426.

Levenson, R. W. (1994). Human emotions: A functional view. In P. Ekman & R. Davidson (Eds.), *The nature of emotion: Fundamental questions* (pp. 123–126). New York: Oxford University Press.

Levy, B. R., Slade, M. D., Kunkel, S. R., & Kasl, S. V. (2002). Longevity increased by positive self-perceptions of aging. *Journal of Personality and Social Psychology, 83,* 261–270.

Moskowitz, J. T. (2003). Positive affect predicts lower risk of AIDS mortality. *Psychosomatic Medicine, 65,* 620–626.

Oatley, K., & Jenkins, J. M. (1996). *Understanding emotions.* Cambridge, MA: Blackwell.

Ostir, G. V., Markides, K. S., Black, S. A., & Goodwin, J. S. (2000). Emotional well-being predicts subsequent functional independence and survival. *Journal of the American Geriatrics Society, 48,* 473–478.

Ostir, G. V., Markides, K. S., Peek, K., & Goodwin, J. S. (2001). The associations between emotional well-being and the incidence of stroke in older adults. *Psychosomatic Medicine, 63,* 210–215.

Panksepp, J. (1998). Attention deficit hyperactivity disorders, psychostimulants, and intolerance of childhood playfulness: A tragedy in the making? *Current Directions in Psychological Science, 7,* 91–98.

Peterson, C., & Seligman, M. E. P. (1984). Causal explanations as a risk factor for depression: Theory and evidence. *Psychological Review, 91,* 347–374.

Reed, M. B., & Aspinwall, L. G. (1998). Self-affirmation reduces biased processing of health-risk information. *Motivation and Emotion, 22,* 99–132.

Rosenberg, E. L. (1998). Levels of analysis and the organization of affect. *Review of General Psychology, 2,* 247–270.

Seligman, M. E. P., & Csikszentmihalyi, M. (2000). Positive psychology: An introduction. *American Psychologist, 55,* 5–14.

Sherrod, L. R., & Singer, J. L (1989). The development of make-believe play. In J. Goldstein (Ed.), *Sports, games and play* (pp. 1–38). Hillsdale, NJ: Erlbaum.

Simons, C. J. R., McCluskey-Fawcett, K. A., & Papini, D. R. (1986). Theoretical and functional perspective on the development of humor during infancy, childhood, and adolescence. In L. Nahemow, K. A. McCluskey-Fawcett, & P. E. McGhee (Eds.), *Humor and aging* (pp. 53–77). San Diego, CA: Academic.

Solomon, R. L., & Corbit, J. D. (1974). An opponent-process theory of motivation: I. Temporal dynamics of affect. *Psychological Review, 81,* 119–145.

Stein, N. L., Folkman, S., Trabasso, T., & Richards, T. A. (1997). Appraisal and goal processes as predictors of psychological well-being in bereaved caregivers. *Journal of Personality and Social Psychology, 72,* 872–884.

Taylor, S. E., Kemeny, M. E., Reed, G. M., Bower, J. E., & Gruenewald, T. L. (2000). Psychological resources, positive illusions, and health. *American Psychologist, 55,* 99–109.

Tooby, J., & Cosmides, L. (1990). The past explains the present: Emotional adaptations and the structure of ancestral environments. *Ethology and Sociobiology, 11,* 375–424.

Trope, Y., & Neter, E. (1994). Reconciling competing motives in self-evaluation: The role of self-control in feedback seeking. *Journal of Personality and Social Psychology, 66,* 646–657.

Trope, Y., & Pomerantz, E. M. (1998). Resolving conflicts among self-evaluative motives: Positive experiences as a resource for overcoming defensiveness. *Motivation and Emotion, 22,* 53–72.

Tugade, M. M., & Fredrickson, B. L. (2002). Positive emotions and emotional intelligence. In L. Feldman-Barrett and P. Salovey (Eds.), *The wisdom of feelings:*

Psychological processes in emotional intelligence (pp. 319–340). New York: Guilford.

Tugade, M., & Fredrickson, B. L. (2004). Resilient individuals use positive emotions to bounce back from negative emotional arousal. *Journal of Personality and Social Psychology, 86,* 320–333.

Waugh, C. E., & Fredrickson, B. L. (2003). Feeling good and feeling close: The effect of positive emotion on self-other overlap. *Manuscript under review.*

Waugh, C. E., Hejmadi, A., Otake, K., & Fredrickson, B. L. (2005). *Cross cultural evidence for the social broadening hypothesis.* Manuscript in preparation.

Wolpe, J. (1958). *Psychotherapy by reciprocal inhibition.* Stanford, CA: Stanford University Press.

6

Benefits of Emotional Intelligence

DAISY D. GREWAL

PETER SALOVEY

There can be no transforming of darkness into light and of apathy into movement without emotion.

—Carl Jung

We know too much and feel too little. At least, we feel too little of those creative emotions from which a good life springs.

—Bertrand Russell

If living a good life is living a life in which one learns and evolves, it is necessary to feel both the joy that accompanies hard-won successes and the unpleasant sting of regret that often follows bad decisions. Emotions are therefore an invaluable source of information and feedback (Frijda, 1996; Lang, Bradley, & Cuthbert, 1998). How can we best utilize the emotions that we notice in ourselves and in others in order to reap the maximum benefits? This is a primary question of interest to researchers who study the concept of emotional intelligence.

Emotional intelligence is not a panacea for all of life's problems, but growing evidence does suggest that the ability to interpret and handle emotions effectively may play an important role in many of life's most important endeavors. The ability to decode and use emotional information accurately may help one to choose a meaningful line of work and succeed within that field, enjoy good physical health, and develop satisfying relationships with friends and loved ones. This chapter provides an overview of how emotional intelligence can lead to positive life outcomes. We begin with a brief history outlining the origins and development of the concept. After defining emotional intelligence in more detail and describing ways in which to measure it, we discuss scientific findings that indicate some of the ways in which emotional intelligence contributes to a good life.

History of the Emotional Intelligence Concept

Salovey and Mayer (1990) began to discuss the idea of emotional intelligence in the late 1980s after pondering the following phenomenon: Why is it that many intelligent individuals who generally behave in adaptive ways, such as certain notable politicians, sometimes suffer lapses in judgment that jeopardize their careers and, in some cases, their personal lives as well? This observation implies that there is more to being a successful politician than just being smart; one may also need the ability to wisely attend to and regulate emotions (Salovey & Mayer, 1994).

A tension between a positive and a negative view of emotions in rational thought dates back centuries to when, for example, the Stoic philosophers of ancient Greece regarded the experience of emotion as too self-absorbed to be a useful guide for insight and wisdom. There was a turning of the tides during the Romantic movement in late 18th- and early 19th-century Europe, when empathy and intuition rooted in emotion were considered important and useful ways to gain insights unattainable through rational thought alone.

A similar debate still continues in the field of human abilities today. Although narrowly focused definitions of intelligence predominated for most of the 20th century, a small but growing minority now views intelligence as composed of multiple and diverse components. Sternberg (1985) helped to broaden the prevailing view of analytic intelligence by arguing that researchers should pay more attention to the creative and practical aspects of intelligence. Another well-known advocate of multiple intelligences, Howard Gardner (1983), described a form of intrapersonal intelligence that is very similar to the current conceptualization of emotional intelligence. Gardner described intrapersonal intelligence:

> The core capacity at work here is access to one's own feeling life—one's range of affects or emotions: the capacity instantly to effect discriminations among these feelings and, eventually, to label them, to enmesh them in symbolic codes, to draw upon them as a means of understanding and guiding one's behavior. (1983, p. 239)

Similarly, Averill argued that emotional skills can be learned and developed as readily as intellectual skills (Averill & Nunley, 1992). The current model of emotional intelligence also grew out of the debate about the rationality of emotion, and in 1990 the first scientific articles introducing the concept were published. Salovey and Mayer (1990; Mayer & Salovey, 1997) outlined an ability that focused on understanding and managing feelings in both the self and other and the ability to use these feelings as tools to facilitate both thought and action. The authors created a framework for how to conceptualize emotional intelligence in such a way that made it possible to organize a serious line of scientific inquiry. Credibility for the concept was reinforced by findings in neuroscience demonstrating that emotional responses are most likely integral to even the most "rational" forms of decision making (e.g., Damasio, 1994). The theoretical conceptualization of emotional intelligence was also reflected in the writing of Goleman's (1995) bestselling book *Emotional Intelligence.* The idea that emotional intelligence, in addition to analytical intelligence, might be an important factor in predicting future success in school, work, and relationships resonated deeply with the general public.

Since the mid-1990s, the amount of scholarly work on emotional intelligence has grown considerably due to the efforts of dedicated researchers who have developed methods for both testing emotional intelligence and evaluating the relationship of emotional intelligence to important life outcomes. In the next few sections, we will concentrate on delineating the current scientific model of emotional intelligence, the more widely used methods of testing it, and empirical evidence showing that emotional intelligence is related to several desirable life outcomes, such as better relationships, success at work, and physical and mental health.

The Four-Branch Model of Emotional Intelligence

What exactly is "emotional intelligence"? Although emotional intelligence is most widely thought of as a singular concept—especially by people less familiar with its scientific roots—our research has shown that it is useful to conceptualize it as consisting of four branches (Mayer & Salovey, 1997). These four branches are (a) perceiving emotions, (b) using emotions to facilitate thought, (c) understanding emotions, and (d) managing emotions in the self and others.

The first branch of emotional intelligence begins with the awareness of emotions in both self and others. Without the ability to detect what one feels accurately, it is nearly impossible to express those feelings. Extreme examples of individuals who lack these skills are those who suffer from alexithymia. These individuals are unable to express what they are feeling verbally, presumably because they lack the ability to identify their feelings as they arise (Apfel & Sifneos, 1979; Bagby, Parker, & Taylor, 1993a, 1993b). More will be said about the lives of alexithymic individuals in the section that describes the relationship between emotional intelligence and mental health.

An inability to detect certain feelings in oneself may also lead to difficulties detecting those same feelings in other people. Such a handicap leaves one with little information with which to perform more complicated emotional tasks, such as consoling a grieving friend. Therefore, at the most basic level, the emotionally intelligent individual must be able to detect and decipher the emotional messages in facial expressions, vocal tones, postures, and cultural artifacts.

The second branch of emotional intelligence focuses on how emotions facilitate cognitive activities, such as problem solving, reasoning, decision making, and creative pursuits. Although research in psychology has traditionally focused on the interference of emotions with cognition, many studies have nevertheless demonstrated that emotions can play a positive role in these cognitive processes. Emotions can help an individual to concentrate on important information (Easterbrook, 1959; Mandler, 1975; Simon, 1982), and certain moods can facilitate different cognitive functions (Palfai & Salovey, 1993; Schwarz, 1990). For example, is it better to be in a sad mood or a happy mood when planning a party? How about when trying to compose a symphony or write a piece of poetry? Although we naturally seem to prefer good moods over bad ones, positive affect may not always be desirable. For example, when trying to work on a task that requires intense concentration and deductive reasoning, a slightly depressed mood can be helpful (Schwarz, 1990).

The third branch of emotional intelligence concerns the understanding of emotions. It represents the ability to label emotions linguistically and to recognize the often subtle and complex relationships between different emotions. Even more important, the emotionally intelligent individual should have the ability to use this knowledge to recognize the hierarchical and temporal relationships among emotions. This individual is aware, for example, of how mild annoyance at someone's behavior might lead to rage if one does not attempt to avoid the offending person or somehow resolve the annoyance. The third branch of emotional intelligence may therefore have important implications for how well people are able to navigate complex interpersonal relationships.

The fourth branch consists of the ability to manage emotions both internally and in the context of interpersonal relationships. The elements of this branch represent what many people most commonly identify with emotional intelligence, perhaps due to Western society's long tradition of valuing control over one's emotions. Managing emotions has important implications in wide-reaching subfields of psychology, among them the social, clinical, and developmental areas. For example, some clinical researchers believe that managing emotions effectively is the key to explaining and preventing certain psychological disorders (Gross & Munoz, 1995). Although the fourth branch of emotional intelligence certainly has implications for why some people may be better at avoiding depression, eliminating negative emotions is only one possible outcome of being able to manage emotions adaptively (Bonanno, 2001; Thompson, 1990). There are times when one might want to increase the powerful emotions one feels in order to help deliver an indignant speech or express profound grief at a funeral, for example. Therefore, the fourth branch of emotional intelligence also includes the voluntary activation of both positive and negative emotions.

The value of all four branches of emotional intelligence most likely depends heavily upon how well the user adapts to the context in which a skill is needed. It is our belief that being emotionally intelligent is more than just possessing the abilities described above but also having the capacity to recognize how to utilize them appropriately in a given situation.

Measurement of Emotional Intelligence

As interest in emotional intelligence has grown since the mid-1990s, so has the number of tests aiming to assess it reliably. Emotional intelligence tests fall into two general categories: self-report inventories and ability-based measures. Self-report inventories assessing various aspects of emotional intelligence have multiplied rapidly due to the fact that they are more easily designed and disseminated than ability-based measures. Two of the more widely used self-report tests are the Emotional Quotient Inventory (Bar-On, 1997) and the Self-Report Emotional Intelligence Test (Schutte et al., 1998).

The Emotional Quotient Inventory (EQ-i) consists of 15 different subscales, including emotional self-awareness, interpersonal skills, stress management, and general mood. The Self-Report Emotional Intelligence Test (SREIT) is based on the four-branch model of emotional intelligence (Mayer & Salovey, 1997). Some items, for example, focus on a person's self-perceived ability to monitor his or her private feelings or the feelings of others. Other items focus on the ability to use emotions to guide one's thinking and actions. Both measures are relatively short and easy to administer. However, the drawback of these and other self-report measures is that they often measure constructs that are difficult to distinguish from aspects of personality (Brackett & Mayer, 2003). We characterize emotional intelligence as a set of skills, rather than relatively fixed personality traits, which by definition are subject to improvement through training and intervention.

Whether self-reported emotional intelligence bears any relation to actually possessing the skills associated with emotional intelligence has yet to be sufficiently investigated (Brackett & Mayer, 2003; Mayer, Caruso, & Salovey, 1999). Just as one might be rather unconvinced that asking participants to answer the question "Do you think you're smart?" would provide accurate estimates of analytic intelligence, one might wonder whether asking people to report on their emotional intelligence helps us to understand their actual abilities. There are circumstances under which it might be interesting to study how accurately individuals assess their strengths and how those self-ratings relate to actual performance and behavior. In view of the drawbacks associated with self-reporting measures, ability-based measures of emotional abilities seem more useful in the assessment of emotional intelligence.

One example of an ability-based measure that captures aspects of emotional intelligence is the Levels of Emotional Awareness Scale (LEAS) (Lane et al., 1990). This scale asks respondents to describe the emotional responses they would have in response to hypothetical scenarios. A recent critical evaluation of the LEAS shows that it measures a construct that is distinct from personality and self-reported measures of emotional intelligence and is helpful in distinguishing individuals who are high in emotional awareness (Ciarrochi, Caputi, & Mayer, 2003). Such individuals can easily and clearly recognize their feelings and are less susceptible to allowing their current moods to influence their judgments (Ciarrochi, Caputi, & Mayer, 2003). They may therefore have an advantage when making important decisions about the future. The first comprehensive ability-based measure designed specifically for assessing the four-branch model of emotional intelligence is the Multifactor Emotional Intelligence Scale (MEIS), which is administered either through interaction with a computer program or via pencil and paper (Mayer, Caruso, & Salovey, 1998, 1999). The MEIS consists of 12 different tasks ranging from recognizing emotions in faces and music to understanding how emotions are likely to change over time. Administering the test to a large sample of adults and adolescents demonstrated that scores on these diverse tasks are positively correlated. Furthermore, additional analyses showed that EI ability increases with age, a finding that would be expected of a construct labeled as an intelligence (Mayer et al., 2001). In 2002, an improved and professionally published test based on the MEIS was released in the form of the Mayer-Salovey-Caruso Emotional Intelligence Test (MSCEIT) (Mayer, Salovey, & Caruso, 2002). The MSCEIT is similar to the MEIS in that it asks respondents to complete a variety of tasks either on a computer or on paper. The eight sets of tasks are grouped into the four domains thought to comprise emotional intelligence: (a) perceiving and expressing emotion; (b) using emotion to facilitate thought; (c) understanding emotion; and (d) managing emotion in the self and in others. Improvements offered by the MSCEIT include a shorter administration time and the elimination of poorly worded items (Mayer, Salovey, Caruso, & Sitarenios, 2003).

Both the MEIS and MSCEIT are scored through reference to consensual norms. This means that scores on the tests are calculated by comparing how closely a respondent's answers correspond to the answers provided by a large, heterogeneous sample of people who previously have taken the test. The MSCEIT can also be scored using expert criteria. In this case, respondents' answers are assessed for their agreement with what experts in emotion research think are the right answers to the questions. Research using the MSCEIT demonstrates that, in general, there is a very high correlation between consensus and expert scores and that both are reliable (Mayer et al., 2003). These findings indicate that most people agree with the experts on what constitutes the most emotionally intelligent response. Furthermore, there is evidence showing that the MSCEIT tests a construct that is different from well-studied measures of personality and, as we shall see, is related to important life outcomes (e.g., Brackett & Mayer, 2003; Lopes, Salovey, & Straus, 2003). Moreover, when administered along with self-report measures of EI, the MSCEIT does not overlap much with self-reported scores, indicating its distinctiveness as a separate measure of actual ability.

Empirical research using ability-based measures of emotional intelligence is currently under way and has produced some interesting results, some of which are described below.

How Might Emotional Intelligence Help Us?

Emotional intelligence has been touted as a solution to many common personal and societal problems (Goleman, 1995). Although many critics of the concept have been quick to point out the lack of evidence of such claims (Matthews, Zeidner, & Roberts, 2002), research in the domain of emotional intelligence has been slowly catching up to its proponents' belief that emotional skills play a significant role in helping people to achieve desirable outcomes. In the following sections, we review the empirical evidence collected thus far that demonstrates how emotional intelligence may be related to the quality of social relationships, performance at work, and mental and physical health.

Social Relationships

Can emotional intelligence help us to develop and sustain better relationships with friends and family? Empirical research using the MSCEIT and its predecessor, the MEIS, seems to demonstrate that this could be the case. The MEIS correlates positively with self-reported empathy and parental warmth and correlates negatively with social anxiety and depression (Mayer, Caruso, & Salovey, 1999). Rubin (1999) found that higher scores on the MEIS are associated with lower levels of antisocial behavior in adolescents (e.g., peer ratings of aggressiveness) and with a higher number of prosocial behaviors by those same students (as rated by the child's schoolteachers). Trinidad and Johnson (2002) demonstrated that middle-school students who had overall higher scores on the MEIS were significantly less likely to have ever tried smoking a cigarette or to have smoked one recently. These students were also less likely to report having consumed alcohol in the past week. Other research has shown that people scoring higher on emotional intelligence are less likely to exhibit violent behavior, such as bullying, and are also less likely to use tobacco, drink alcohol to excess, or take illicit drugs (Brackett & Mayer, 2003; Brackett, Mayer, & Warner, 2004; Rubin, 1999, 2002).

In addition, individuals who score high in emotional intelligence, as measured with the MSCEIT, report more positive interactions and relations with other people (Lopes, Salovey, Côté, & Beers, 2004). Furthermore, there is evidence that the fourth branch of the MSCEIT, which tests managing emotions, provides insight into how well people navigate their social worlds. A diary study of social interaction with a sample of German college students demonstrated that higher scores on branch four were positively correlated with the perceived quality of social interaction with members of the opposite sex (Lopes, Brackett, Nezlek, Schütz, Sellin, & Salovey, 2004).

A second study in the same investigation yielded similar results: Higher scores on the managing-emotions subscale of the MSCEIT positively correlated with participants' self-reports of positive interactions with friends. Furthermore, the scores were also positively related to the ratings of interaction quality made by these friends. Participants who scored higher on the MSCEIT were also rated by their friends as more likely to provide emotional support when needed. The effects of emotional intelligence remained important even when statistically controlled for personality factors, suggesting that something above and beyond personality traits accounted for the results.

There is also reason to believe that the other, more-basic abilities involved in emotional intelligence, in particular emotional awareness, may play an important role in sustaining close relationships. Although these findings are not based on measures of emotional intelligence, they assess constructs similar to the branches outlined in the scientific model and are therefore relevant to our discussion. For example, spouses who report higher happiness levels are also better able to detect their partner's emotional cues and exhibit higher levels of empathetic accuracy (Noller & Ruzzene, 1991). In contrast, unhappy spouses appear to interpret neutral or mildly negative emotional messages as hostile. Such recurrent interpretations sometimes lead to a repetitive pattern of conflict that couples find difficult to break (Gottman, 1994). A study of marital forgiveness examined feelings of forgiveness in 90 couples that had been married for a long time and 70 currently divorced men and women (Fitness, 2001). Participants were asked to write about an offense that had occurred with their current or past partner and then were asked to explain whether they had decided to forgive their partners and why. Participants also completed the Trait Meta-Mood Scale (Salovey et al., 1995), a self-report measure believed to tap into various constructs related to perceived emotional intelligence, including how clearly one can identify one's feelings. Individuals reporting higher emotional clarity also reported less difficulty in forgiving a partner and also greater marital happiness, even when controlling for gender and age. These findings suggest that emotional skills and abilities can play an important role in helping people to manage conflict and experience positive emotions in their relationships with others.

Work

A question that often surfaces regarding emotional intelligence is whether emotional skills affect job performance. Traditionally, our culture stresses academic and analytical intelligence as the foundation on which a successful career is built. Although general intelligence undoubtedly has an important influence on being able to perform the types of tasks required for many jobs, success at work probably involves more than this. In today's often complex working world, being able to cooperate with coworkers and managers is critical. Therefore, we would expect to find that people who are more emotionally intelligent receive more positive ratings by both supervisors and coworkers. Some research using ability-based measures of emotional intelligence supports this idea. Rice (1999) conducted a study wherein a shortened version of the MEIS was administered to 164 employees in an insurance company, each of whom was assigned to 26 customer claim teams. Rice asked a department manager to rate the effectiveness of both the teams and their leaders. Statistical analyses showed that MEIS scores were positively correlated with team leaders' degree of effectiveness. Furthermore, the average MEIS scores for each team were positively related to the manager's ratings of the team's performance in customer service. More emotionally intelligent teams also spent more time handling each consumer complaint, perhaps because dealing effectively with customer complaints in an emotionally intelligent fashion requires a certain amount of time and patience.

A more recent workplace study has yielded even more impressive findings linking emotional intelligence to important job outcomes (Lopes, Grewal, Kadis, Gall, & Salovey, in press). In this study, 44 analysts and clerical workers in a Fortune 500 insurance company completed the MSCEIT and were asked to rate their peers on a variety of interpersonal and emotional skills. Scores on the MSCEIT were positively related to both peer and supervisor ratings of interpersonal skills, stress tolerance, and leadership potential. Higher emotional intelligence scores also correlated with merit raises and job status, demonstrating that emotional ability may play a role in determining not only how well one gets along with coworkers but how high one climbs up the corporate ladder. The results of this study held up even after statistically controlling for a variety of other factors, including age, gender, verbal intelligence, and personality factors. Such findings demonstrate that emotional intelligence represents a concept separate from personality that has a unique contribution to make to the prediction of professional success.

Mental and Physical Health

Depression is one of the most widespread and debilitating disorders of our time. The rates of depression in America have been steadily increasing in the decades since World War II (Klerman & Weissman, 1989) despite rapid, simultaneous increases in the standard of living for the majority of Americans. Trying to solve the depression problem remains a pressing concern for many mental health professionals. Because depression is characterized primarily by a predominance of negative affect and little positive affect, might there be a relationship between knowing how to manage one's emotions and the amount of depression one experiences? A small study conducted with Yale undergraduates revealed that higher scores on the MSCEIT were associated with lower self-reports of depression and anxiety and higher overall satisfaction with college (Head, 2002). More research is needed to determine how exactly emotional intelligence might be related to depression, but the results so far are promising.

Other evidence also indicates that low emotional intelligence is associated with some forms of mental illness. Consider alexithymia, a condition wherein individuals have difficulties processing emotional information (Taylor, 2001). Although it would be unfair to characterize alexithymia purely as a form of low emotional intelligence, alexithymic individuals are deficient in many important emotional skills. For example, they often have difficulties with tasks associated with the first branch of emotional intelligence. They have difficulty identifying feelings in themselves and others and are consequently perceived as lacking empathy. Moreover, they also score high on measures of anxiety, depression, and neuroticism and are prone to panic attacks and posttraumatic stress disorder (PTSD) (Taylor, 2001). A 26-item self-report measure called the Toronto Alexithymia Scale (TAS) is used to assess the degree of alexithymia in individuals, and scores on the TAS-20 are negatively correlated with scores on the MSCEIT (e.g., Grewal et al., 2004).

Alexithymia is not the only evidence of a link between low emotional intelligence and mental illness. A study with patients suffering from borderline personality disorder (BPD) showed that individuals with this disorder often misread emotions in both themselves and in other people and have great difficulty regulating their emotions (Levine, Marziali, & Hood, 1997). BPD is characterized by severe problems in interpersonal relations, high rates of suicidal behavior, and intense personal distress. Some of the more successful treatments for BPD focus on helping individuals to integrate their emotional experiences and regulate their intense mood swings (Heard & Linehan, 1994), skills we associate with the first and fourth branches of emotional intelligence, respectively. Further research is needed to try and determine further how a lack of certain skills related to emotional intelligence may put people at risk for various mental disorders (Taylor, 2001).

Other research may help to illuminate how interference in the development of emotion-related skills may lead to later maladjustment. Child abuse is a known risk factor for the later development of mental disorders (e.g., Kendler et al., 2000), however the reasons underlying this link have not been well understood. A recent study seems to indicate that abused children may have difficulties correctly identifying emotional information in faces, a skill identified within the first branch of emotional intelligence (Pollak & Tolley-Schell, 2003). Children who had suffered abuse during their lives were shown a series of digitally morphed faces expressing varying degrees of happiness, fear, sadness, or anger and were asked to identify the emotions being expressed at different points in time. Their responses were compared to a group of children who had never experienced abuse. All of the children responded in the same way to faces depicting happiness, sadness, or fear. However, the abused children identified angry faces more quickly. The abused children also identified more of the ambiguous faces as being angry, revealing a bias toward interpreting neutral stimuli as hostile. The experimenters interpreted these data as demonstrating how abused children develop a hypersensitivity to angry cues. Although in some ways this sensitivity is adaptive considering the environment in which they grew up, as the children continue to mature and encounter different situations, this bias toward interpreting emotional cues as negative may cause problems and lead to conflict with others and mental illness.

Emotional intelligence may also play an important role in physical health. As we have previously discussed, being able to identify emotions in oneself, a task pertaining to the first branch of emotional intelligence, is the first step in being able to express feelings to others. Research by Pennebaker and his colleagues indicates that being able to express emotions through writing might have important health benefits. Pennebaker has conducted numerous studies investigating the effects of writing about emotional traumas on physical health. Pennebaker discovered that college students who were assigned to write about traumatic emotional experiences made fewer visits to the university health center in subsequent months as compared to peers who were assigned to write about a trivial topic (Pennebaker, Colder, & Sharp, 1990). His research has also demonstrated that disclosing strong emotional experiences may enhance immune system activity and lead to a decrease in self-reported physical symptoms, subjective distress, and depression (Pennebaker, Kiecolt-Glaser, & Glaser, 1988).

Although we cannot conclude that openly expressing emotions is always a good thing, the aforementioned research does seem to support the view that reduced ability to identify and express feelings in appropriate circumstances may impede physical health. Furthermore, there may be reason to believe that managing emotions might also be extremely important in maintaining good health. Goldman, Kraemer, and Salovey (1996) found that individuals who believe that they cannot repair or regulate their negative feelings effectively tend to seek out more attention from doctors when experiencing periods of stress. These individuals may be trying to seek help in regulating their moods, or it could also be the case that people who manage their emotions poorly are more likely to become physically ill and therefore seek medical attention. Our emotions—and more specifically the skills related to emotional intelligence—may have important implications for keeping our bodies and minds healthy.

Is Being Emotionally Intelligent Always Better?

Western psychology has often classified emotions as entities that interfere with desirable thought processes (Shaffer, 1936; Young, 1940). We must be wary of falling into the opposite trap of declaring everything emotional as good. There might be reason to believe that being superbly attuned to all affective states is not necessarily always adaptive. A person might run the risk of becoming overwhelmed or even paralyzed by negative emotion or unnecessarily bogged down with emotional information from the external world. There might be times when being oblivious to emotional states is adaptive. For example, being too perceptive of your partner's shortcomings, which could plausibly induce negative moods and a tendency toward anger, might cause decreased satisfaction within the relationship (e.g., Murray & Holmes, 1996).

Furthermore, emotional intelligence involves being attuned to social norms and complying with what most people find acceptable. One would therefore expect emotionally intelligent individuals to exhibit behaviors that most people would find acceptable and desirable in interpersonal relationships. This is one of the reasons that a high degree of agreement between consensus and expert scores on the MSCEIT seems reasonable and expected. However, there are instances when being part of the crowd might not necessarily be the most desirable attribute, such as with highly creative individuals.

Highly creative people often exhibit behaviors and traits that distinguish them from their peers. Personality traits that involve emotions, such as neuroticism and extroversion, often distinguish highly creative people from others. These creative individuals tend to be more emotionally sensitive, anxious, emotionally labile, and impulsive than other people (Feist, 2002). Furthermore, Averill's (1999) work on emotional creativity has shown that the ability to experience unusual or novel emotional experiences might aid the creative process. Being acutely attuned to social norms may hinder the ability to experience such novelty. Therefore, creative expression is a domain in which being emotionally intelligent might not be a helpful attribute.

Recent empirical evidence supports this notion (Grewal et al., 2004). A study was conducted in which participants were asked to spend 40 minutes composing an original fictional scene between two characters. Then participants completed the MSCEIT along with a battery of other self-reporting measures assessing various emotional traits. Independent raters judged the writing samples collected from participants along a variety of dimensions, including creativity. Preliminary analyses suggest negative correlations between judgments of creativity and participants' scores on branch two (using emotions) of the MSCEIT. Although emotional intelligence might aid creative people to stay motivated or work themselves into the "right" mood to create, it may not necessarily be useful in helping people to attain high levels of creative expression.

Summary and Future Directions

In this chapter, we defined and outlined the ability model of emotional intelligence, focusing on the four branches we feel represent distinct but related competencies: (a) perceiving emotions; (b) using emotions to facilitate thought; (c) understanding emotions; and (d) managing emotions. We described the self-report and ability-based measures most commonly used to assess emotional intelligence, including the Mayer-Salovey-Caruso Emotional Intelligence Test (MSCEIT), which has shown appropriate reliability as well as discriminant and convergent validity (Mayer et al., 2003). Although research testing the validity of the MSCEIT has only recently begun, preliminary evidence shows that it can predict important life outcomes in the domains of social relationships, workplace performance, and mental health. We also reviewed evidence of outcomes to which emotional intelligence might not contribute positively, such as creativity.

Much more work is needed in the field of emotional intelligence. There is important and interesting research needed to investigate the cross-cultural validity of emotional intelligence tests, for example. This will eventually help researchers to examine cultural differences in the application of emotional skills. There is also more work to be done on how emotional intelligence might be related to family relationships, marriage, parenting, financial success, health behaviors, and other domains where we might expect emotional skills to play an adaptive role. In order to thrive, the field of emotional intelligence requires the efforts of bright and enthusiastic researchers interested in helping to refine current ability-based measures of emotional intelligence with the ultimate goal of using those measures to study further the predictive validity of emotional intelligence, over and above other constructs. We hope that the promising results contained within this chapter may help to lure a new generation of researchers to join us on the exciting path of examining the rewards of the emotionally intelligent life.

Preparation of this chapter was supported by grants from the National Cancer Institute (R01-CA68427), the National Institute of Mental Health (P01-MH/DA56826), the National Institute of Drug Abuse (P50-DA13334), and the Donaghue Women's Health Investigator Program at Yale to Peter Salovey. We wish to thank Emma Seppala for her helpful comments on earlier drafts of this chapter.

References

Apfel, R. J., & Sifneos, P. E. (1979). Alexithymia: Concept and measurement. *Psychotherapy and Psychosomatics, 32*, 180–190.

Averill, J. R. (1999). Individual differences in emotional creativity: Structure and correlates. *Journal of Personality, 67*, 331–371.

Averill, J. R., & Nunley, E. P. (1992). *Voyages of the heart: Living an emotionally creative life.* New York: Free Press.

Bagby, R. M., Parker, J. D. A., & Taylor, G. J. (1993a). The twenty-item Toronto Alexithymia Scale: I. Item selection and cross-validation of the factor structure. *Journal of Psychosomatic Research, 38*, 23–32.

Bagby, R. M., Parker, J. D. A., & Taylor, G. J. (1993b). The twenty-item Toronto Alexithymia Scale: II. Convergent, discriminant, and concurrent validity. *Journal of Psychosomatic Research, 38*, 33–40.

Bar-On, R. (1997). *Emotional Intelligence Quotient Inventory: A measure of emotional intelligence.* Toronto, ON: Multi-Health Systems.

Bonanno, G. (2001). Self-regulation of emotions. In T. J. Mayne & G. Bonnano (Eds.). *Emotions: Current issues and future directions* (pp. 251–285). New York: Guilford.

Brackett, M. A., & Mayer, J. D. (2003). Convergent, discriminant, and incremental validity of competing measures of emotional intelligence. *Personality and Social Psychology Bulletin, 29,* 1147–1158.

Brackett, M. A., Mayer, J. D., & Warner, R. M. (2004). Emotional intelligence and the prediction of behavior. *Personality and Individual Differences, 36,* 1387–1402.

Ciarrochi, J., Caputi, P., & Mayer, J. D. (2003). The distinctiveness and utility of a measure of trait emotional awareness. *Personality and Individual Differences, 34,* 1477–1490.

Damasio, A. R. (1994). *Descartes' error: Emotion, reason, and the human brain.* New York: Putnam.

Easterbrook, J. A. (1959). The effects of emotion on cue utilization and the organization of behavior. *Psychological Review, 66,* 183–200.

Feist, G. J. (2002). The influence of personality on artistic and scientific creativity. In R. J. Sternberg (Ed.), *The handbook of creativity* (pp. 273–296). Cambridge: Cambridge University Press.

Fitness, J. (2001). Betrayal, rejection, revenge, and forgiveness: An interpersonal script approach. In M. Leary (Ed.), *Interpersonal rejection* (pp. 73–103). New York: Oxford University Press.

Frijda, N. H. (1996). *The emotions.* Cambridge: Cambridge University Press.

Gardner, H. (1983). *Frames of mind.* New York: Basic.

Goldman, S. L., Kraemer, D. T., & Salovey, P. (1996). Beliefs about mood moderate the relationship of stress to illness and symptom reporting. *Journal of Psychosomatic Research, 41,* 115–128.

Goleman, D. (1995). *Emotional intelligence.* New York: Bantam.

Gottman, J. M. (1994). *What predicts divorce? The relationship between marital processes and marital outcomes.* Hillsdale, NJ: Erlbaum.

Grewal, D., Icvecic, Z., Lopes, P. N., Brackett, M. A., & Salovey, P. (2004). *Emotions and the artist: The relationship between emotional intelligence and creativity.* Manuscript in preparation.

Gross, J. J., & Munoz, R. F. (1995). Emotion regulation and mental health. *Clinical Psychology: Science and Practice, 2,* 151–164.

Head, C. (2002). *The relationship between emotional intelligence and symptoms of anxiety and depression.* Unpublished senior thesis, Yale University.

Heard, H. L., & Linehan, M. M. (1994). Dialectical behavior therapy: An integrative approach to the treatment of borderline personality disorder. *Journal of Psychotherapy Integration, 4,* 55–82.

Kendler, K. S., Bulik, C. M., Silberg, J., Hettema, J. M., Myers, J., & Prescott, C. (2000). Childhood sexual abuse and psychiatric and substance use disorders in women: An epidemiological and co-twin control analysis. *Archives of General Psychiatry, 57,* 953–959.

Klerman, G. L., & Weissman, M. M. (1989). Increasing rates of depression. *Journal of the American Medical Association, 261,* 2229–2235.

Lane, R. D., Quinlan, D. M., Schwartz, G. E., Walker, P., & Zeitlin, S. B. (1990). The levels of emotional awareness scale: A cognitive-developmental measure of emotion. *Journal of Personality Assessment, 55,* 124–134.

Lang, P. J., Bradley, M. M., & Cuthbert, B. N. (1998). Emotion, motivation, and anxiety: Brain mechanisms and psychophysiology. *Biological Psychiatry, 44,* 1248–1263.

Levine, D., Marziali, E., & Hood, J. (1997). Emotion processing in borderline personality disorders. *Journal of Nervous and Mental Disease, 195,* 240–246.

Lopes, P. N., Brackett, M. A., Nezlek, J. B., Schütz, A., Sellin, I., & Salovey, P. (2004). Emotional intelligence and social interaction. *Personality and Social Psychology Bulletin, 30,* 1018–1034.

Lopes, P. N., Grewal, D., Kadis, J., Gall, M., & Salovey, P. (in press). Evidence that emotional intelligence is related to job performance, interpersonal facilitation, affect and attitudes at work, and leadership potential. *Psicothema.*

Lopes, P. N., Salovey, P., Côté, S., & Beers, M. (2004). Emotional regulation abilities and the quality of social interaction. *Emotion, 5,* 113–118.

Lopes, P. N., Salovey, P., & Straus, R. (2003). Emotional intelligence, personality, and the perceived quality of social relationships. *Personality and Individual Differences, 35,* 641–658.

Mandler, G. (1975). *Mind and emotion.* New York: Wiley.

Matthews, G., Zeidner, M., & Roberts, R. D. (2002). *Emotional intelligence: Science and myth.* Cambridge, MA: MIT Press.

Mayer, J. D., Caruso, D. R., & Salovey, P. (1998). *Multifactor Emotional Intelligence Scale (MEIS).* (Available from John D. Mayer, Department of Psychology, University of New Hampshire, Conant Hall, Durham, NH 03824)

Mayer, J. D., Caruso, D., & Salovey, P. (1999). Emotional intelligence meets traditional standards for an intelligence. *Intelligence, 27,* 267–298.

Mayer, J. D., & Salovey, P. (1997). What is emotional intelligence? In P. Salovey & D. Sluyter (Eds.), *Emotional development and emotional intelligence: Educational implications* (pp. 3–31). New York: Basic.

Mayer, J. D., Salovey, P., & Caruso, D. (2002). *The Mayer-Salovey-Caruso Emotional Intelligence Test (MSCEIT).* Toronto, Ontario: Multi-Health Systems.

Mayer, J. D., Salovey, P., Caruso, D., & Sitarenios, G. (2001). Emotional intelligence as a standard intelligence. *Emotion, 1,* 232–242.

Mayer, J. D., Salovey, P., Caruso, D. R., & Sitarenios, G. (2003). Measuring emotional intelligence with the MSCEIT V2.0. *Emotion, 3,* 97–105.

Murray, S. L., & Holmes, J. G. (1996). The construction of relationship realities. In J. O. Fletcher (Ed.)., *Knowledge structures in close relationships: A social psychological approach* (pp. 91–120). Mahwah, NJ: Erlbaum.

Noller, P., & Ruzzene, M. (1991). Communication in marriage: The influence of affect and cognition. In G. L. O. Fletcher & F. Fincham (Eds.), *Cognition in close relationships* (pp. 203–233). Hillsdale, NJ: Erlbaum.

Palfai, T. P., & Salovey, P. (1993). The influence of depressed and elated mood on deductive and inductive reasoning. *Imagination, Cognition, and Personality, 13,* 57–71.

Pennebaker, J. W., Colder, M., & Sharp, L. K. (1990). Accelerating the coping process. *Journal of Personality and Social Psychology, 58,* 528–537.

Pennebaker, J. W., Kiecolt-Glaser, J. K., & Glaser, R. (1988). Disclosure of traumas and immune function: Health implications for psychotherapy. *Journal of Consulting and Clinical Psychology, 56,* 239–245.

Pollak, S. D., & Tolley-Schell, S. (2003). Selective attention to facial emotion in physically abused children. *Journal of Abnormal Psychology, 112,* 323–338.

Rice, C. L. (1999). *A quantitative study of emotional intelligence and its impact on team performance.* Unpublished master's thesis, Pepperdine University, Malibu, CA.

Rubin, M. M. (1999). *Emotional intelligence and its role in mitigating aggression: Correlational study of the relationship between emotional intelligence and aggression in urban adolescents.* Unpublished manuscript, Immaculata College, Immaculata, PA.

Salovey, P., & Mayer, J. D. (1990). Emotional intelligence. *Imagination, Cognition, and Personality, 9,* 185–211.

Salovey, P., & Mayer, J. D. (1994). Some final thoughts about personality and intelligence. In R. J. Sternberg & P. Ruzgis (Eds.), *Personality and intelligence* (pp. 303–318). Cambridge: Cambridge University Press.

Salovey, P., Mayer, J. D., Goldman, S. L., Turvey, C., & Palfai, T. P. (1995). Emotional attention, clarity, and repair: Exploring emotional intelligence using the Trait Meta-Mood Scale. In J. W. Pennebaker (Ed.), *Emotion, disclosure, and health* (pp. 125–154). Washington, DC: American Psychological Association.

Schutte, N. S., Malouff, J. M., Hall, L. E., Haggerty, D. J., Cooper, J. T., Golden, C. J., & Dornheim, L. (1998). Development and validation of a measure of emotional intelligence. *Personality and Individual Differences, 25,* 167–177.

Schwarz, N. (1990). Feelings as information: Informational and motivational functions of affective states. In E. T. Higgins & E. M. Sorrentino (Eds.), *Handbook of motivation and cognition* (Vol. 2, pp. 527–561). New York: Guilford.

Shaffer, L. F. (1936). *The psychology of adjustment: An objective approach to mental hygiene.* Boston: Houghton Mifflin.

Simon, H. A. (1982). Comments. In M. S. Clark & S. T. Fiske (Eds.). *Affect and cognition: The 17th annual Carnegie Symposium on Cognition* (pp. 333–342). Hillsdale, NJ: Erlbaum.

Sternberg, R. J. (1985). *Beyond IQ: A triarchic theory of human intelligence.* Cambridge: Cambridge University Press.

Taylor, G. J. (2001). Low emotional intelligence and mental illness. In J. Ciarrochi, J. P. Forgas, & J. D. Mayer (Eds.), *Emotional intelligence in everyday life: A scientific inquiry* (pp. 150–167). Philadelphia: Psychology Press.

Thompson, R. (1990). Emotion and self-regulation. In R. Thompson (Ed.), *Socioemotional development: Nebraska Symposium on Motivation* (pp. 367–467). Lincoln: University of Nebraska Press.

Trinidad, D. R., & Johnson, C. A. (2002). The association between emotional intelligence and early adolescent tobacco and alcohol use. *Personality and Individual Differences, 32,* 95–105.

Young, K. (1940). *Personality and problems of adjustment.* New York: Appleton-Century-Crofts.

7

Strategies for Achieving Well-Being

JANE HENRY

This chapter considers a variety of strategies people use to improve their well-being over the long term. It begins by examining the main strategies found in psychotherapy and contrasting these with approaches advocated in self-help and spiritual practice. The chapter goes on to compare the approaches adopted by mental health professionals with strategies derived from studies of people who exhibit well-being and strategies people judge to have helped them personally.

Psychotherapeutic Approaches

Perhaps the dominant method currently used by professionals to help people develop more constructive thoughts and behaviors is some kind of talking therapy. This holds for consultations with clinical psychologists, psychotherapists, counselors, and a variety of other mental health and development professionals, including nurses, social workers, organizational trainers, life coaches, and educational psychologists.

Mental health caregivers often aim to improve the situation by focusing on what is wrong and teaching people to control, cope with, or "cure" the problem. This type of intervention derives from studies of pathology aimed at helping clinical populations. Many of the practices now applied with normal populations and the "worried well" derive from earlier work with clinical populations. For example, Rose (1990) argues that this approach to development has expanded to areas such as personnel, training, life tragedies, and more mundane aspects of life. If you are infertile, in debt, or a victim of crime, you are quite likely to be sent off to the counselor to talk about the problem and possibly assumed to be in denial if you are reluctant to do so. Rose suggests that this has led to an unhelpful neuroticization of discourse, which is disempowering.

The pathological approach to self-improvement is so deeply ingrained in psychology that both the American and the British psychological associations have institutionalized it, in that they have professional groups of clinical psychology, counseling psychology, and psychotherapy, all essentially oriented to looking at how to fix pathology, not how to enhance well-being. Positive psychology offers an important counterbalance to this bias in the discipline.

There are literally hundreds of different schools of psychotherapy, often operating from very different theoretical orientations that are applied in clinical, educational, organizational, and other settings. Table 7.1 contrasts some of the different practices by illustrating the approaches and methods employed in some of the main therapeutic schools. Other psychotherapeutic approaches include narrative, brief therapy, constructivist, and integrative approaches.

The different mental health professions often tend to favor different schools, with psychiatrists stressing a psychobiological approach, clinical psychologists tending to favor cognitive-behavioral therapies, a fair number of psychotherapists

Table 7.1.   Common Psychotherapeutic Approaches

School	Approach	Methods
Behavioral	Positive reinforcement	Counterconditioning
	Behavioral psychotherapy	Desensitization
		Aversion therapy
	Behavioral modification	Positive reinforcement
		Skill development
Cognitive	Cognitive behavior	Thought catching
	Cognitive therapy	Reality testing
	Rational emotive therapy	Activity scheduling
		Cognitive rehearsal
		Disputation
Psychodynamic	Psychoanalysis	Clinical interview
	Object relations	Life story
	Psychostructural	Free association
		Active imaging
		Transference
Humanistic/Experiential	Gestalt	Genuineness
	Person-centered	Positive regard
	Psychosynthesis	Affective self-disclosure
		Expressive
		Cathartic
Systemic	Family therapy	Group discussion
	Group therapy	Interpersonal dialogue
	Cognitive analytic therapy	Observation
		Interpretation and comment
		Practical intervention

retaining a psychodynamic orientation, and a few counselors operating from a more humanistic standpoint.

The *psychobiological* approach, favored by psychiatrists, assumes that the problem is basically biological, often some neurochemical imbalance, so its answer is to prescribe drugs such as Prozac to rectify the imbalance. The approach favored by most clinical psychologists is *cognitive-behavioral.* Here the problem is assumed to be one of faulty thinking, so the prescription is to change bad habits of thought with healthier forms of thinking. Clients are encouraged to test the reality of their assumptions and challenge and dispute their reasoning to arrive at more positive and appropriate interpretations of situations and strategies for dealing with them. In some cases, behavioral strategies, such as desensitization for phobias, may also be employed. *Psychodynamic* approaches are still quite popular among psychotherapists in the United Kingdom and some counselors in the United States. Here, socialization is assumed to have been lacking, so a lot of attention is given to discussion of family relations in an attempt to understand how past experiences influence current patterns of behavior. In addition, processes of transference are thought to provide one route to help make up for deficiencies in past relationships. In contrast, *humanistic* (or experiential) models lay more stress on emotions and the need to disclose your feelings and possibly to act them out expressively to help deal with unfinished business; catharsis is encouraged. Finally, there are various *systemic* group methods, such as family therapy. Many psychotherapeutic approaches assume the problem is in the individual's head and try to tackle the problem by doing something solely with the individual. Family therapy assumes that the problem arises from the dynamics of the group and attempts are made to improve these through group discussion, observation, and intervention.

Though the theories underlying the different talking therapies seem very different, there are commonalities in the process. Clients present an emotionally charged problem, and they discuss the nature and cause of the problem and what to do about it with the therapist/counselor/coach. Hopefully this leads to the problem being reframed in a helpful manner and more constructive behavior.

However, talking therapy does not seem to be a route that appeals to everyone. Studies of the number of people that stick with a course of therapy find it has quite high dropout rates. Studies in the United Kingdom have found that a lot of people either do not bother to turn up for their first appointment or do not finish the series (Phillips & Fagan, 1982; Turvey, 1997). In addition, psychotherapy is not cheap so not everyone can afford this form of treatment. European studies suggest that only a small proportion of those needing help for psychological problems receive professional support. Hannay (1979) found that of a third of the population reporting clinical symptoms, 70% did nothing, under a fifth saw a doctor, and around a tenth saw a friend. Even those who do receive therapy may not receive much; a general practitioner's office in the United Kingdom typically allocates six sessions with a counselor. Dosage outcome studies suggest that this might be insufficient for over half of clients (Howard et al., 1986). Thus, whether by circumstance or inclination, most people are forced to find other ways of improving their well-being.

Self-Help

Judging by the popularity of television programs such as "Oprah" and "Dr. Phil" and the size of the mind and body section in your local bookstore, there is enormous interest in ways of changing and developing oneself and a desire to learn how to improve well-being. There is also an interesting contrast between strategies advocated in the self-help literature and in the therapeutic and professional development literature. In the self-help literature, there seems to be much less emphasis on talking about your problem(s) and much more emphasis on looking to the future and elaborating where you would like to be. Instead of trying to analyze the problem and attempting to fix it, you are often encouraged to start from a vision of where you would like to be and work out what steps you can take to get there. There is often an emphasis on *positive thinking*, developed from Coue through Carnegie to the present-day emphasis on positive affirmations. You also find more attention paid to intuitive, nonverbal, and narrative approaches, like visualization and storytelling, approaches that might be expected to be more sensitive to emotions and implicit understandings. In addition, embodied strategies that aim to get at the mind through the body are common, for example, psychophysical approaches such as focusing and biogenetics. The self-help area, like positive psychology, also includes attention to modeling success such as Covey's (1990) attempts to derive principles from his studies of successful people or the neurolinguistic programming (NLP) patterns of productive communication derived from studying successful therapists (Dilts, 1990).

There are other interesting differences between professional and self-help strategies. Professional approaches tend to be expert-led by a trained practitioner, whereas some of the very successful approaches in the self-help area are self-managed. These include Alcoholics Anonymous and co-counseling, procedures that operate according to certain simple principles and rules and without an expert leader.

The attention to modeling success, positive thinking, a future orientation, embodied, and more-intuitive routes to personal development seems very different from the strategies advocated traditionally by many professional clinicians. Positive psychologists share the concern with modeling success, valuing a positive attitude and the benefits of a future orientation.

Well-Being and Positive Psychology

Decades of work on well-being has shown that certain behaviors and beliefs consistently correlate with measures of life satisfaction.

Social support is one factor that shows a positive correlation with life satisfaction (Myers, 2000). People who are married and cohabiting (Diener, Gohm, Suh, & Oishi, 2000) and people who belong to groups generally tend to report themselves more satisfied with life than those who are less socially embedded (Argyle, 1987). People who are socially supported also do better on various health measures, and they tend to recover more quickly from illness. People also tend to rate themselves happier in the present when they are with friends than when they are alone (Argyle, 1999). If you were trying to derive a strategy to enhance well-being from this research, you might advise people to keep up with their friends, go out and socialize, or go to an evening class rather than dwelling on their problems.

Another strand of work on well-being stems from Csikszentmihalyi's work on flow. His studies suggest that people are contentedly absorbed when they are engaged in an activity that appeals to them and offers some challenge but which is achievable. The state of mind attained when one is so engaged has been found to be common across different activities and is termed *flow*. The activities often have a physical component—gardening, playing with children, or dancing—involving the body as well as the mind. On the whole, more passive activities, like watching TV, are less likely to lead to the state of flow. During flow, attention is directed outward, not in toward oneself, as in counseling and therapy. The implication for those wishing to enhance their well-being might be to think about what they like doing and make a point of spending time doing such activities and less time watching TV (Csikszentmihalyi, 1999; Csikszentmihalyi & Csikszentmihalyi, 1988).

As is clear from the other chapters in this book, positive psychologists have begun to advocate various strategies based on an approach that values positive experiences, encourages positive attitudes, and orients to building strengths as a buffer against weakness rather than one that focuses on fixing deficiencies. These include work on psychological strengths (Peterson, this volume), emotional intelligence (Grewal & Salovey, this volume), positive emotions (Fredrickson, this volume), optimism (Seligman, 1991), hope (Snyder, Rand, & Sigmon, 2002), gratitude (Emmons, this volume), and well-being (Fava, 1999).

Spiritual

Both psychotherapeutic and positive psychology's approaches to enhancing well-being are of relatively recent origin compared to the long-standing Eastern concern with mastering consciousness. If we date talking therapy from Freud, it has about a 100-year history compared with the millennia that spiritual practitioners in the East have been focusing on inner science. During this time, they have developed detailed psychologies of how attitude and experience are interlinked and an extensive array of practices designed to improve well-being.

When young, I asked many different practitioners what they would advocate for depression, curious to hear their responses. Not surprisingly, psychotherapists tended to recommend talking about the problem, but Buddhists were more likely to say things like "wait for it to pass" or "try looking above the horizon." Though I found the latter wanting at the time, it now seems positively sage.

Most of the Western approaches to personal development are concerned with changing thoughts—the contents of consciousness—whereas spiritual approaches like Buddhism seem more concerned with redirecting attention and refining the instrument of perception. This offers a strategy that bypasses much of the usual Western psychological focus on problems and goals in favor of allowing one's mind to work in a better way, through the aid of practices such as meditation and mindfulness.

The personal development literature and much positive psychology tends to assume that trying to make yourself a better/happier/more-fulfilled person is a reasonable goal. Eastern spiritual approaches tend to be more concerned with surrendering to some higher good, releasing expectations, and living in the present. Detachment from fleeting emotions, forgiveness, compassion, and selfless action feature prominently in many spiritual traditions.

By directing attention toward focusing on the present and detaching from identification with troubles, one gives both problems and desires less attention than in therapy or self-help and perhaps avoids the danger of fanning the flames of pointless rumination and childish emotion. Instead, one is encouraged to be here now and to view the world from a more-encompassing perspective.

Of course meditation, mindfulness, and contemplation are not the only Eastern spiritual practices in existence. One characteristic of Hindu approaches is their acceptance of diversity. They have developed different yogas, or ways of perfecting the self. Intellectuals may be attracted to jnana yoga's focus on knowledge. The altruistic may prefer karma yoga, a way of service; the more active may be attracted to hatha yoga, which involves learning to control the body through various exercises; and the emotionally inclined may be drawn to bhakti, a practice centered around devotion, for example, to a guru. These different approaches allow people to develop in manners that suit their particular temperaments.

Comparison

Table 7.2 points up the rather different orientations and approaches found in mainstream psychotherapy, self-help, well-being research, and spiritual practice. Clinical psychologists, counselors, mental health professionals, and

Table 7.2.   Comparison of Different Strategies for Improving Well-Being

	Therapy	Self-Help	Well-Being	Spiritual
Processes	Insight	Recognize pattern	Active participation	Detachment
	Catharsis	Positive attitude	Appropriate challenge	Acceptance
	Social skills	Practical skills	Social support	Identify higher good
	Coping strategies	Take action	Belong to group Build on strengths	Compassion
Concern	Analyze problem	Positive approach	Active involvement	Quieting mind
	Self-awareness	Preferred future outcome	Social embeddedness Positive orientation	Refine perception
Approaches	Cognitive	Positive thinking	Active involvement	Mindfulness
	Behavioral	Value intuition	Belong to social group	Meditation
	Humanistic	Modeling success	Meaning system	Service
	Experiential	Desired future	Optimistic outlook	Devotion
	Counseling		Utilize strengths	
	Psychodynamic			
	Systemic			

psychotherapists often encourage a strategy of self-awareness and insight, particularly analyzing problems as a route to improving well-being. (Professional development adopts a similar strategy in its advocacy of reflecting on the nature of the problem, noting what you can learn from it, and if need be developing a new competency.) Self-help and popular psychology often advocate the rather different tactic of elaborating the positive, going for your preferred outcome and incorporating intuitive and embodied approaches, such as visualization and movement. Three of the strategies derived from studies of well-being and positive psychology are the importance of social support, active absorption in the world, and building on your strengths. Spiritual practices that are beginning to be given attention by psychologists in the West include quieting the mind and living in the present as routes to change and development. In reality, the picture may be less clear-cut as practitioners in one area draw on ideas developed in others, as in therapists who advocate mindfulness, for example.

Self-Report Studies

This section reports on approaches that ordinary people judged to be helpful in improving their well-being over the long term. The findings are based on a series of studies I have conducted aimed at identifying what approaches nonclinical populations find helpful and what they find less so. In these studies, participants are asked questions about their development over time, specifically, how they think they have changed, what if anything has helped them to improve their well-being over an extended time period like 10 years, what strategies they tried that have failed to help, and what they would still like to change about themselves that has proved difficult to alter.

To date, most of the samples have comprised managers, psychologists, and educators who have been attending a course, conference, or seminar at the time the research was conducted. Some of the data come from open-ended questionnaires incorporating questions similar to those cited above, and some was obtained during workshops convened to answer questions along similar lines. The sample reported on here comprises approximately 40% women, 60% men, is mainly aged 18 to 50, with around 60% from the United Kingdom, 30% from Europe, and about 10% of the sample from the rest of the world. Some groups have included people with a professional interest in development; others comprise people who are quite naive about professional discourse in this area.

Almost without exception, people report positive changes of one kind or another, but the changes reported confound maturational and self-directed changes. For example, confidence is one thing that comes with age for many of this largely British sample. Women in particular report becoming more assertive over time. As people mature, they often get less bothered about things. Some people get clearer about what they want in life, which helps them to become more focused, passionate, and purposeful. Others report getting more accepting of themselves and their foibles.

The things people get less bothered about seem to vary with temperament. The angry get less so, the melancholic likewise. Those with a medium to high thinking preference on the Myers Briggs Type Indicator (MBTI®) (low agreeableness on the Big Five) eventually realize they have to listen to people more and may begin to become more tolerant of those who are different from themselves. Many people seem to become more balanced over time. Some behaviors seem much harder to change for certain personality types. For example, many of those with a high feeling preference on the MBTI seem to find it hard to get over what they view as excessive sensitivity, and many of those with a high MBTI perceiving preference find it difficult to submit work on time.

Helpful Strategies

Table 7.3 summarizes the variety of methods that people have cited as helpful in achieving lasting personal change and improving their well-being over the long term. Most people mentioned only a few strategies, whether filling out the questionnaire or raising issues in a workshop. More may have been cited had more time been allowed for the exercise.

One of the most common approaches cited is some form of quieting the mind and following intuitive hunches. This took different forms, ranging from formal meditation to the more informal, like "I just go to bed, and I know it will sort itself in the morning." For one person, it was going fishing; for others it was listening to their intuition and "following their bliss," as Campbell (1995) would say. Quieting the mind seems to offer an intuitive way to resolve issues and receive guidance that can offer an alternative to analysis and dialogue. Allied to this type of approach, some found it helpful to let go, accept and work with their foibles rather than strive after goals.

Another strategy that comes out strongly is some form of physical activity. Some people cite walking; for a number of others, dancing seems to work; and for others, running or being in nature. Just being among trees was thought to enhance well-being in some cases. Running would increase endorphin levels, but it seemed that physical activity and being in nature are not just matters of changing mood to enhance well-being in the short term. Maybe making time

Table 7.3.   Effective Ways of Achieving Lasting Personal Change

Quieting the mind/ Intuitive	listening to oneself, following one's bliss, contemplation, meditation, spiritual approaches
Self-Acceptance	kind to and gentle with self, cease to care what others think, forget self, letting go
Physical/Nature	walking, exercise, bodywork, movement, running, yoga, being amid trees, being barefoot
Social support	support of sympathetic other(s), reassurance, close friends, social immersion
Reflect/Reframing	learning through others' similar problems, clash of beliefs prompting rethinking, self-analysis, pair and group counseling/therapy
Balance/Mastery	learn to say no, take on less, realism, discipline, clarifying priorities, being present-centered
Circumstance	rise to the occasion, survive crisis, personal circumstances force change
Other	listening to others, becoming more tolerant, love
Orientation/Action	transforming
Confidence/Daring	be assertive, face fear, take risks, commit, delegate, surrender, self-reliance
Expression	expressing feelings via images, acting out, concretizing feelings, music, poetry, sculpture
Future	having a clear vision of where you want to be
Positive	remembering successes, affirming positive outcomes
Humor	laughing, watching funny programs
Drugs	chocolate, ecstasy, prescription drugs
Purpose	doing the right thing, seeing bigger purpose

for such activities suggests a switch to a more balanced lifestyle, but whatever the reason, there appears to be a longer-term beneficial effect from physical activity and time in nature which was credited with lifting and preventing depression, enabling people to see things in perspective, and making them happier.

As we would expect from the well-being studies, social support is another helpful strategy, in guises such as being with close friends and sympathetic others, both of which seem to make people feel more content.

Another strategy is daring. For some, this is a question of facing fear, as in the person who is afraid of flying who opts to go parachuting. For others, it is more a question of feeling the pain, facing unpleasant emotions and situations rather than running away. For some, perhaps the indecisive, it is making a leap, committing to something they want to try. For others, it is more a matter of surrendering or giving up unrealistic goals. All of these strategies move people to try something different. People also benefited from having dared to stand up for themselves, being more assertive, self-reliant, and/or self-disciplined. People who used to look to others for advice felt better about themselves once they started relying more on themselves and were less lazy.

Some people value reflection and reframing. This could happen informally—learning from others with similar problems and rethinking one's position after coming across somebody who thinks differently—or as a result of engagement in a more-formal process, such as co-counseling or group therapy.

For some people, clarifying their priorities and getting a clear picture of where they want to be is important; for others, learning to delegate and being more realistic are the big lessons. Others value learning to express their needs or feelings—in some cases by concretizing feelings through drama, art, or a poem. Others learn late in life to start listening, becoming more tolerant and ceasing to expect to get their way as much. Developing balance and mastery also featured. This could entail learning to say no and being more present-centered.

Various other strategies have been cited occasionally. These include humor, drugs, and the influence of a special person. As regards laughter, one person found that a daily dose of laughing with "The Simpsons" (the TV program) worked wonders in removing depressive tendencies. A couple of people swore that the recreational drug Ecstasy really changed them for the better. A few people felt that they had been transformed in an instant following an interaction with a spiritual guru.

Though some people found being more positive to be helpful, few people mentioned the attainment of positive qualities like courage or hope as helpful strategies. There may also be differences in the acceptability of voicing such qualities in Europe and the United States. Perhaps people would cite such qualities more often if they featured more prominently in modern rhetoric.

In most groups I have looked at, many different strategies were cited, though only a few were seen as having made a long-term impact on any given individual.

But there are also some differences in the issues raised by members of different professions. Managers, for example, cite circumstances as a common catalyst for change more frequently than do educators and psychologists. This is where they felt that life forced change upon them by thrusting them into situations where they had to sink or swim.

So far, quieting the mind has proved to be the most commonly cited approach. Around a third of my respondents have cited an approach such as quieting the mind, accepting the self, and learning to be more other-oriented, which are perhaps reminiscent of spiritual approaches to improving well-being. Though in line with ancient Eastern disciplines, until recently quieting the mind has not been given much attention by mental health professionals. Admittedly, researchers such as Kabat-Zinn and Teasdale are experimenting with mindfulness as a therapeutic strategy (Kabat-Zinn et al., 1992; Teasdale, Seagal, & Williams, 1995).

Around a fifth of the sample cite a tactic reminiscent of behaviors exhibited by those with high levels of subjective well-being, such as getting physically active and absorbed in activities in the world, garnering social support, and to a lesser degree, finding a purpose and meaning in life. There is plenty of research to show that social support is linked to well-being (Taylor, Dickerson, & Klein, 2002), and there are papers that say that being out in or even seeing nature is beneficial (Ulrich, 1984) and that exercise is great for endorphins (McCann & Holmes, 1984). Nevertheless, on the whole, therapists are not encouraged to suggest that clients keep up with their friends and exercise as routes out of depression.

Another fifth of the sample cite strategies reminiscent of those found in clinical and counseling practices, such as reflecting on and reframing understandings, developing more mastery and better balance in life, and to a lesser degree learning to express oneself. Around a tenth cited strategies that could be reminiscent of approaches found in self-help and positive psychology, i.e., developing a positive attitude, being future-oriented, and taking action. Another tenth adopted other approaches, varying from rising to the new opportunities that life presents, to the use of drugs (recreational or prescription), to humor.

What is striking about these results is the frequency with which nonanalytical approaches to improving long-term well-being were valued. These include quieting the mind, accepting and letting go, physical exercise, being in nature, and social support. This seems at odds with professional discourse on personal development.

Unhelpful Strategies

People were also asked about approaches they had tried that proved unhelpful in their attempts to achieve lasting change and improve their well-being over the long term.

Table 7.4.   Methods Cited as Failing to Bring About
Personal Change or Improvement

Exhortation
Reading
Talking about problem
Analyzing
Planning
Time management
Advice
Insight
Negative feedback
Reliving emotions
Obsessing over an issue
Doing nothing

On top of the list of unhelpful strategies is exhortations like "cheer up, love." For a lot of people, reading about how to deal with problems, talking about and analyzing problems, and planning were also judged to be unhelpful. This is unfortunate as reading, talking about problems, analyzing their causes, and planning for the future are central to most caring professionals' repertoire of methods for personal development. A number of these participants seem to have found that turning their attention away from their problems and sometimes away from themselves had proved more productive in the long run.

There are some things with which a fair proportion of the sample wanted a better way of dealing. Time management is one such issue, as many people felt too busy, but a number found traditional advice in this area insufficient to engender change.

One caveat is necessary: As less time was devoted to discussing ineffective strategies, Table 7.4 is based on fewer cases than the tables for the helpful strategies given above, and as a consequence needs to be treated with more caution.

Discussion

If these results are broadly representative of the range of strategies that nonclinical populations find aid their own development, they present an interesting contrast with the dominant rhetoric employed for this purpose among mental health professionals. Mainstream approaches to personal development currently seem to suggest that personal issues are best helped through discussion of their problematic nature with an expert helper, such as a clinician, counselor, or other mental health professional. Though this type of approach was valued by around a fifth of my participants, most opted to cite other approaches as effective in improving their long-term well-being. Why might there be this discrepancy between strategies advocated by professionals and approaches found to be helpful by ordinary people?

It may be that these results are atypical as the sample is not representative, though the author has found broadly similar results in a variety of settings since the 1990s. Generally, participants appear to have been very forthcoming in disclosing information about themselves, so it seems unlikely that reticence can account for the range of strategies raised.

Alternatively, it may be that psychologists and other development professionals have been overemphasizing a particular route to development and neglecting other more-social, embodied, and positive approaches (Henry, 1998). Seligman and Csikszentmihalyi (2000) have suggested that a postwar historical bias has left psychology largely oriented toward ameliorating pathology and neglecting the merits of building on the positive. Not only psychology but much of the wider personal development industry is oriented toward fixing deficiency and failure. The information-processing model of knowledge acquisition dominates educational and organizational training. This frames personal failings largely in terms of skill deficiencies to be rectified by inputting the missing competencies into the trainee's head and directs much educational and organizational development toward focusing on means of addressing failure rather than building on strengths. Indeed until very recently, this focus on the half-empty view of the glass has been common among a variety of such professionals, where it appears natural to frame development issues in essentially pathological terms.

However, in these changing times, some of the newer technologies and movements, like coaching and life strategies, are more obviously focused on kick-starting constructive action. A trend toward positive engagement is also apparent in other areas of applied psychology, such as organizational development, where consultants now advocate benchmarking good practices and developing shared visions rather than focusing solely on troubleshooting problems.

Appeal

As regards personal development, it seems that a fair number of people find the standard emphasis on self-awareness and insight into the problem in most talking therapies not to their liking. The dropout rate cited earlier suggests such therapy has limited appeal.

My studies suggest that there is a relationship among cognitive style, what people find difficult to change, and the kind of technique found to be helpful. Those with a preference for feeling on the MBTI seem to find disassociation strategies particularly helpful, for example. This makes sense as they are more primed to be engulfed by feelings.

There is other evidence that some people, notably people inclined to excessive negative rumination, are not helped by a discussion of their problems, or at least not initially. Nolen-Hoeksema has shown that people who are sad find their mood lowered when asked to think about themselves but lifted by a neutral distraction, such as thinking of a cool breeze on a warm day (Lyubomirsky, Caldwell, & Nolen-Hoeksema, 1998). When the introspective versus distraction tasks are followed by an assignment asking people to note their ideas about their past, present, and future, the depressed produce less-negative responses after even a short period of distraction (Lyubomirsky & Nolen-Hoeksema, 1995). She notes also that depression is more common in the young and middle-aged than in the elderly (Kerman & Weissman, 1989). She puts this phenomenon down to the tendency of older people to distract themselves with work when troubled rather than inquiring deeply into its cause as younger people often do (Nolen-Hoeksema & Morrow, 1993). She recommends breaking out of negative rumination by seeing supportive friends, exercising, doing something useful, or distracting yourself in some other way before attempting to analyze a problem, so one is better placed to see things in perspective. The participants in my studies seem to concur. However, for many of them, quieting the mind, social support, and physical activity were not just useful tools for disassociating; rather, time spent in this way seemed to obviate their need for discussion of previously troubling issues, lessen the chance of their reappearance, and increase subjective well-being.

Talking therapy may be contraindicated altogether in certain posttraumatic cases and where there is a risk of adverse restimulation setting off a downward spiral of negative thinking. In many countries, posttraumatic counseling is almost mandatory if you are a crime victim or in a serious fire, train crash, or other trauma. Yet research suggests that reliving the problem makes the situation worse for some people. It has been suggested that perhaps only a fifth of those counseled posttrauma benefit (Bisson, 1994, 1997). Here, too, people may benefit from directing their attention away from the trauma toward things they value and enjoy.

Elsewhere, insight into a problem may be insufficient to effect change. Prochaska's work suggests that although insight may be useful early in the change process, later support which helps embed new behavior and more constructive habits appears to be more critical (Prochaska & DiClemente, 1982). So where people know what they want and are committed to trying, social support may be the more critical factor.

Process

The high value that talking therapy places on insight and self-awareness is mirrored in the stress on reflection and self-knowledge found in personal, professional, educational, and management development and training more generally, but is this emphasis sufficient to explain what is going on? In evaluating the merit of therapy, therapists have tended to stress the importance of the insight that the client obtains. Clients, however, tend to lay greater emphasis on the support they get from the therapist, so therapists and clients appear to have somewhat different perceptions of what is useful (Garfield, 1994; Llewelyn, 1988).

Research on therapeutic outcomes suggests that it is hard to determine whether any particular psychotherapy produces better outcomes than others to any significant degree. In addition, paraprofessionals seem to obtain just about as good outcomes as do professionals (Faust & Zlotnick, 1995). It appears that some other common factor(s) account for most of the improvement (Barkham & Newnes, 1995; Bergin & Lambert, 1994). One candidate is the therapeutic alliance between the therapist and the client. Client expectation is also an important factor in predicting positive outcomes. Frank (1982) has long argued that therapy is a process that restores hope in the client. Others have suggested that the process offers a way of transforming meaning (Power & Brewin, 1997) and assimilating problematic experiences (Stiles et al., 1990).

Cognitive psychology suggests other reasons for questioning the central role accorded to explicit understanding in personal development generally. We know that the accounts that people give of their own motivations are not terribly reliable (Nisbett & Wilson, 1977), and our memories are no better (Loftus, 1994). So the stories that people present in therapy may be just that, stories bearing little relation to reality. Such stories may still have therapeutic value, but there are other reasons for caution. Explicit knowledge is known to lag behind implicit learning, and some situations are too complex for people to be able to state explicitly what they are doing (Lewicki et al., 1992). It seems likely that certain aspects of motivation and decision making about ourselves are similarly complex and unavailable for conscious perusal. There is also some evidence that verbalization can interfere with intuitive thinking and decision satisfaction. Schooler, Ohlsson, and Brooks (1993) invited people to choose a poster or a college course and asked half the group to verbalize why they were making the decisions they were and the other half to select by gut feel without rationalization. Six months later, more of those who had chosen intuitively were happier with their decision than those who were required to verbalize their rationale during the decision-making process. This work argues for greater attention to intuitive as opposed to explicit strategies for development.

It is also worth bearing in mind Taylor and Brown's (1994) work on the adaptive potential of positive illusions. This series of studies suggest that happy people tend to have falsely positive estimations of themselves and their future prospects, compared to their more-depressed counterparts. An optimistic outlook is known to be associated with higher confidence, subjective well-being, and positive health. This line of work is one of many highlighting the merits of concentrating on the positive (highlighted elsewhere in this book) rather than focusing on failure.

Development

The discussion above offers some reasons the large number of people in my studies valuing intuitive, embodied, and socially embedded strategies over explicit problem analysis may have good reason for doing so. There is also research to support their efficacy. For example, work on the relaxation response documents some benefits of quieting the mind (Benson, 1975), and mindfulness and meditation are now proving their worth as therapeutic tools (Kabat-Zinn, 1996). There is an extensive literature on the beneficial effects of social support (Taylor, Dickerson, & Klein, 2002), and physical exercise is known to raise endorphins and improve mental functioning (McCann & Holmes, 1984).

Good clinicians may already draw attention to their clients' strengths and encourage them to be active and social, but such tactics are not necessarily featured in manuals of good practice. It would be preferable if development rhetoric recognized the importance of more active, social, and intuitive routes to achieving the good life more explicitly. The work of positive psychologists and others detailing the merits of positive, embodied, and embedded approaches to development is already helping to legitimize practice in this area. However, positive psychology still inclines to a cognitively oriented approach to improving well-being, which champions the need for clear goals and planned action within a positive frame. One question raised by this study is how clinicians and mental health professionals can best help people who are less attracted to explicit analysis and who favor more intuitive, social, and active routes to change.

Further research is needed on aspects of counseling and therapy associated with positive improvement in well-being over the long term, rather than an absence of relapse. Here, as in many of areas of psychology, longitudinal research would be particularly welcome.

Conclusion

The findings in this study suggest that a wider range of processes help people to develop well-being than those typically advocated by clinicians and mental health professionals. One of the most popular was quieting the mind. A significant proportion of the sample valued approaches based on engaging with the world, being socially embedded, and in some cases building a positive attitude, finding purpose, and orienting toward the future. Many of the strategies that people found to be helpful are in line with key principles and practices advocated in positive psychology.

One implication is that clinicians, counselors, and mental health professionals might incorporate development strategies that recognize the importance of quieting the mind, physical activity, engagement with the world, social support, and building on strengths rather than just reflection. Spiritual practitioners have long advocated quieting the mind; doctors urge us to get out and exercise more; social scientists and health professionals have long noted the benefits of social support; and positive psychologists are busy developing approaches that build on strengths. The studies reported here suggest that these routes to well-being are important ones. The suggestion of widening the range of strategies employed is not an argument against talking therapies per se but rather one of balance. Notions of counseling and competency dominate our approaches to personal development and are increasingly prevalent in other domains. Yet it seems from my studies and other research that, for many people, more embodied, embedded, and less analytic strategies have proved to be effective routes to improving long-term well-being and are valued more highly than approaches centered around talking about their problems.

This chapter draws on some material in Henry (1994).

References

Argyle, M. (1987). *The psychology of happiness.* London: Methuen.

Argyle, M. (1999). *Empirical studies of well-being.* Presentation to CEP Consciousness and Well-Being Conference, Oxford.

Barkham, M., & Newnes, C. (1995). Outcomes in psychotherapy [Special issue]. *Changes, 13*(3), 161–224.

Benson, H. (1975). *The relaxation response.* New York: Morrow.

Bergin, A. E., & Lambert, M. J. (1994). The effectiveness of psychotherapy. In A. E. Bergin & S. L. Garfield (Eds.), *Handbook of psychotherapy and behavior change* (4th ed., pp. 143–189). New York: Wiley.

Bisson, J. (1994). Psychological debriefing and the prevention of post-traumatic stress: More research is needed. *British Journal of Psychiatry, 165*(6), 717–720.

Bisson, J. (1997). Randomised controlled trial of psychological debriefing for victims of acute trauma. *British Journal of Psychiatry, 171,* 78–81.

Campbell, J. (1995). *Myths to live by.* London: Souvenir Press.

Covey, S. (1990). *The seven habits of highly effective people.* New York: Fireside.

Csikszentmihalyi, M. (1999). *Flow and the evolution of consciousness.* Presentation to CEP Consciousness and Well-Being Conference, Oxford.

Csikszentmihalyi, M., & Csikszentmihalyi, I. (1988). *Optimal experience: Studies of flow in consciousness.* Cambridge: Cambridge University Press.

Diener, E., Gohm, C. L., Suh, E., & Oishi, S. (2000). Similarity of the relations between marital status and subjective well-being across cultures. *Journal of Cross-Cultural Psychology, 31,* 419–436.

Dilts, R. (1990). *Changing belief systems with NLP.* Cupertino, CA: Meta.

Faust, D., & Zlotnick, C. (1995). Revisiting the comparative benefit of professional & paraprofessional therapists. *Clinical Psychology and Psychotherapy, 2*(3), 157–167.

Fava, G. (1999). Well-being therapy: Conceptual and technical issues. *Psychotherapy and Psychosomatics, 68,* 171–179.

Frank, J. D. (1982). Therapeutic components shared by all therapies. In J. H. Harvey & M. M. Parks (Eds.), *The Master lecture series: Vol. 1. Psychotherapy research and behavior change* (pp. 73–122). Washington, DC: American Psychological Association.

Garfield, S. L. (1994). Research on client variables. In A. E. Bergin & S. L Garfield (Eds.), *Handbook of psychotherapy and behavior change* (4th ed., pp. 190–228). New York: Wiley.

Hannay, D. R. (1979). *The symptom iceberg.* London: Routledge & Kegan Paul.

Henry, J. (1998). Privileged practice in personal development. *Lifelong Learning in Europe, 3*(3), 161–165.

Henry, J. (1994). A comparison of strategies for achieving well-being in non-clinical populations. *Ricerche de Psicologia, 27,* 135–158.

Howard, K. I., Kopta, S. M., Krause, M. S., & Orlinsky, D. E. (1986). The dose-effect relationship in psychotherapy. *American Psychologist, 41,* 159–164.

Kabat-Zinn, J. (1996). Mindfulness meditation: What it is and what it isn't, and its role in health care and medicine. In Y. Haruki, Y. Ishii, & M. Suzuki (Eds.), *Comparative and psychological study in meditation* (pp. 161–170). Netherlands: Eburon.

Kabat-Zinn, J., et al. (1992). Effectiveness of a meditation-based stress-reduction program in the treatment of anxiety disorders. *American Journal of Psychiatry, 149,* 936–943.

Kerman, G. K., & Weissman, M. M. (1989). Increasing rates of depression. *Journal of the American Medical Association, 262,* 2229–2235.

Lewicki, P., Hill, T., & Czyzewska, M. (1992). Non-conscious acquisition of information. *American Psychologist, 47,* 796–801.

Llewelyn, S. P. (1988). Psychological therapy as viewed by clients and therapists. *British Journal of Clinical Psychology, 27,* 223–237.

Loftus, E. F. (1994). The repressed memory controversy. *American Psychologist, 49*(5), 443–445.

Lyubomirsky, S., Caldwell, N. D., & Nolen-Hoeksema, S. (1998). Effects of rumination and distracting responses to depressed mood on retrieval of autobiographical memories. *Journal of Personality and Social Psychology, 75,* 166–177.

Lyubomirsky, S., & Nolen-Hoeksema, S. (1995). Effects of self-focused rumination and negative thinking and interpersonal problem solving. *Journal of Personality and Social Psychology, 69,* 176–190.

McCann, I. L., & Holmes, D. S. (1984). Influence of aerobic exercise on depression. *Journal of Personality and Social Psychology, 27,* 1142–1147.

Myers, D. (2000). The funds, friends and faith of happy people. *American Psychologist, 55*(1), 56–67.

Nisbett, R. E., & Wilson, T. D. (1977). Telling more than we can know: Verbal reports on mental processes. *Psychological Review, 75,* 522–536.

Nolen-Hoeksema, S., & Morrow, J. (1993). Effects of rumination and distraction on naturally occurring depressed mood. *Cognition and Emotion, 7,* 561–579.

Phillips, F. L., & Fagan, P. J. (1982). *Attrition: Focus on the intake and first therapy interviews.* Presented at the 90th Annual APA Convention.

Power, M., & Brewin, C. R. (1997). *The transformation of meaning in psychological therapies: Integrating theory and practice.* London: Wiley.

Prochaska, O., & DiClemente, C. C. (1982). Transtheoretical therapy: Towards a more integrative model of change. *Psychotherapy: Theory, Research and Practice, 19,* 276–288.

Rose, N. (1990). *Governing the soul.* London: Routledge.

Schooler, J. W., Ohlsson, S., & Brooks, K. (1993). Thoughts beyond words when verbalization overshadows insight. *Journal of Experimental Psychology, 122,* 166–183.

Seligman, M. (1991). *Learned optimism.* New York: Knopf.

Seligman, M., & Csikszentmihalyi, M. (2000). Positive psychology [Special issue]. *American Psychologist, 55*(1), 1–196.

Snyder, C. R., Rand, K. L., & Sigmon, D. R. (2002). Hope theory: A member of the positive psychology family. In C. R. Snyder & S. J. Lopez (Eds.), *The positive psychology handbook* (pp. 257–276). Oxford: Oxford University Press.

Stiles, W. B., Elliot, R., Llewelyn, S. P., Firth, J. A., Cozens, J. A., Margerison, F. R., Shapiro, D. A., & Hardy, G. E. (1990). Assimilation of problematic experiences by clients in psychotherapy. *Psychotherapy, 27,* 411–420.

Taylor, S. E., & Brown, J. D. (1994). Positive illusion and mental well-being revisited: Separating fact from fiction. *Psychological Bulletin, 116*(1), 21–27.

Taylor, S. E., Dickerson, S. S., & Klein, L. C. (2002). Towards a biology of social support. In C. R. Snyder & S. J. Lopez (Eds.), *The positive psychology handbook* (pp. 556–569). Oxford: Oxford University Press.

Teasdale, J., Seagal, Z., & Williams, M. (1995). How does cognitive therapy prevent depressive relapse and why should attentional control (mindfulness) training help? *Behaviour Research and Therapy, 33*(1), 25–39.

Turvey, T. (1997). *Clinical outcomes of an adult clinical psychology service 1988–1995.* Paper presented to BPS Clinical Psychology Section Conference, Edinburgh.

Ulrich, R. S. (1984). View through a window may influence recovery from surgery. *Science, 224,* 420–421.

PART III

LIFELONG POSITIVE DEVELOPMENT

The third part of this volume consists of five chapters dealing with long-term developmental issues. Instead of focusing on momentary experiences, they ask the questions: What is a good life? How does one achieve it? Although each author approaches these questions from a different theoretical position, the conclusions they reach are astonishingly convergent. Jochen Brandtstädter argues that satisfaction with one's lot over the lifespan, and especially in the later years, is contingent on developing meaningful goals that lend coherence to one's daily actions. He reviews strategies for setting goals and for adjusting them when conditions change. Flexible goal adjustment prevents the helplessness and depression resulting from frustrated purpose and makes it possible for older persons to maintain a positive view as previously salient goals become less and less realistic. When aversive states cannot be avoided objectively, through instrumental action, the cognitive system can step in and achieve symbolic control over material obstacles.

Antonella Delle Fave, whose team at the University of Milan has spent decades collecting cross-cultural material concerning quality-of-life issues, develops a similar theme. She reports on children in India and Nepal, as well as in various European samples, who despite often severe disabilities perceive their quality of life to be either good or excellent. The construct of "functional optimism" helps to explain how these children are able to bring order and structure to their disrupted lives by making their experiences comprehensible, manageable, and meaningful. It is not unusual for some individuals to transform even the most tragic situations into opportunities for personal growth.

Given that development can be successfully pursued through hardship and disablement, Delle Fave questions quality-of-life measures that rely solely on objective indicators. If what constitutes a good life depends on how one responds to external conditions, then researchers should be measuring the style of the responses in addition to the conditions themselves. If poverty, neglect, and illness are eradicated, this can improve the quality of life. But if a person cannot find meaning in daily experience, no improvement is likely to occur. Thus, disadvantaged populations can teach us important lessons about enhancing the quality of life through subjective, rather than through objective, means.

The importance of determining one's destiny by constructing personally meaningful goals, introduced by Brandtstädter at the beginning of this section, continues in the work of Jari-Erik Nurmi and Katariina Salmela-Aro. They present a wealth of evidence to the effect that well-being is enhanced when people are committed to goals that match their needs—especially when they are in control of them and when the goals involve psychological outcomes, such as self-acceptance or affiliation, rather than material outcomes, such as financial success. Each stage of life presents its own characteristic "opportunity spaces" for developing meaningful goals. An important point that is echoed by several other authors is that goals focused exclusively on the self are less likely to lead to a positive quality of life than goals that take other people into consideration. Nurmi and Salmela-Aro conclude with the suggestion that research on goal setting could inform counseling strategies for improving the quality of life.

The same argument is developed further by Tim Kasser, whose research focuses on the ill effects of materialistic goals. His conclusion is that the great economist John Maynard Keynes was not far off when he claimed that the love of money is a form of mental illness. The more that people value materialistic goals, he finds, the less happy they are likely to be and the more damaging their behavior is to the social and natural environment. Materialistic values tend to drive out prosocial or spiritual values, and they lead to objectification—treating other people as tools to be manipulated rather than as individuals with their own needs. In line with most other contributions to this volume, Kasser is not content with just reporting the facts but suggests ways to apply the knowledge derived from research to improving the quality of life. He outlines a variety of means to combat the consumerism that exacerbates materialism, ranging from a redefinition of how the Gross Domestic Product is computed, to changing laws and influencing the media.

We are given by Kennon Sheldon a good illustration of how one's values may affect conclusions based on scholarly research. The topic that Sheldon addresses is the relationship between chronological age and well-being. As long as we assume that a good life requires great health, fluid mental processes, material gains, and career success, old age does not look very good, and we might conclude that the quality of life declines with time. But if one defines a good life in terms of subjective experience, as a sense of self-determination, happiness, and life satisfaction, research leads to the opposite conclusion. Older respondents—even within the same family—tend to report more of these positive states than do younger ones.

The book ends with an afterword by Martin Seligman, in which he outlines the main elements of the vision that has resulted in the movement we now know as positive psychology. A good life, he writes, is one that allows for pleasure, engagement, and meaning. Following this definition might help clinical psychology to break the "65% barrier," which now prevents therapists from even trying to cure mental disease but resigns them to use palliatives to mask and reduce pain.

The hope he extends is that of learning to be like Abraham Lincoln or Winston Churchill, who despite severe depression were able to forge lives that were in many respects exemplary and beneficial to humankind.

The chapters in this volume agree on some extraordinarily important issues. First and perhaps foremost, we do not depend for our happiness on good luck or inherited resources—whether genetic or financial. The measure of freedom and autonomy that our complex brains afford—whether we like it or not—makes it possible for each person to carve out a life worth living, despite the most dire external circumstances. Being able to approach one's lot with optimism, savoring the moment instead of ruminating about what could have been, is a first step. After that, a commitment to realistic yet ambitious, unselfish, nonmaterial goals helps to give meaning to one's actions and leads to a richer life. And all of this is a clear continuation of the "experiential turn" that psychologists such as William James and John Dewey initiated a century or so ago: the realization that psychology should deal first and foremost with lived experience and only secondarily with more "objective" phenomena like behaviors, traits, and physical or mental abilities. If positive psychology succeeds in reintegrating even these few perspectives into the main discipline, it will have earned for itself an important place in the history of thought.

At the same time, it is important that in this process we do not overshoot the mark. The danger is that the realization of how important subjective states are might lead to a neglect of those objective conditions that contribute to the quality of life. For instance, it is important to know that one can be happy even under a totalitarian dictatorship. Or in a soulless consumer society. Or when ravaged by poverty and disease. But it would be a grave error on that account to conclude that all ills are just "in the head" and abdicate responsibility for trying to correct the external situations that dialectically influence, and are influenced by, the person's subjective experience. These, however, are concerns that need not worry us overmuch at this time. What is important now is to take seriously the corrective contributions that positive psychology is poised to make—contributions that are likely to enrich our understanding of human behavior for many years to come.

8

Adaptive Resources in Later Life

Tenacious Goal Pursuit and Flexible Goal Adjustment

JOCHEN BRANDTSTÄDTER

The question of what conditions promote desirable forms of development over a lifespan has often been approached by listing criteria such as inner harmony, meaningful activity, personal fulfillment, accomplishment, agency, belongingness, leading a life of purpose, and the like. "Happiness" and "satisfaction" are often considered to be the consequence or quintessence of such conditions. Serious theoretical work, however, begins with asking what personal and contextual conditions can promote or impede such desired states.

Much that is interesting and important can be said in that regard (see, e.g., Becker, 1992; Nussbaum & Sen, 1993; Ryff & Singer, 1998; Seligman, 2002). However, the more concrete and specific the answers become, the less they can claim to be valid for all people at all ages and times. What makes life worth living depends to a large extent on what people themselves consider to be desirable (Brandtstädter, 1992; Greve, 2001). Unfortunately, personal notions of the good life—and social conceptions of optimal development as well—are often rendered questionable by the course of life. A considerable part of our life activity consists in dealing with unintended or unpredicted consequences of earlier choices and actions; this of course reflects the "bounded rationality" (Simon, 1983) of human agents. Not only is our causal and procedural knowledge fallible and limited; even our own motives and desires, and their modifications over the course of life, are not fully transparent and predictable to us.

Questions of optimal development and successful aging thus cannot simply be conceived in terms of efficiency in the achievement of personal goals; a comprehensive theoretical account must also heed the processes and mechanisms through which the person copes with, and eventually comes to accept, divergences between the desired and factual paths of life. In the following, I

143

will discuss a theoretical perspective that focuses on the dynamics of goal pursuit and goal adjustment and their implications for well-being in later life.

Goals as Sources of Meaning— and Depression

A brief digression into the history of ideas may help to bring the key issues into perspective. Philosophical teachings since antiquity have revolved around two opposed views of the good life, which can be denoted as "offensive" and "defensive" notions of happiness, respectively (Tatarkiewicz, 1976). *Offensive notions* consider happiness and satisfaction as essentially consisting in the successful achievement of personal goals; *defensive notions,* by contrast, have emphasized the importance of making oneself resistant to the vicissitudes of life. Among those advocating the latter stance were Stoic philosophers such as Seneca and Epictetus, who considered ambitious desires to be a source of distress; these philosophers considered the readiness to accommodate to necessity as a key condition of wisdom and *eudaimonia* (see also Long, 1974). While offensive notions of optimal development and successful aging are clearly more *en vogue* among psychologists today, defensive notions seem to contain a valid insight, too. Taken together, both positions sensitize us to the ambivalent role that goals and ambitions play in a person's economy of satisfaction and happiness.

On the one hand, goals and personal projects lend structure, coherence, and meaning to life; in fact, having goals is itself a good predictor of life satisfaction (see Brunstein, Schultheiss, & Maier, 1999; Emmons, 1996). This holds only as long as goals are perceived as meaningful and attainable, however. Goals are experienced as meaningful to the extent that they are related to overarching identity projects or life themes (Csikszentmihalyi & Beattie, 1979); such "upward" links are activated when we ask ourselves *why* we pursue a particular goal. The degree to which we can identify with our life and activity first and foremost depends on these associative relations. Beliefs related to the attainability of goals, by contrast, constitute "downward" links that relate goals to representations of means and strategies of goal implementation. Such links are activated when we ask *how* a given goal can be implemented (see also Brandtstädter, 1998; Kruglanski, 1996). When downward links cannot be established, goals can become a source of frustration and depression. This however holds only as long as goals are seen as meaningful and attractive and as long as the commitment to them persists; generally, difficulties of goal attainment have a stronger negative influence on subjective well-being when the person's commitment to the goal is high (see also Brunstein et al., 1999).

These preliminary considerations suggest important metacriteria of optimal development and successful aging. On the one hand, any personal or contextual factor that enhances the feasibility of goals, as well as their integration into systems of meaning, promotes a sense of self-esteem, well-being, and satisfaction. This also includes contextual resources and personal capacities to prevent, and eventually to compensate for, losses and constraints in action resources. The feasibility of goals, however, is linked to personal and contextual action resources that may change on ontogenetic and historical dimensions of time. Accordingly, flexibility in accommodating goals to action resources and contextual constraints appears to be another key condition for maintaining a positive view of self and personal development over the life course.

Goal Pursuit and Goal Adjustment: The Dual-Process Model

It thus appears that resilience and subjective well-being across the lifespan essentially hinges on the interplay of two different types of adaptive processes: first, activities through which the actual situation or course of personal development is brought into congruence with personal goals and life themes; second, the adjustment of goals and ambitions to contextual and personal resources of action or to changes in available action resources. We denote these two adaptive modes as *assimilative* and *accommodative,* respectively (Brandtstädter & Renner, 1990; Brandtstädter & Rothermund, 2002a, 2002b; Brandtstädter, Wentura, & Rothermund, 1999). The two modes are antagonistically related: People will maintain their goals and commitments as long as these appear to be attainable without disproportionate effort or cost, and they will adjust their commitments and aspirations only when attainability beliefs are weak or have been eroded by futile attempts to reach the goals. The dynamics of assimilation and accommodation obviously depend on two critical parameters: first, the degree of perceived control over the goal (which depends on "capacity beliefs" as well as on "strategy beliefs"; see Skinner, 1995); and second, the personal value or importance of the goal. Feelings of helplessness and depression typically arise when a highly important goal is perceived as unattainable. The dual-process model posits, however, that the erosion of attainability beliefs activates accommodative modes of coping that reduce the attractive valence of the blocked goal (Brandtstädter & Greve, 1994; Brandtstädter et al., 1999; see also Wrosch, Scheier, Carver, & Schulz, 2003). The model also suggests that states of depression and helplessness may enhance the process of accommodation, which eventually results in dissolving the barren commitment.

Despite their antagonism, assimilative and accommodative modes can mutually complement and support each other in concrete episodes of coping. Under reduced action resources, for example, disengaging from some goals may facilitate the maintenance of other, more-central goals. There are situations where assimilative and accommodative processes may be simultaneously activated; conflicts between holding on and letting go typically occur when goal-related efforts reach resource limits. Such critical constellations often arise in old age, when questions of how, and into which goals and projects, scarce lifetime reserves and action resources should be invested become an acute concern. In fact, later life can be considered as a paradigm field for the dual-process model, although we do not see the scope of the theory limited to that particular segment of the lifespan.

Subjective Well-Being in Later Life: Some Empirical Observations

It seems fitting at this point to briefly review some empirical observations about well-being and subjective life quality in later life. Old age is commonly seen as a period when the balance between developmental gains and losses tips toward the negative, and this picture also emerges in self-ratings of elderly people (cf. Brandtstädter, Wentura, & Greve, 1993; Heckhausen, Dixon, & Baltes, 1989). Although there is high individual variation in most parameters of aging, the loss of adaptive reserves and action resources appears to be a general feature of the aging process; irreversible losses accumulate in later life (Seligman & Elder, 1986). Adding to this picture the widespread negative stereotypes about aging and the aged and their potentially insidious effects on the elderly person's self-view (see Rothermund & Brandtstädter, 2003), one might expect that such gloomy prospects should undermine a sense of well-being, efficacy, and personal worth.

This plausible assumption has received surprisingly little empirical support, however. There is no consistent evidence for a dramatic decline in indicators of well-being and subjective life quality in the transition to old age, at least up to the terminal phases of life when critical events such as illness or bereavement accumulate (cf. Brandtstädter et al., 1993; Diener, Suh, Lucas, & Smith, 1999; Staudinger, Marsiske, & Baltes, 1995; Stock, Okun, Haring, & Witter, 1983). Findings from my own longitudinal projects illustrate this general pattern (see Brandtstädter, 2002a). The data were obtained from a sample of more than 800 participants in the initial age range of 54 to 78 years. Figure 8.1 depicts cross-sequential differences and 8-year longitudinal changes in life satisfaction, as measured by the Life Satisfaction Inventory (Neugarten, Havighurst, & Tobin, 1961). Data are T-scaled with mean = 50 and SD = 10.

Although the regression of satisfaction on age reveals a curvilinear component, the picture, on the average, is one of considerable stability. At an age roughly corresponding to the average life expectancy, we observe indications of a terminal drop (see also Lawton, 1991); even in the oldest cohort, however, the number of cases showing an increase in well-being over the longitudinal interval is only slightly lower than the number of cases for the opposed trend (see also Brandtstädter, 2002a).

We have found similar patterns for measures of self-esteem and (with signs reversed) for measures of depression. The convergence of longitudinal and cross-

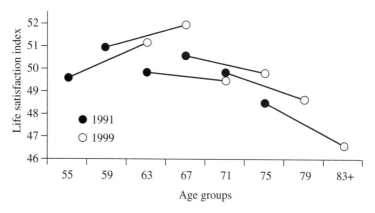

Figure 8.1.   Life Satisfaction and Age: Cross-Sequential Findings
Source: Brandstädter, 2002a.

sectional effects renders explanations in terms of generation or cohort effects less plausible, which however does not preclude the possibility that historical changes, such as increasing individualism and the "waning of the commons" (Seligman, 1990), may contribute to rising levels of depression and dissatisfaction in the population.

There is of course much individual variation around the general pattern; reported well-being varies among the elderly as it does in younger groups. Those who are less depressed or more satisfied with their lives report a greater sense of efficacy and control; they perceive their future as more open and are less prone to feelings of obsolescence (e.g., Brandtstädter & Rothermund, 2003). The resilience of the aging self vis-à-vis constraints and losses, however, remains impressive; it raises the more general question as to the protective processes that the self-system engages to preserve a sense of continuity, efficacy, and personal worth despite the losses and constraints that typically accompany old age.

Clearly, the prospects of being old are aversive as long as they are evaluated from a "younger" frame of reference. When we look at old age from a temporal distance, we tend to base our evaluations on our current goals and self-definitions. What we tend to overlook, however, is that this evaluative frame also changes over the life course; a key proposition of the dual-process model is that it tends to change in ways that help to maintain a positive outlook on self and personal development.

Assimilative Processes

Assimilative activities comprise all types of intentional behaviors through which people try to achieve or maintain a desired course of personal development; they are integral to the lifelong process of intentional self-development and are part of the process through which cultural systems maintain and regenerate themselves (see Brandtstädter & Lerner, 1999). Self-cultivation, self-perfection, expanding personal competencies, and maintaining desired levels of functioning or standards of living are basic intentional vectors that drive assimilative efforts. People engage in selective and self-regulatory mechanisms in order to assimilate their behavior to self-evaluative standards and normative expectations; they try to assimilate their bodily appearance to a desired bodily self through jogging, dieting, visiting beauty farms, or whatever appears to be effective. Briefly, our life activity to a large extent consists in the attempt to realize representations of a desired or "ought" self. The corresponding self-regulatory intentions emerge as soon as the person has formed such normative self-representations, or "self guides" (Higgins, 1996). Assimilative efforts are guided by personal and social notions of the good life as well as by individually and contextually accessible knowledge about how to implement such normative expectations; these conditions and constraints may change on ontogenetic and historical dimensions of time. The intentional focus of assimilation, too, tends to change over the lifespan. In early adulthood, assimilative efforts predominantly strive for an expansion of action resources and for the achievement of future-related goals and projects; in later life, assimilative efforts increasingly center on the maintenance of resources and personally valued competencies and on the prevention and compensation of losses (see also Cross & Markus, 1991).

A common feature of assimilative activities is the tenacious adherence to particular goals, performance standards, or desired projections of life. Assimilative efforts become increasingly taxing, however, under conditions of constrained action resources. When they approach resource limits, there may first be a reactant mobilization of reserve capacities, and intermediary goals of optimizing the use of scarce resources and compensating for functional deficits may emerge (Brandtstädter et al., 1999; cf. Klinger, 1975; Wortman & Brehm, 1975). Not surprisingly, then, the notion of compensation looms large in current notions of successful aging (e.g., Baltes & Baltes, 1990; Dixon & Bäckman, 1995).

Compensatory and optimizing activities mark a late phase of assimilative efforts where the aspect of tenaciously maintaining previous goals and standards becomes particularly salient. A principle of diminishing returns, however, sets limits to such efforts. In functional domains where losses and constraints accumulate, compensatory effort investment may first increase, but then drop more or less gradually as the costs of compensatory efforts outweigh the benefits (for evidence, see Brandtstädter & Rothermund, 2003). When goals and desired self-representations can no longer be achieved or maintained, a situation arises that—according to prevailing clinical notions—should precipitate feelings of helplessness and depression. According to the dual-process model, however, this is the critical point where accommodative tendencies come into play.

Accommodative Processes

Facets of accommodation include disengagement from blocked goals, downgrading of ambitions, rescaling of self-evaluative standards, and shifting of comparison perspectives. In contrast to the assimilative mode, the key characteristic of the accommodative mode is the flexible adjustment of previously adopted goals and standards to situational constraints and to available action resources. Although inhibiting further effort expenditure with respect to goals that have drifted beyond the subject's span of control, the accommodative process does not terminate assimilative activities altogether, but rather helps to redirect them to new and more promising areas of life and development. The coadjustment of goals and action resources that results from the balanced interplay of assimilation and accommodation thus also helps to keep the person within a "flow channel" (Csikszentmihalyi & Rathunde, 1998).

It should be noted, however, that accommodative processes—in contrast to assimilative activities—cannot be considered as intentionally originated. Just as we cannot intentionally select our beliefs and preferences, we cannot dissolve from barren commitments or reduce the attractiveness of blocked goals simply by an act of will. Of course we may eventually decide to drop the goal and turn to other projects, but such a decision would already be the outcome of accommodation. This is a theoretically important point that has led us to investigate more closely the microprocesses that underlie accommodation, as well as the conditions that may differentially enhance or impede the shift from assimilation to accommodation.

The phenomena of depression, rumination, grief, or regret remind us that the shift from assimilative to accommodative modes of coping is not always a smooth one. Some personal and situational conditions that are relevant in that regard shall be briefly mentioned (see also Brandtstädter & Greve, 1994; Brandtstädter & Rothermund, 2002b).

People will find it most difficult to disengage from ambitions and goals that are central to their identities or life plans and for which equivalent substitutes cannot easily be found. Accordingly, a multifaceted self-structure that embraces a variety of different goals or projects will enhance accommodation and thus should contribute to the resiliency of the self-system in situations of loss and impairment (see also Linville, 1987). As already intimated, self-beliefs of control and efficacy figure most prominently among the factors that affect the balance between assimilation and accommodation. The dual-process model partly converges with positions that emphasize the importance of perceived control for subjective well-being and as a coping resource, but it also points to possible negative side effects. While a strong sense of control and efficacy generally leads people to persist longer in assimilative efforts, it may put them at a disadvantage when they face irreversible loss (see also Janoff-Bulman & Brickman, 1982; Thompson, Cheek, & Graham, 1988). By impeding or delaying the shift toward accommodation, such a disposition may lead to an "escalating commitment" to blocked goals and barren projects, which can have catastrophic consequences in personal development and organizational contexts as well (Staw, 1997). Such side effects may also account for some of the counterintuitive findings of a positive correlation between measures of perceived control and depression (see Coyne, 1992).

These assumptions also seem to afford a better understanding of the phenomenon of depression. Besides the loss of control over personally important goals, the inability to disengage from blocked goals and to relinquish barren life paths appears to make people vulnerable to feelings of helplessness and depression (see also Carver & Scheier, 2003). Such feelings apparently are symptomatic of difficulties in resolving conflicts between holding on and letting go; they arise when upward links of goals are still activated although goals cannot be linked to implementation activities. Accommodation theory, however, does not consider depression to be simply the final outcome of failed coping efforts. As will become more clear in the following, depressives states and their functional correlates, such as rumination and feelings of helplessness, may have an inherent potential of enhancing the shift toward accommodation and the reorientation toward new goals (see also Klinger, 1975; Nesse, 2000). Figure 8.2 summarizes the considerations so far. As indicated in the scheme, we assume that assimilative and accommodative processes involve radically different modes of information processing.

Information Processing in the Two Modes

In the assimilative mode, the cognitive system is tuned toward the successful implementation of goals; attention is focused on information that is relevant for goal pursuit, and task-unrelated, distracting stimuli are warded off (e.g., Kuhl, 1987). At the same time, cognitions that support goal pursuit and help to maintain an intended course of action become more available. As long as the system operates in the assimilative mode, it responds to obstacles that may arise during goal pursuit by a mobilization of effort; the increased cost of goal pursuit is often "compensated" by a reactant increase in goal pursuit (see also Wright & Brehm, 1989).

As the system shifts toward accommodation, this goal-focused, or "implemental," cognitive set (Gollwitzer, 1990) is inhibited and superseded by mechanisms that tend to eliminate the hedonic differences between the goal state and the current situation, which motivated the assimilative effort: Cognitive content that helps to deconstruct the attractiveness of the blocked goal and that enhances a positive reappraisal of the given situation becomes more available. The attentional field widens and the cognitive system becomes responsive to stimuli and competing action tendencies that have been warded off in the assimilative phase. In sum, a heuristic-divergent, bottom-up mode of information processing supersedes the more top-down, convergent mode that characterizes assimilation (Brandtstädter & Rothermund, 2002b). Support for this latter assumption

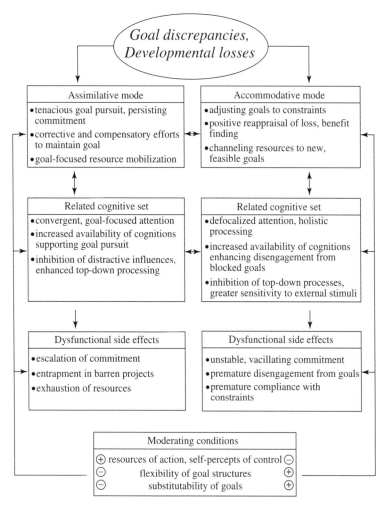

Figure 8.2.   Assimilative and Accommodative Processes: Facets, Basic Mechanisms, and Differential Conditions
Note: + and – indicate enhancing and inhibiting effects, respectively. *Source:* Brandstädter, & Rothermund, 2002b.

comes from experimental studies in which we used incidental recall for distractor stimuli as a dependent variable (Brandtstädter & Rothermund, 2002a). Participants in these experiments worked on two sets of anagrams; the task stimuli (letter strings to be rearranged) were surrounded on the computer screen by distractor words that were unrelated to the task. Anagrams in the first set were solvable throughout; in the second series, the experimental group received unsolvable anagrams, whereas the control group continued with solvable tasks. Recall for distractors was assessed after completing the second set. We expected that the gradual erosion of task-related control beliefs in the unsolvable series would mediate enhanced recall for distractors in the experimental group; results were consistent with this assumption. Findings from animal studies likewise suggest that the blocking of goal-related activity may enhance performance in tasks requiring attention to external cues (e.g., Rodd, Rosellini, Stock, & Gallup, 1997).

The functional states that correspond to the two mindsets thus differ in characteristic ways: Whereas the hedonic contrast between current situational conditions and intended goal states is accentuated in the assimilative mode, it is deemphasized or neutralized in the accommodative mode; attention regulation and the availability of cognitions change in accordance. This functional state renders the cognitive system susceptible to particular types of biases. Whereas people tend to overestimate their control when entering the phase of goal implementation (see Taylor & Gollwitzer, 1995), a more realistic assessment of their own capacities appears characteristic for, and enhances, the disengagement from blocked goals and the shift toward more promising projects. Notions of "depressive realism" (Alloy & Abramson, 1988) fit into this general picture, although we consider a more "realistic," or even negatively biased, assessment of their own action resources not simply as a depressive symptom but rather as a condition that enhances the shift toward accommodation. As intimated above, there are situations where both adaptive tendencies may conflict; these situations occur when assimilative efforts are pushed to limits and begin to exhaust action resources. Ruminative thinking may help to resolve this conflict; while rumination can enhance problem solving (see Martin & Tesser, 1989), it may support positive reappraisals of initially aversive situations when attainability beliefs are eroded. The characteristic cognitive sets that correspond to the two adaptive modes map on a broader range of phenomena that are relevant for the dynamics of subjective well-being. According to the dual-process model, the tendency to find "benefit in adversity" (Affleck & Tennen, 1996) is not a general one, but should be more strongly expressed in situations that appear to be irreversible and not open to active change; a positive reappraisal of aversive states would appear to be dysfunctional as long as there are chances to alter the situation (for converging findings, see Lyubomirsky & Ross, 1999). This asymmetry should also be enhanced by the reduced availability of upward counterfactuals under conditions of no control (see also Roese, 1997). The same holds for affective adaptations to aversive changes; the "hedonic treadmill" (Kahneman, 1999, 2000a, 2000b) should operate more effectively when the change cannot be reversed and positive alternatives are not easily attainable. Similarly, people should be more willing to accept negative self-descriptions when the corresponding attributes appear open to improvement (see Duval & Silvia, 2002; Rothermund, Bak, & Brandtstädter, 2005).

With regard to the perception of dangers, the dual-process model predicts a sensitizing effect when the person feels able to avert the impending danger, whereas an opposed defensive bias should emerge when the person feels unable to avert the danger (for experimental evidence, see Brandtstädter, Voß, & Rothermund, 2004). The tendency to overpredict the strength and duration of negative emotions in the case of failure ("durability bias"; Gilbert, Pinel, Wilson, Blumberg, & Wheatley, 1998; see also Kahneman, 2000a, 2000b) can possibly be reconstrued as a joint effect of the cognitive sets that characterize assimilative/pre-accommodative and post-assimilative/accommodative phases. According to this account, however, duration biases should be more strongly expressed when an aversive outcome appears not open to ameliorative change.

Implications for Successful Aging

Assimilative and accommodative processes are protective mechanisms through which the self-system constructs personal continuity over the life course (Brandtstädter & Greve, 1994). Assimilative processes aim at the active realization of desired courses of development and aging; accommodative processes, by contrast, help people to disengage from barren life paths and accept irreversible losses without permanent regret.

On a dispositional level, we have found stable individual differences in these two modes of coping and life management. To assess such differences, we have used two scales: Tenacious Goal Pursuit (TGP) as a measure of assimilative persistence and Flexible Goal Adjustment (FGA) as a measure of accommodative flexibility.[1] TGP and FGA assess independent facets of coping competence and show low negative or zero correlations in most studies. Both scales, however, show convergent positive correlations with indicators of subjective life quality, such as life satisfaction, optimism, emotional stability, and (low) depression (e.g., see Becker, 1995; Brandtstädter & Renner, 1990; Freund & Baltes, 2002). At the same time, the scales exhibit opposed regressions on chronological age, which are suggestive of an increasing dominance of, or preference for, accommodative over assimilative modes of coping (cf. Brandtstädter, 1992; Heckhausen & Schulz, 1995). Considering the accumulation of irreversible losses and the curtailment of action resources and lifetime reserves in later life, this finding conforms with theoretical predictions.

A broad array of findings from questionnaire studies and experiments, as well as from interviews with elderly people, attests to the particular importance of accommodative flexibility in adjusting to losses and impairments in later life (see also Brandtstädter, 2002b). While the scales of TGP and FGA are both strong predictors of life quality at all age levels, the latter has repeatedly shown two specific effects. First, accommodative flexibility buffers the negative impact of age-typical losses and constraints on subjective well-being. Second, it enhances the availability of uplifting cognitions in situations of threat and loss.

Accommodative Flexibility
as an Interactive Buffer

The dual-process model posits that when goals become nonattainable, accommodative mechanisms are activated that gradually deconstruct the attractiveness of these goals. By enhancing that process, accommodative flexibility should shield self-esteem and well-being from experiences of loss. A corresponding buffering effect consistently emerged in moderated regression analyses in which the FGA variable was entered as a moderator.

For example, aversive conditions, such as physical impairment or chronic pain, have been found to affect subjective life quality and well-being to a lesser degree among persons scoring high in accommodative flexibility (e.g., Brandtstädter et al., 1993; Schmitz, Saile, & Nilges, 1996). Flexible individuals likewise are less negatively affected by the shrinking of lifetime reserves (Brandtstädter & Wentura, 1994; Brandtstädter, Wentura, & Schmitz, 1997). Accommodative flexibility also dampens spillover effects from aversive experiences in specific domains of life to a person's general sense of well-being; for example, among flexible individuals, satisfaction in a particular domain (e.g., marital satisfaction) tends to be less closely associated with general life satisfaction (cf. Brandtstädter & Baltes-Götz, 1990; Felser, Schmitz, & Brandtstädter, 1998). According to the dual-process model, the buffering function of accommodative flexibility should become particularly salient when the person is faced with strong and irreversible losses or impairments. Consistent with this assumption are findings by Boerner (in press); working with a sample of visually handicapped people, she found that accommodative flexibility contributes more to subjective life quality among people with strong visual impairments.

Although accommodative changes in goal importance are driven by an erosion of attainability beliefs, and although they are not under personal control and should not be equated with cognitive maneuvers to maintain a sense of control (in the sense of "secondary control"; see Heckhausen & Schulz, 1995; Rothbaum, Weisz, & Snyder, 1982), they appear to contribute to stabilizing a sense of efficacy and control. As Brandtstädter and Rothermund (1994) observed, longitudinal changes in perceived control within a particular goal domain have a less negative impact on generalized control beliefs if the personal importance of the respective goal decreases within the same interval. The explanation in terms of the dual-process model seems straightforward: Notions of efficacy and control conceptually imply positive beliefs about the attainability of personally important goals; accordingly, when important goals are no longer attainable, decreases in goal importance should help to preserve a general sense of efficacy. This rationale may also account for the surprisingly high stability of generalized self-percepts of control and efficacy in later life, which has been documented in many studies (e.g., Gatz & Karel, 1993; Lachman, 1986). The mentioned findings also point to a general tendency to adjust preferences in ways that emphasize gain and deemphasize loss. In our panel studies, we consistently found inverse relationships between perceived distance from developmental goals and ratings of goal importance, as well as between longitudinal change scores for both ratings. Different explanations may come to mind for this pattern; we tend to see it as an expression of a tendency to deemphasize loss on a particular goal dimension by reducing its importance. This interpretation is supported by the observation that the inverse relationship between distance and importance ratings is less strongly expressed among depressed people (cf. Brandtstädter & Baltes-Götz, 1990; Brandtstädter, Rothermund, & Schmitz, 1998).

In line with these observations, flexible goal adjustment also appears to enhance the process of coping with, and adjusting to, developmental transitions that require a reorganization of goals and life plans. People scoring high in FGA, for example, appear to have fewer problems in adjusting their goals and in maintaining subjective well-being after retirement (Trépanier, Lapierre, Baillargeon, & Bouffard, 2001). Age-linked biological changes, too, affect the feasibility of goals; for example, goals related to motherhood become unattainable for postmenopausal women. Not surprisingly, women tend to disengage from such goals when they have passed the critical biological limit (Heckhausen, Wrosch, & Fleeson, 2001); such disengagements should pose fewer problems when satisfying alternative goals or equivalent substitutions are available. Nurmi and Salmela-Aro (2002; see also Salmela-Aro, Nurmi, Saisto, & Halmesmäki, 2001) point to an important qualification, however. Their observations hint that in developmental transitions involving new role demands or developmental tasks (such as the transition from school to work or the transition to motherhood), only goal changes that are in accordance with the demands of the current situation contribute to well-being.

Accommodative Flexibility and Palliative Thoughts

The considerations so far suggest that accommodative flexibility is an important developmental asset that becomes particularly valuable when it comes time to cope with the adaptive challenges of later life. Obviously, the "satisfaction treadmill" works better among people who harbor this particular adaptive strength, at least when it comes to coping with loss and aversive change.

Further support for these conclusions comes from the observation that accommodative flexibility enhances the availability of uplifting thoughts. Neutralization of aversive states is a basic feature of adaptation; the dual-process model assumes that if such neutralization cannot be achieved by instrumental actions, the cognitive system tends to produce it mentally. Parenthetically, this may explain why presumed "mood congruency" effects in memory and cognition are not consistently found for negative mood states (see Isen, 1999). Flexible people should be particularly prone to generating palliative cognitive content in threatening situations. This hypothesis has been borne out in several studies. In one study (Wentura, Rothermund, & Brandtstädter, 1995), participants (*n* = 120, age range 56 to 80 years) read brief descriptions of a stressful episode that comprised threatening as well as uplifting elements (sample scenario: "You recently visited your *doctor* for a check-up. He told you that your hearing has become *worse* since the last visit, but that it is still *better* than for most people of your age"). Semantic priming techniques were used to assess the degree to which (in the given example) *doctor* as a prime stimulus enhanced recognition of target words from the threatening or uplifting phrase (*worse, better*). As theoretically expected, recognition performance for positive target stimuli was better among participants scoring high in FGA. In a similar vein, accommodative flexibility supports a positive view of aging and growing old. Among flexible people, the attribute *old* has been found to prime increasingly positive associations (such as *good, happy*) with advancing age (Rothermund, Wentura, & Brandtstädter, 1995).

In interview studies with elderly people, accommodative attitudes toward aging were expressed in statements such as "Things that I can't change—I don't worry about them as much"; "After a certain amount of time, you come to terms with it, because other things are always happening, which are nice"; "You have to be humble enough to say, 'You aren't 40 any more! Taking a break is normal!'" It is obviously not resignation or depression that transpires from such statements. On the contrary, content analyses revealed that participants who frequently expressed accommodative thoughts of this type were more content with their aging and more likely to find continuity and meaning in their lives (Schmitz, 1998).

Accommodation of Meaning Perspectives

Adaptive challenges in later life are boosted by the fading of lifetime reserves. Time is a resource of action as well as of meaning; to a large degree, our activities gain motivating meaning from future-related goals and projects. Accommodative shifts of meaning perspectives, however, may alleviate losses in "future meaning" in later life (Reker, Peacock, & Wong, 1987). In old age, people often tend to integrate their personal biography into a larger context of meaning; as life is a temporally closed gestalt, however, its "meaning" cannot easily be found within a life-immanent time horizon. There are sources of meaning, however, the valence of which does not depend on outcomes in the future. Moral and religious ideals and altruistic and socioemotional goals (friendship, love, intimacy) may be considered as examples of these more-intrinsic, time-transcendent dimensions of meaning.

Findings from different lines of research suggest that such perspectives of meaning gain importance under fading resources of action and shrinking lifetime reserves. Older people (and, more generally, individuals who anticipate separation from familiar surroundings) tend to spend their time preferentially with close people; marriage partners, children, and grandchildren become central sources of meaning (cf. Carstensen, 1993; Dittmann-Kohli & Westerhof, 2000; Fredrickson & Carstensen, 1990). In later life, past experiences and achievements gain importance as bases for the construction of identity and personal continuity (e.g., Sherman, 1991); whereas a dominant orientation toward the past is often a symptom of depressive tendencies among younger people, this relationship weakens with advancing age (Brandtstädter & Wentura, 1994). We also observe an increased emphasis on social norms and moral ideals and a stronger commitment to projects that transcend the personal horizon of the lifetime, such as care for future generations (see also Brandtstädter et al., 1997). Such shifts in meaning perspectives have been explained as defensive processes that serve to neutralize fear and uncertainty and that are triggered when life's finitude becomes salient (e.g., Rosenblatt, Greenberg, Solomon, Pyszczynski, & Lyon, 1989). From the present theoretical perspective, they appear as a result of accommodative processes that are activated by the shrinking of lifetime reserves and action potentials and that eventually lead to significant changes in frames of rationality and in personal constructions of what makes life worth living.

Summary

People strive to manage their lives and to control their development and aging in order to strike a favorable balance of gains and losses across the lifespan. They do so, however, within developmental settings that are partly opaque and beyond their control; historical and ontogenetic changes affect the attainability of goals and personal projects. Well-being and self-esteem over the life course thus depend not only on efficient goal pursuit, but also on the readiness to adjust goals to changing circumstances and to disengage without permanent regret from life paths that have not been, or can no longer be, accomplished.

The model of assimilative and accommodative processes has been proposed as a framework that integrates these perspectives. At the core of this theory is the antagonism between intentional activities that aim for the actualization of desired self-projections and developmental outcomes (assimilative mode) and processes through which goals, self-evaluative standards, and life plans are adjusted to contextual constraints and age-related changes in action resources (accommodative mode). Throughout the life course, a sense of efficacy and well-being hinges on the balanced interplay of these modes, which of course is also affected by the cultural discourse about what we can, and cannot, change in human development and aging (see also Seligman, 1994).

This theoretical perspective also affords a better understanding of the conditions that help the individual to maintain a sense of well-being and efficacy in later life. Although old age typically involves a curtailment of action resources in many areas of life and functioning, there is no general decline in subjective life quality and well-being, at least not until the terminal phases of life. Converging evidence from different lines of research points to the particular importance of accommodative processes in coping with the changes of later life. I have discussed findings that suggest that flexibility in adjusting goals to changing action resources is a developmental strength that buffers the negative emotional impact of loss, enhances positive reappraisals of aversive changes, and helps to maintain a sense of efficacy and a meaningful outlook on personal development even under conditions of shrinking action resources and lifetime reserves.

Note

1. Sample items from the FGA: "I find it easy to see something positive even in a serious mishap"; "In general, I am not upset very long about a missed opportunity." Sample items from the TGP: "The harder a goal is to achieve, the more appeal it has to me"; "When faced with obstacles, I usually double my efforts."

References

Affleck, G., & Tennen, H. (1996). Construing benefits from adversity: Adaptational significance and dispositional underpinnings. *Journal of Personality, 64*, 899–922.

Alloy, L. B., & Abramson, L. Y. (1988). Depressive realism: Four theoretical perspectives. In L. B. Alloy (Ed.), *Cognitive processes in depression* (pp. 223–265). New York: Guilford.

Baltes, P. B., & Baltes, M. M. (1990). Psychological perspectives on successful aging: The model of selective optimization with compensation. In P. B. Baltes & M. M. Baltes (Eds.), *Successful aging: Perspectives from the behavioral sciences* (pp. 1–34). New York: Cambridge University Press.

Becker, L. C. (1992). Good lives: Prolegomena. *Social Philosophy and Policy, 9*, 15–37.

Becker, P. (1995). *Seelische Gesundheit und Verhaltenskontrolle*. Göttingen: Hogrefe.

Boerner, K. (in press). Adaptation to disability among middle-aged and older adults: The role of assimilative and accommodative coping. *Journal of Gerontology: Psychological Sciences*.

Brandtstädter, J. (1992). Personal control over development: Some developmental implications of self-efficacy. In R. Schwarzer (Ed.), *Self-efficacy: Thought control of action* (pp. 127–145). New York: Hemisphere.

Brandtstädter, J. (1998). Action perspectives on human development. In R. M. Lerner (Ed.), *Handbook of child psychology: Vol. 1. Theoretical models of human development* (5th ed., pp. 807–863). New York: Wiley.

Brandtstädter, J. (2002a). Protective self-processes in later life: Maintaining and revising personal goals. In C. von Hofsten & L. Bäckman (Eds.), *Psychology at the turn of the millennium: Vol. 2. Social, developmental, and clinical perspectives* (pp. 133–152). Hove, UK: Psychology Press.

Brandtstädter, J. (2002b). Searching for paths to successful development and aging: Integrating developmental and action-theoretical perspectives. In L. Pulkkinen & A. Caspi (Eds.), *Paths to successful development: Personality in the life course* (pp. 380–408). Cambridge: Cambridge University Press.

Brandtstädter, J., & Baltes-Götz, B. (1990). Personal control over development and quality of life perspectives in adulthood. In P. B. Baltes & M. M. Baltes (Eds.), *Successful aging: Perspectives from the behavioral sciences* (pp. 197–224). New York: Cambridge University Press.

Brandtstädter, J., & Greve, W. (1994). The aging self: Stabilizing and protective processes. *Developmental Review, 14,* 52–80.

Brandtstädter, J., & Lerner, R. M. (Eds.). (1999). *Action and self-development: Theory and research through the life span.* Thousand Oaks, CA: Sage.

Brandtstädter, J., & Renner, G. (1990). Tenacious goal pursuit and flexible goal adjustment: Explication and age-related analysis of assimilative and accommodative strategies of coping. *Psychology and Aging, 5,* 58–67.

Brandtstädter, J., & Rothermund, K. (1994). Self-percepts of control in middle and later adulthood: Buffering losses by rescaling goals. *Psychology and Aging, 9,* 265–273.

Brandtstädter, J., & Rothermund, K. (2002a). Intentional self-development: Exploring the interfaces between development, intentionality, and the self. In L. J. Crockett (Ed.), *Agency, motivation, and the life course* (pp. 31–75). Lincoln: University of Nebraska Press.

Brandtstädter, J., & Rothermund, K. (2002b). The life-course dynamics of goal pursuit and goal adjustment: A two-process framework. *Developmental Review, 22,* 117–150.

Brandtstädter, J., & Rothermund, K. (2003). Intentionality and time in human development and aging: Compensation and goal adjustment in changing developmental contexts. In U. M. Staudinger & U. Lindenberger (Eds.), *Understanding human development: Dialogues with lifespan psychology* (pp. 105–124). Boston: Kluwer Academic.

Brandtstädter, J., Rothermund, K., & Schmitz, U. (1998). Maintaining self-integrity and self-efficacy through adulthood and later life: The adaptive functions of assimilative persistence and accommodative flexibility. In J. Heckhausen & C. S. Dweck (Eds.), *Motivation and self-regulation across the life span* (pp. 365–388). New York: Cambridge University Press.

Brandtstädter, J., Voß, A., & Rothermund, K. (2004). Perception of danger signals: The role of control. *Experimental Psychology,* 24–32.

Brandtstädter, J., & Wentura, D. (1994). Veränderungen der Zeit- und Zukunftsperspektive im Übergang zum höheren Erwachsenenalter: entwicklungspsychologische und differentielle Aspekte. *Zeitschrift für Entwicklungspsychologie und Pädagogische Psychologie, 26,* 2–21.

Brandtstädter, J., Wentura, D., & Greve, W. (1993). Adaptive resources of the aging self: Outlines of an emergent perspective. *International Journal of Behavioral Development, 16,* 323–349.

Brandtstädter, J., Wentura, D., & Rothermund, K. (1999). Intentional self-development through adulthood and later life: Tenacious pursuit and flexible adjustment of goals. In J. Brandtstädter & R. M. Lerner (Eds.), *Action and self-development: Theory and research through the life span* (pp. 373–400). Thousand Oaks, CA: Sage.

Brandtstädter, J., Wentura, D., & Schmitz, U. (1997). Veränderungen der Zeit- und Zukunftsperspektive im Übergang zum höheren Alter: quer- und längsschnittliche Befunde. *Zeitschrift für Psychologie, 205,* 377–395.

Brunstein, J. C., Schultheiss, O. C., & Maier, G. W. (1999). The pursuit of personal goals: A motivational approach to well-being and life adjustment. In J. Brandtstädter & R. M. Lerner (Eds.), *Action and self-development: Theory and research through the life span* (pp. 169–196). Thousand Oaks, CA: Sage.

Carstensen, L. L. (1993). Motivation for social contact across the life-span: A theory of socioemotional selectivity. In J. E. Jacobs (Ed.), *Developmental perspectives on motivation* (pp. 209–254). Lincoln: University of Nebraska Press.

Carver, C. S., & Scheier, M. F. (2003). Three human strengths. In L. G. Aspinwall & U. M. Staudinger (Eds.), *A psychology of human strengths: Fundamental questions and future directions for a positive psychology* (pp. 87–102). Washington, DC: American Psychological Association.

Coyne, J. C. (1992). Cognition in depression: A paradigm in crisis. *Psychological Inquiry, 3,* 232–234.

Cross, S., & Markus, H. (1991). Possible selves across the life span. *Human Development, 34,* 230–255.

Csikszentmihalyi, M., & Beattie, O. (1979). Life themes: A theoretical and empirical exploration of their origins and effects. *Journal of Humanistic Psychology, 19,* 45–63.

Csikszentmihalyi, M., & Rathunde, K. (1998). The development of the person: An experiential perspective on the ontogenesis of psychological complexity. In R. M. Lerner (Ed.), *Handbook of child psychology: Vol. 1. Theoretical models of human development* (5th ed., pp. 635–684). New York: Wiley.

Diener, E., Suh, E. M., Lucas, R. E., & Smith, H. L. (1999). Subjective well-being: Three decades of progress. *Psychological Bulletin, 125,* 276–302.

Dittmann-Kohli, F., & Westerhof, G. J. (2000). The personal meaning system in a life-span perspective. In G. T. Reker & K. Chamberlain (Eds.), *Exploring existential meaning: Optimizing human development across the life span* (pp. 107–122). Thousand Oaks, CA: Sage.

Dixon, R. A., & Bäckman, L. (Eds.). (1995). *Compensating for psychological deficits and declines: Managing losses and promoting gains.* Mahwah, NJ: Erlbaum.

Duval, T. S., & Silvia, P. J. (2002). Self-awareness, probability of improvement, and the self-serving bias. *Journal of Personality and Social Psychology, 82,* 49–61.

Emmons, R. A. (1996). Striving and feeling: Personal goals and subjective well-being. In P. M. Gollwitzer & J. A. Bargh (Eds.), *The psychology of action: Linking cognition and motivation to behavior* (pp. 313–337). New York: Guilford.

Felser, G., Schmitz, U., & Brandtstädter, J. (1998). Stabilität und Qualität von Partnerschaften: Risiken und Ressourcen. In K. Hahlweg, D. H. Baucom, R. Bastine, & H. J. Markman (Eds.), *Prävention von Trennung und Scheidung:*

Internationale Ansätze zur Prädiktion und Prävention von Beziehungsstörungen (pp. 83–103). Stuttgart: Kohlhammer.

Fredrickson, B. L., & Carstensen, L. L. (1990). Choosing social partners: How old age and anticipated endings make people more selective. *Psychology and Aging, 5,* 335–347.

Freund, A. M., & Baltes, P. B. (2002). Life-management strategies of selection, optimization, and compensation: Measurement by self-report and construct validity. *Journal of Personality and Social Psychology, 82,* 642–662.

Gatz, M., & Karel, M. J. (1993). Individual change in perceived control over 20 years. *International Journal of Behavioral Development, 16,* 305–322.

Gilbert, D. T., Pinel, E. C., Wilson, T. D., Blumberg, S. J., & Wheatley, T. P. (1998). Immune neglect: A source of durability bias in affective forecasting. *Journal of Personality and Social Psychology, 75,* 617–638.

Gollwitzer, P. M. (1990). Action phases and mind-sets. In E. T. Higgins & R. M. Sorrentino (Eds.), *Handbook of motivation and cognition: Foundations of social behavior* (Vol. 2, pp. 53–92). New York: Guilford.

Greve, W. (2001). Successful human development: Psychological conceptions. In N. J. Smelser & P. B. Baltes (Eds. in Chief), *International encyclopedia of the social and behavioral sciences* (Vol. 10, pp. 6970–6974). Oxford: Elsevier Science.

Heckhausen, J., Dixon, R. A., & Baltes, P. B. (1989). Gains and losses in development throughout adulthood as perceived by different adult age groups. *Developmental Psychology, 25,* 109–121.

Heckhausen, J., & Schulz, R. (1995). A life-span theory of control. *Psychological Review, 102,* 284–304.

Heckhausen, J., Wrosch, C., & Fleeson, W. (2001). Developmental regulation before and after a developmental deadline: The sample case of "biological clock" for child-bearing. *Psychology and Aging, 16,* 400–413.

Higgins, E. T. (1996). The "self digest": Self-knowledge serving self-regulatory functions. *Journal of Personality and Social Psychology, 71,* 1062–1083.

Isen, A. M. (1999). Positive affect. In T. Dalgleish & M. J. Power (Eds.), *Handbook of cognition and emotion* (pp. 521–539). Chichester, UK: Wiley.

Janoff-Bulman, R., & Brickman, P. (1982). Expectations and what people learn from failure. In N. T. Feather (Ed.), *Expectations and actions: Expectancy-value models in psychology* (pp. 207–237). Hillsdale, NJ: Erlbaum.

Kahneman, D. (1999). Objective happiness. In D. Kahneman, E. Diener, & N. Schwarz (Eds.), *Well-being: Foundations of hedonic psychology* (pp. 3–25). New York: Russell Sage.

Kahneman, D. (2000a). Evaluation by moments: Past and future. In D. Kahneman & A. Tversky (Eds.), *Choices, values, and frames* (pp. 693–708). New York: Russell Sage Foundation/Cambridge University Press.

Kahneman, D. (2000b). Experienced utility and objective happiness: A moment-based approach. In D. Kahneman & A. Tversky (Eds.), *Choices, values, and frames* (pp. 673–692). New York: Russell Sage Foundation/Cambridge University Press.

Klinger, E. (1975). Consequences of commitment to and disengagement from incentives. *Psychological Review, 82,* 1–25.

Kruglanski, A. W. (1996). Goals as knowledge structures. In P. M. Gollwitzer & J. A. Bargh (Eds.), *The psychology of action: Linking cognition and motivation to behavior* (pp. 599–618). New York: Guilford.

Kuhl, J. (1987). Action control: The maintenance of motivational states. In F. Halisch & J. Kuhl (Eds.), *Motivation, intention and volition* (pp. 279–291). Berlin: Springer.

Lachman, M. E. (1986). Personal control in later life: Stability, change, and cognitive correlates. In M. M. Baltes & P. B. Baltes (Eds.), *The psychology of control and aging* (pp. 207–236). Hillsdale, NJ: Erlbaum.

Lawton, M. P. (1991). A multidimensional view of quality of life in frail elders. In J. E. Birren, J. E. Lubben, J. C. Rowe, & D. E. Deutchman (Eds.), *The concept and measurement of quality of life in the frail elderly* (pp. 3–27). San Diego, CA: Academic.

Linville, P. W. (1987). Self-complexity as a cognitive buffer against stress-related illness and depression. *Journal of Personality and Social Psychology, 52,* 663–676.

Long, A. A. (1974). *Hellenistic philosophy: Stoics, epicureans, sceptics.* London: Duckworth.

Lyubomirsky, S., & Ross, L. (1999). Changes in attractiveness of elected, rejected, and precluded alternatives: A comparison of happy and unhappy individuals. *Journal of Personality and Social Psychology, 61,* 380–391.

Martin, L. L., & Tesser, A. (1989). Toward a motivational and structural theory of ruminative thought. In J. S. Uleman & J. A. Bargh (Eds.), *Unintended thought* (pp. 306–326). New York: Guilford.

Nesse, R. M. (2000). Is depression an adaptation? *Archives of General Psychiatry, 57,* 14–20.

Neugarten, B. L., Havighurst, R. J., & Tobin, S. S. (1961). The measurement of life satisfaction. *Journal of Gerontology, 16,* 134–143.

Nurmi, J.-E., & Salmela-Aro, K. (2002). Goal construction, reconstruction and depressive symptoms in a life-span context: The transition from school to work. *Journal of Personality, 70,* 387–422.

Nussbaum, M., & Sen, A. (Eds.). (1993). *The quality of life.* Oxford: Clarendon.

Reker, G. T., Peacock, E. J., & Wong, P. T. (1987). Meaning and the purpose in life and well-being: A life-span perspective. *Journal of Gerontology, 42,* 44–49.

Rodd, Z. A., Rosellini, R. A., Stock, H. S., & Gallup, G. G., Jr. (1997). Learned helplessness in chickens (*Gallus gallus*): Evidence for attentional bias. *Learning and Motivation, 28,* 43–55.

Roese, N. J. (1997). Counterfactual thinking. *Psychological Bulletin, 121,* 133–148.

Rosenblatt, A., Greenberg, J., Solomon, S., Pyszczynski, T., & Lyon, D. (1989). Evidence for terror management theory: I. The effects of mortality salience on reactions to those who violate or uphold cultural values. *Journal of Personality and Social Psychology, 62,* 681–690.

Rothbaum, F., Weisz, J. R., & Snyder, S. S. (1982). Changing the world and changing the self. A two-process model of perceived control. *Journal of Personality and Social Psychology, 42,* 5–37.

Rothermund, K., Bak, P., & Brandtstädter, J. (2005). Biases in self-evaluation:

Effects of attribute controllability. *European Journal of Social Psychology, 35,* 281–290.

Rothermund, K., & Brandtstädter, J. (2003). Age stereotypes and self-views in later life: Evaluating rival assumptions. *International Journal of Behavioral Development, 27,* 549–554.

Rothermund, K., Wentura, D., & Brandtstädter, J. (1995). Selbstwertschützende Verschiebungen in der Semantik des Begriffs "alt" im höheren Erwachsenenalter. *Sprache & Kognition, 14,* 52–63.

Ryff, C. D., & Singer, B. (1998). The contours of positive human health. *Psychological Inquiry, 9,* 1–28.

Salmela-Aro, K., Nurmi, J.-E., Saisto, T., & Halmesmäki, E. (2001). Goal reconstruction and depressive symptoms during the transition to motherhood: Evidence from two cross-lagged longitudinal studies. *Journal of Personality and Social Psychology, 81,* 1144–1159.

Schmitz, U. (1998). *Entwicklungserleben älterer Menschen. Eine Interviewstudie zur Wahrnehmung und Bewältigung von Entwicklungsproblemen im höheren Alter.* Regensburg, Germany: Roderer.

Schmitz, U., Saile, H., & Nilges, P. (1996). Coping with chronic pain: Flexible goal adjustment as an interactive buffer against pain-related distress. *Pain, 67,* 41–51.

Seligman, M. E. P. (1990). Why is there so much depression today? The waxing of the individual and the waning of the commons. In R. E. Ingram (Ed.), *Contemporary psychological approaches to depression* (pp. 1–9). New York: Plenum.

Seligman, M. E. P. (1994). *What you can change and what you can't: The ultimate guide to self-improvement.* New York: Knopf.

Seligman, M. E. P. (2002). *Authentic happiness.* New York: Free Press.

Seligman, M. E. P., & Elder, G. (1986). Learned helplessness and life-span development. In A. B. Sorensen, F. E. Weinert, & L. R. Sherrod (Eds.), *Human development and the life course: Multidisciplinary perspectives* (pp. 377–428). Hillsdale, NJ: Erlbaum.

Sherman, E. (1991). *Reminiscence and the self in old age.* New York: Springer.

Simon, H. A. (1983). *Reason in human affairs.* Oxford: Basil Blackwell.

Skinner, E. A. (1995). *Perceived control, motivation, and coping.* Thousand Oaks, CA: Sage.

Staudinger, U. M., Marsiske, M., & Baltes, P. B. (1995). Resilience and reserve capacity in later adulthood: Potentials and limits of development across the life span. In D. Cicchetti & D. J. Cohen (Eds.), *Developmental psychopathology: Vol. 2. Risk, disorder, and adaptation* (pp. 801–847). New York: Wiley.

Staw, B. M. (1997). The escalation of commitment: An update and appraisal. In Z. Shapira (Ed.), *Organizational decision making* (pp. 191–215). Cambridge: Cambridge University Press.

Stock, W. A., Okun, M. A., Haring, M. J., & Witter, R. A. (1983). Age and subjective well-being: A meta-analysis. In R. J. Light (Ed.), *Evaluation studies: Review annual* (Vol. 8, pp. 279–302). Beverly Hills, CA: Sage.

Tatarkiewicz, W. (1976). *Analysis of happiness.* The Hague, Netherlands: Martinus Nijhoff.

Taylor, S. E., & Gollwitzer, P. M. (1995). Effects of mindset on positive illusions. *Journal of Personality and Social Psychology, 69*, 213–226.

Thompson, S. C., Cheek, P. R., & Graham, M. A. (1988). The other side of perceived control: Disadvantages and negative effects. In S. Spacapan & S. Oskamp (Eds.), *The social psychology of health* (pp. 69–93). Newbury Park, CA: Sage.

Trépanier, L., Lapierre, S., Baillargeon, J., & Bouffard, L. (2001). Ténacité et flexibilité dans la poursuite de projets personnels: Impact sur le bien-être à la retraite. *Canadian Journal on Aging, 20,* 557–576.

Wentura, D., Rothermund, K., & Brandtstädter, J. (1995). Experimentelle Analysen zur Verarbeitung belastender Informationen: Differential- und alternspsychologische Aspekte. *Zeitschrift für Experimentelle Psychologie, 42,* 152–175.

Wortman, C. B., & Brehm, J. W. (1975). Responses to uncontrollable outcomes: An integration of reactance theory and the learned helplessness model. In L. Berkowitz (Ed.), *Advances in experimental social psychology* (Vol. 8, pp. 278–336). New York: Academic.

Wright, R. A., & Brehm, J. W. (1989). Energization and goal attractiveness. In L. A. Pervin (Ed.), *Goal concepts in personality and social psychology* (pp. 169–210). Hillsdale, NJ: Erlbaum.

Wrosch, C., Scheier, M. F., Carver, C. S., & Schulz, R. (2003). The importance of goal disengagement in adaptive self-regulation: When giving up is beneficial. *Self and Identity, 2,* 1–20.

9

The Impact of Subjective Experience on the Quality of Life

A Central Issue for Health Professionals

ANTONELLA DELLE FAVE

Health and the Biopsychosocial Model

Researchers and practitioners are devoting increasing attention to the role of subjectivity in the evaluation of well-being. The issue has been traditionally investigated in term of objective indicators, such as income, health, and housing conditions. However, there is evidence that economic indicators do not provide an adequate evaluation of the developmental resources and goal attainment of a person, or of the success of a nation (Biswas-Diener & Diener, 2001; Marmot & Wilkinson, 1999). As several studies show, it is also important to identify and measure subjective indicators of well-being, referring to individuals' judgments about their own state, satisfaction with life, social relationships, work and health, future goals, and personal achievements (Diener, 2000; Diener & Suh, 1997; Veenhoven, 2002).

In the domain of health psychology, several studies emphasize the necessity to consider quality of life as a relative concept, to be interpreted from the subjective perspective (Fitzpatrick, 2000; Nordenfelt, 1994). Moreover, quality of life should not be considered only in relation to health: It is a broader construct, involves areas and activities of daily life which are not necessarily dependent on the body's condition, and can be pursued despite physical limitations (Albrecht, 1996; Weinberg, 1988). All individuals, according to their health conditions, social roles, personalities, and idiosyncratic styles of interaction with environmental opportunities, develop personal evaluations of what a good quality of life means.

Most researchers presently agree that health is a multidimensional construct which includes physical, social, and psychological dimensions. This perspective was first asserted in the Declaration of Human Rights (1948) and again emphasized at the World Health Organization (WHO) meeting at Alma Ata (1986), where the idea of considering health not simply as an absence of pathology but as a state of physical and psychological well-being was claimed. During the same period, a new approach to the diagnosis and treatment of disease was formalized: the biopsychosocial model (Engel, 1977, 1982). Engel pointed out the limitations of the Western biomedical model of medicine, which is focused on symptoms and physical impairments, and proposed a broader approach, centered on the patient as a person, a carrier of a specific cultural background, an individual with a subjective interpretation and experience of health and disease.

The first effort to integrate the biomedical model with the social perspective was substantiated in the International Classification of Impairments, Disabilities and Handicaps (ICIDH; World Health Organization, 1980/1993), which acknowledged the role of social environmental factors in the production of disease and disablement (Thuriaux, 1989). However, except for this general statement, ICIDH did not assess specific features of the social world that may influence people's level of ability and performance in daily life (Chapireau & Colvez, 1998). This classification also overlooked the psychological components of health. After a substantial revision process (Thuriaux, 1995), a new version of the international classification was elaborated (ICIDH-2), which fully embodied the biopsychosocial model: Each dimension of disease and disablement was conceptualized as a dynamic interaction among individual features and the social and physical environment.

In its definitive official version, the new classification has been labeled the ICF (International Classification of Functioning; World Health Organization, 2001). This shift in terminology, far from being a purely linguistic convention, is a relevant conceptual change. It stresses the necessity of evaluating any health condition from a constructive and substantially positive perspective: the perspective of functioning. The ICF aims at investigating what people actually can do in their daily lives and in their social environments. It shifts the focus from the consequences of disease (such as impairments and activity limitations) to the components of health, in terms of physical resources, daily activity performance, and social participation. It also emphasizes the active role of the person in interacting with the environment. It is clear that two persons with the same degree of health can have different levels of functioning. This depends on variables that differ from physical conditions, but that are nevertheless connected with health: individual psychological features, family and social support, material and economic resources, educational background, cultural representations, and social policies (Ingstad, 1999; Simeonsson, Lollar, Hollowell, & Adams, 2000; Üstün et al., 2001).

Culture and Health

Advancements in cross-cultural psychology (Dasen, Berry, & Sartorius, 1988) and the research trend in indigenous psychologies (Kim & Berry, 1993) have shown that the social representations of the body and its pathologies are strongly influenced by cultural norms and beliefs. Social representations and behavioral models in the domain of health widely differ across cultures and according to pathologies. Wallander, Varni, Babani, Banis, and Wilcox (1988) identified a set of intrapersonal, interpersonal, and environmental factors which interact in moderating the effects of chronic illness. In a survey of children's health in India, Saraswathi (1992) showed that the physical and psychological growth of a child is deeply influenced by the environment (both natural and cultural), the family structure (income, size, age of members), and the mother's condition (age, job, education level, decisional status within the family). Tripathi and Agarwal (2000) specifically investigated the quality of life of Indian children with chronic pathologies. They pointed out that mothers' attitudes and beliefs, the quality of daily family interactions, and the opportunities for action and learning that these children are offered have a tremendous impact on their physical and psychological development. For example, children with debilitating diseases, such as tuberculosis or severe sensory impairment, are often considered unable to attain a productive role in life, being therefore neglected and understimulated by their caregivers (Agarwal, 1995). The ultimate consequence of this attitude is that chronically ill children show poor performance in various cognitive tasks and lower academic achievement when compared with children in the same age group. They also develop a significantly poorer self-concept (Dorner & Elton, 1973).

The multidimensional aspects of health and disease have to be considered in order to promote effective intervention strategies (Berry, Segall, & Kagitçibasi, 1997; Werner, 1987). Disabled and sick persons will only be disadvantaged in social, cultural, or attitudinal environments in which their conditions bring about disadvantageous consequences (Bickenbach, Chatterji, Badley, & Üstün, 1999). Despite limitations in health services, logistic facilities, and material resources, in traditional cultures people with disabilities or chronic illnesses are often more integrated into the society than in industrialized countries. Social cohesion and lower levels of individualism paradoxically enhance the chances for at least some people to actively participate in the daily life of their communities (Brown, Varma, Malhotra, Jiloha, Conover, & Susser, 1998; Tanaka-Matsumi & Draguns, 1997).

Psychological Components of Health

Individuals can be more or less effective in actively exploiting the environmental opportunities for action available to them. Several studies have emphasized the subjective perspective in coping with disease and the individual strategies developed to overcome the related constraints, highlighting the positive and constructive components of individual life history and daily experience. Positive consequences of illness are frequently noted by sick people and by people having recovered from illness. Such consequences, more common than often realized, include improved interpersonal relationships, positive personality and life changes, disengagement from unattainable goals, and shifts toward new ones (Leedham, Meyerowitz, Muirhead, & Frist, 1995; Mendola, Tennen, Affleck, McCann, & Fitzgerald, 1990; Sodergren & Hyland, 2000).

More specifically, a satisfying quality of life seems to be related to a good balance at the personal and interpersonal levels. Albrecht and Devlieger (1999) interviewed people with severe disabilities by means of semistructured interviews. They found that more than half of the participants perceived themselves as having a good to excellent quality of life. This finding clearly shows that individual development and social integration can be successfully pursued despite, or maybe through, disability. Physical constraints can help to discover new goals, interests, and meanings in daily life.

Several researchers have investigated the psychological factors involved in the construction of a positive perception of disability and illness. Antonovsky (1993) developed the *salutogenesis approach:* Individuals can attain a good quality of life despite adverse health conditions by building an inner sense of coherence. People are able to bring order and structure to the ambiguous and disruptive situation of disease or disability by making it comprehensible, manageable, and meaningful. From this perspective, the meaning-making process, which is the way in which people actively organize their own experiences in time (Kegan, 1994), plays a key role in developing a positive adaptation to disease and disability: In time, individuals can attribute different meanings to the same situation, according to progressively more complex principles in organizing their experiences and their personal perceptions of life and the environment (Kunnen & Bosma, 2000).

Other researchers have focused on the role of intentional goal setting in pursuing health behaviors. Prochaska (1994) proposed a stage model of behavioral change: Individuals have first to become aware of their health goals (the contemplation stage) and then develop an intentional strategy to attain them, coping with possible relapses and actively contributing to the maintenance of the achieved results. Bandura (1992, 1998) identified the key role of self-efficacy in pursuing health and in coping with disease. More specifically, self-efficacy fosters the perception of internal control in facing stressful events, in dealing with worsening health conditions, and in pursuing health goals. It facilitates the intentional mobilization of individual resources and skills in the long term. Self-efficacious people are relatively unaffected by failures, and they show high levels of perseverance in pursuing their goals. Gollwitzer, Wicklund and Hilton (1982) stressed the importance of the commitment to self-defining goals: Individuals strive to achieve personal identity in various realms. The commitment toward self-completion and self-definition elicits persistent efforts to acquire the attributes or skills that people consider to be relevant to their identities in each realm. This is also true of health goals. Gollwitzer and Oettingen (1998) specifically investigated two processes underlying goal achievement in the domain of health. The first one is the *threat appraisal process:* Individuals evaluate their own conditions and the potential risk factors in order to make appropriate decisions and identify adequate strategies to cope with diseases or to maintain health. The second one is the *goal attainment process,* and it follows the threat appraisal phase: Individuals actualize the previously identified coping strategies, and even improve them, in pursuit of a progressively better adaptation and quality of life.

These models emphasize the role of intentionally processing information in pursuing health goals. At the same time, most of them include a crucial variable in the decisional process: optimism. *Optimism* can be described as a quite stable component of the explanatory style a person adopts in interpreting life events through causal attributions (Abramson, Seligman, & Teasdale, 1978; Peterson, 1991; Peterson, Schulman, Castellon, & Seligman, 1992). Within this framework, optimism can be considered to be an individual characteristic that people possess in different degrees and that can be at least indirectly related to a genetic component (Schulman, Keith, & Seligman, 1993). Scheier and Carver (1992) identified it with a personality variable labeled *dispositional optimism.* Taylor and Gollwitzer (1995) emphasized that optimism represents an important resource in the goal attainment process in that it supports efforts toward goal achievement. However, optimism can be deleterious in the domain of health, specifically during the threat appraisal process, in that it may prevent individuals from realistically evaluating their conditions and from undertaking appropriate behaviors. Schwarzer (1994) distinguished between *defensive optimism* and *functional optimism.* The former includes the unrealistic overvaluation of individual control of the disease and a biased risk perception. In contrast, functional optimism involves self-efficacy and the belief in personal capability to cope with the demands of the situation, and it is therefore an adaptive component of health behavior.

From this perspective, optimism and realism seem to be dichotomous and mutually exclusive concepts. However, Schwarzer (1998) proposed an integrated and more exhaustive model, in which these two dimensions are orthogonal. Only positive levels of realism and optimism combined together can be adaptive in any situation. Most likely, in the phase of threat appraisal, the prominence of realism over optimism can help the individual correctly to perceive risks and problems. This fosters a shift from defensive (or unrealistic) optimism to functional optimism. Still, positive beliefs concerning one's own capabilities to cope with disease, disability, or physical limitations promote self-efficacy and a more effective exploitation of personal resources even in evaluating threats and risks (Aspinwall & Brunhart, 1996).

Most studies on optimism emphasize its cognitive aspects. However, emotions, motivations, and cognitive processes coexist in human information processing, and the subjective experience is eventually shaped by their complex interplay, both in the short and in the long term. "Optimism is not simply cold cognition" (Peterson, 2000, p. 45); rather, it has emotional and motivational components that can deeply influence the cognitive evaluation of situations. Several researchers have highlighted these aspects while investigating the role of optimism in coping with traumatic or life-threatening events and in pursuing health. Taylor (1983) found that women who had experienced breast cancer developed positive beliefs about their health that in most cases were illusory. More specifically, many women reported that they could personally control the course of the disease or that they had completely recovered, despite clinical evidence of disease progression. The same was true of people with HIV or AIDS (Reed, Kemeny, Taylor, Wang, & Visscher, 1994). Far from being maladaptive, positive though illusory expectations, paired with the identification of a meaning in the experience of illness, appear to be physiologically protective (Bower, Kemeny, Taylor, & Fahey, 1998; Taylor, Kemeny, Reed, Bower, & Gruenewald, 2000).

Several studies have shown the relationship between emotional states and health: Negative mood states increase people's susceptibility to illness (Cohen, Doyle, Skoner, Fireman, Gwaltney, & Newsom, 1995); negative emotional arousal affects the cardiovascular system (Friedman, 1992); and emotions have direct influence on the functioning of the immune system (Salovey, Rothman, Detweiler, & Steward, 2000). Effectiveness in regulating and understanding one's own emotions has pervasive effects on individual development and global well-being (Halle, 2003).

Optimal Experiences, Health, and Development

Although a growing number of studies focuses on the perceived positive consequences of disabilities and chronic diseases, the subjective perception of functioning during daily activities and social contexts was scarcely investigated. In our studies, we explored the quality of experience that people with disabilities reported in their lives, with particular attention to the situations they associated with optimal experience, or flow (Csikszentmihalyi, 1975; Csikszentmihalyi & Csikszentmihalyi, 1988). *Optimal experience* is characterized by the perception of high environmental challenges matched by adequately high personal skills and by high levels of concentration, involvement, enjoyment, control, and intrinsic motivation (Deci & Ryan, 1985).

Cross-cultural investigations have shown that most daily activities can be associated with optimal experience (Massimini & Delle Fave, 2000). However, the situation should be sufficiently challenging to require active engagement and to promote satisfaction in the use of personal skills. Thanks to the positive and complex features of optimal experience, individuals preferentially cultivate throughout their lives the associated activities; this process, defined as *psychological selection* (Csikszentmihalyi, & Massimini, 1985), leads to a progressive skill refinement in specific domains. Such selective development of competencies shapes an individual's life theme (Csikszentmihalyi & Beattie, 1979; Delle Fave & Massimini, 2000), which comprises the basic life goals and lifelong targets each person uniquely selects for preferential cultivation.

In order to investigate optimal experiences and the developmental trajectories of people with disabilities, we used both the Flow and the Life Theme questionnaires. The first instrument (Delle Fave & Massimini, 1991; Massimini, Csikszentmihalyi, & Delle Fave, 1988) allowed us to assess the occurrence of optimal experience in daily life, its psychological features, the associated activities, and the quality of experience in work and family contexts. Participants' wishes (both realistic and unrealistic) were also explored. The second instrument provided information on participants' positive and negative life influences, present challenges, future life goals, and the specific roles played by school, work, and family as the main socialization factors in their lives.

We administered the Flow Questionnaire and the Life Theme Questionnaire to people with congenital or early occurring diseases and to people who had acquired disabilities during adolescence or adulthood as a consequence of chronic or progressive diseases or traumas and accidents. The findings showed that optimal activities play a prominent role in people with disabilities' chances of integration into active lives, in that their cultivation contributes to maximizing the residual sensory-motor skills and to implementing vicarious motor abilities and sensory channels. The enjoyment, high challenges, and intrinsic motivation reported in doing such activities are substantial prerequisites for their preferential replication and for the achievement of higher levels of complexity in behavior through the progressive increase of related skills and the acquisition of new information. This is especially true of productive activities, such as work and study, and of activities requiring complex skills, such as sports and arts (Negri, Massimini, & Delle Fave, 1992). Our results also highlighted the crucial role of challenging and socially meaningful opportunities for action in the process of individual development and cultural integration. As concerns acquired disabilities, the previous cultivation of activities associated with optimal experiences before the occurrence of the disabilities fostered their preferential replication after the traumas (whenever possible) or the active search for alternative opportunities for optimal experiences (Delle Fave, 1996a; Delle Fave & Maletto, 1992).

The findings showed that development can be successfully pursued through disablement. Physical constraints can help people to discover new opportunities in daily life, as well as foster personal growth and enhance individual strengths and resources (Delle Fave & Massimini, 2003a). Although in the Life Theme Questionnaire most participants reported disablement as a negative life influence, they also stressed their efforts to effectively overcome the related social and be-havioral constraints by focusing on the positive and constructive components of their life histories and daily experiences (Delle Fave & Massimini, 2004). They emphasized the challenges associated with disability, but described them more as opportunities for personal growth than as obstacles and limitations. In some cases, the acquired disability was described among the positive life influences, thus confirming the findings of other studies investigating the positive conse-quences of illness.

We also conducted a comparative cross-cultural study on optimal experience and individual development among Nepalese children and young people with disabilities, in collaboration with a local CBR (community-based rehabilitation) project in the area of Bhaktapur, Katmandu Valley (SCN-CBR, 2000). Data were gathered through the Flow Questionnaire and the Life Theme Questionnaire. All of the participants except one reported optimal experiences during their lives and associated them with the opportunities for action available in their culture, in the domains of work, study, and leisure (Delle Fave & Massimini, 2004; Lombardi & Delle Fave, 2002). This was largely due to the effective intervention of CBR workers: Children and young people were actively supported in the cultivation of challenging and enjoyable activities. Their individual preferences, abilities, and health conditions were taken into account, and the developmental and thera-peutic role of individual integration into the cultural context was emphasized. Participants were also asked about life influences, present challenges, future goals, and the role of family, school, and rehabilitation programs in their lives. Results showed the importance of educating youth with disabilities to pursue challenges in meaningful and complex activities, thus overriding the limitations associated with their physical constraints. The cross-cultural comparison showed more similarities than differences in the rehabilitation and socialization process: In particular, results highlighted that the availability of material re-sources does not guarantee development in the absence of social support.

The key role of optimal experiences in fostering personal growth and social integration was also detected in the field of mental health: The cross-cultural application of this concept in psychotherapy and psychiatric rehabilitation has produced encouraging results in international cooperation programs (Delle Fave & Massimini, 1990, 1992; Massimini, Csikszentmihalyi, & Carli, 1987).

The Quality of Experience of Health Professionals

Several studies have recently investigated the quality of experience that health professionals associate with their job and its influence on work performance, relationships with patients, and patients' well-being. In particular, physicians' empathy and positive disposition toward patients fosters patients' satisfaction, with consequently positive outcomes in the domains of both prevention and treatment (Majani, Pierobon, Giardini, & Callegari, 2000). Conversely, physicians reporting burnout symptoms are self-critical concerning their accomplishments, frequently perceiving suboptimal patient care practices (Shanafelt, Bradley, Wipf, & Back, 2002).

A positive doctor-patient relationship has been widely recognized as a crucial factor in medical care: It enhances patients' compliance and effective coping with symptoms (Di Caccavo, Ley, & Reid, 2000; Jackson, Chamberlin, & Kroenke, 2001). In-patients receiving medical or surgical care prominently attributed satisfaction with their medical care to positive interpersonal relations and to the adequate communication of health care information (Nguyen Thi, Briançon, Empereur, & Guillemin, 2002; Williams, 1994). Physicians who pay attention to their patients' perceived quality of life and adopt a biopsychosocial approach are more effective both in communicating and in getting the collaboration of their patients in health-related decisions (Baile, Buckman, Lenzi, Glober, Beale, & Kudelka, 2000; Glass, 1996; Williams, Freedman, & Deci, 1998).

We recently conducted a study of a group of surgeons, anesthesiologists, and gynecologists in order to investigate the opportunities for optimal experience that they perceived in daily life (Delle Fave & Massimini, 2003b). Over one third of the participants associated work with optimal experience, mainly referring to performing a surgical operation, doing research work, and interacting with patients. More specifically, the operating-room setting was described as a prominent occasion for optimal experience or as a peculiarly challenging, engaging, and intrinsically rewarding task, an arena where physicians test their medical and technical knowledge, interpersonal skills, and emotional balance. Similar findings were reported by Csikszentmihalyi (1985). We also investigated the job motivations of the participants, as well as the most positive and most negative situations perceived at work. Intrinsic motivation was reported as the main reason for choosing the medical profession (74% of the answers). Among the most positive work experiences, the participants quoted a good relationship with colleagues and patients. On the opposite, they associated the most negative experiences at work with failures, pressure, and conflicts with colleagues. These results, on the one hand, highlighted the key role of doctor-patient relationships in physicians' satisfaction. On the other hand, they were consistent with the findings obtained in other studies, which showed that burnout among physicians is primarily related to difficult relationships in the *équipe* (Deckard, Meterko, & Field, 1994) and to work overload (Campbell, Sonnad, Eckhauser, Campbell, & Greenfield, 2001).

We also collected information from 31 nurses and delivery assistants (Delle Fave, 1996b). When asked about opportunities for optimal experiences during daily life, 26% of them named work. They also reported intrinsic motivation as the main reason for choosing their jobs (54% of the answers). A nurse's job is complex and challenging, socially meaningful, and rich in opportunities for action. It promotes individual and social skills, as well as technical competencies, therefore showing great potential as an opportunity for optimal experiences. These study results should be taken into account in medical education and health services.

Doctors and nurses represent a primary resource for promoting health at the community level. Nevertheless, the quality of life they experience at work is often overlooked, with negative effects on their performance and on the well-being of their fellow citizens. Training curricula should be designed so as to support the autonomy, engagement, and self-determination of health professionals (Ryan & Deci, 2000; Williams & Deci, 1998) and to improve their quality of experience at work through the improvement of their work environment at the levels of structure, organization, and social context.

Conclusions

Only recently has the issue of subjective perspective and experience been raised in the health domain and rarely in cross-cultural comparisons. The ICF emphasizes the role of personal factors in influencing the lives of people with diseases or disabilities, but it does not propose any classification of them. In the ICF, information concerning personal factors is represented by only one open-ended question, within a section titled "other contextual factors." Personal factors are explicitly not classified. Despite the growing popularity of the biopsychosocial perspective and the evidence of its effectiveness, the biomedical, problem-centered model is still the prevailing one. Patients are treated for their pathologies, disregarding how their cultural contexts and subjective experiences can influence the onset and the outcome of disease (Mathew, Ravichandran, May, & Morsley, 2001). Even in non-Western countries, the person-centered approach, though typical of most traditional medical systems throughout the world (Beardsley & Pedersen, 1997), has been replaced by the problem-centered approaches and techniques that characterize modern medicine, disregarding the local social structure, knowledge, and strategies for coping with disease (Woelk, 1992).

The cultural system, its structure, and values interact with the individual in an interdependent process of circular causality. Culture can undermine or promote the quality of life of people with disabilities or diseases. In their turn, individuals can be more or less effective in actively taking and developing the environmental opportunities for action available to them, through adaptive coping strategies, specific traits such as optimism, and the ability to find meaning in the experience of illness. Listening to people's subjective reports and paying attention to their personal ways of interacting with the environment are still invaluable instruments for designing effective intervention programs in the domain of health.

Intervention should focus on human flexibility and the potential for complexity, regardless of the actual health conditions: Individual resources are often overlooked. Even in difficult circumstances, people can devote themselves to the cultivation of activities which they perceive as challenging and enjoyable. More specifically, researchers and policy makers should more systematically address some critical issues in order to design effective health promotion strategies:

- the development of models of individual optimal functioning and their relevance in chronic diseases and disability
- the implementation of methodologies for the sampling of subjective experience
- the evaluation of both objective and perceived effectiveness of the cultural environment in fostering the autonomy and integration of people with disabilities and chronic diseases
- the assessment of family support in promoting patients' independence and socialization through objective and subjective measures
- the development of intervention programs promoting the well-being of patients on the basis of their perceived needs and resources
- the promotion of health professionals' self-determination and quality of experience in job settings through intervention at the organizational and educational levels

References

Abramson, L. Y., Seligman, M. E. P., & Teasdale, J. D. (1978). Learned helplessness in humans: Critique and reformulation. *Journal of Abnormal Psychology, 87*, 49–74.

Agarwal, A. (1995). Mass-media and health promotion in Indian villages. *Psychology and Developing Societies, 7*, 217–236

Albrecht, G. L. (1996). Using subjective health assessments in practice and policy making. *Health Care Analysis, 4*, 284–292.

Albrecht, G. L., & Devlieger, P. J. (1999). The disability paradox: High quality of life against all odds. *Social Science and Medicine, 48*, 977–988.

Antonovsky, A. (1993). Complexity, conflict, chaos, coherence, coercion and civility. *Social Science and Medicine, 37*, 969–974.

Aspinwall, L. G., & Brunhart, S. M. (1996). Distinguishing optimism from denial: Optimistic beliefs predict attention to health threats. *Personality and Social Psychology Bulletin, 22*, 993–1003.

Baile, W.-F., Buckman, R., Lenzi, R., Glober, G., Beale, E. A., & Kudelka, A. P. (2000). SPIKES: A six-step protocol for delivering bad news: Application to the patient with cancer. *Oncologist, 5*, 302–311.

Bandura, A. (1992). Exercise of personal agency through the self-efficacy mechanism. In R. Schwarzer (Ed.), *Self-efficacy: Thought control of action* (p. 3–38). Washington, DC: Hemisphere.

Bandura, A. (1998). Health promotion from the perspective of social cognitive theory. *Psychology and Health, 13*, 623–649.

Beardsley, L., & Pedersen, P. (1997). Health and culture-centered intervention. In J. W. Berry, M. H. Segall, & C. Kagitçibasi (Eds.), *Handbook of cross-cultural psychology: Vol. 3. Social behavior and applications* (pp. 413–448). Needham Heights, MA: Allyn and Bacon.

Berry, J. W., Segall, M. H., & Kagitçibasi, C. (Eds.). (1997). *Handbook of cross-cultural psychology: Vol. 3. Social behavior and applications.* Needham Heights, MA: Allyn and Bacon.

Bickenbach, J. E., Chatterji, S., Badley, E. M., & Üstün, T. B. (1999). Models of disablement, universalism and the International Classification of Impairments, Disabilities and Handicaps. *Social Science & Medicine, 48,* 1173–1187.

Biswas-Diener, R., & Diener, E. (2001). Making the best of a bad situation: Satisfaction in the slums of Calcutta. *Social Indicators Research, 55,* 329–352.

Bower, J. E., Kemeny, M. E., Taylor, S. E., & Fahey, J. L. (1998). Cognitive processing, discovery of meaning, CD4 decline, and AIDS-related mortality among bereaved HIV-seropositive men. *Journal of Consulting and Clinical Psychology, 66,* 979–986.

Brown, A. S., Varma, V. K., Malhotra, S., Jiloha, R. C., Conover, S. A., & Susser, E. S. (1998). Course of acute affective disorders in a developing country setting. *Journal of Nervous and Mental Disease, 186,* 207–213.

Campbell, D. A., Sonnad, S. S., Eckhauser, F. E., Campbell, K. K., & Greenfield, L. J. (2001). Burnout among American surgeons. *Surgery, 130,* 696–705.

Chapireau, F., & Colvez, A. (1998). Social disadvantage in the International Classification of Impairments, Disabilities, and Handicaps. *Social Science and Medicine, 47,* 59–66.

Cohen, S., Doyle, W. J., Skoner, D. P., Fireman, P., Gwaltney, J. M., & Newsom, J. T. (1995). State and trait negative affect as predictors of objective and subjective symptoms of respiratory viral infections. *Journal of Personality and Social Psychology, 68,* 159–169.

Csikszentmihalyi, M. (1975). *Beyond boredom and anxiety.* San Francisco: Jossey-Bass.

Csikszentmihalyi, M. (1985). Reflections on enjoyment. *Perspectives in Biology and Medicine, 28,* 489–497.

Csikszentmihalyi, M., & Beattie, O. (1979). Life themes: A theoretical and empirical exploration of their origins and effects. *Journal of Humanistic Psychology, 19,* 677–693.

Csikszentmihalyi, M., & Csikszentmihalyi, I. (Eds.). (1988). *Optimal experience: Psychological studies of flow in consciousness.* New York: Cambridge University Press.

Csikszentmihalyi, M., & Massimini, F. (1985). On the psychological selection of bio-cultural information. *New Ideas in Psychology, 3,* 115–138.

Dasen, P. R., Berry, J. W., & Sartorius, N. (Eds.). (1988). *Health and cross-cultural psychology: Toward applications.* Newbury Park, CA: Sage.

Deci, E. L., & Ryan, R. M. (1985). *Intrinsic motivation and self-determination in human behavior.* New York: Plenum.

Deckard, G., Meterko, M., & Field, D. (1994). Physician burnout: An examination of personal, professional, and organizational relationships. *Medical Care, 32,* 745–754.

Delle Fave, A. (1996a). Il processo di "trasformazione di Flow" in un campione di soggetti medullolesi (Flow transformation in a sample of people with medullar lesions). In F. Massimini, P. Inghilleri, & A. Delle Fave (Eds.), *La selezione psicologica umana* (pp. 615–634). Milan, Italy: Coop. Libraria IULM.

Delle Fave, A. (1996b). Flow e attività tradizionali femminili: La continuità nella selezione e ritenzione delle informazioni (Flow and traditional female activities: Continuity in the selection and acquisition of information). In F. Massimini, P. Inghilleri, & A. Delle Fave (Eds.), *La selezione psicologica umana* (pp. 599–614). Milan, Italy: Coop. Libraria IULM.

Delle Fave, A., & Maletto, C. (1992). Processi di attenzione e qualità dell'esperienza soggettiva nei non vedenti (Attention processes and quality of subjective experience in blind people). In D. Galati (Ed.), *Vedere con la mente: Processi cognitivi, affettivi e strategie adattative* (pp. 321–353). Milan, Italy: Franco Angeli.

Delle Fave, A., & Massimini, F. (1990). Esperienza ottimale e riabilitazione psichiatrica (Optimal experience and psychiatric rehabilitation). *Psicoterapia e Scienze Umane, 2*, 53–71.

Delle Fave, A., & Massimini, F. (1991). Modernization and the quality of daily experience in a southern Italy village. In N. Bleichrodt & P. J. D. Drenth (Eds.), *Contemporary issues in cross-cultural psychology* (pp. 110–119). Amsterdam: Swets & Zeitlinger.

Delle Fave, A., & Massimini, F. (1992). Experience sampling method and the measurement of clinical change: A case of anxiety disorder. In M. W. deVries (Ed.), *The experience of psychopathology* (pp. 280–289). New York: Cambridge University Press.

Delle Fave, A., & Massimini, F. (2000). Living at home or in institution: Adolescents' optimal experience and life theme. *Paideia. Cadernos de Psicologia e Educaçao, 19*, 55–66.

Delle Fave, A., & Massimini, F. (2003a). Making disability into a resource. *Psychologist, 16*, 9–10.

Delle Fave, A., & Massimini, F. (2003b). Optimal experience in work and leisure among teachers and physicians: Individual and bio-cultural implications. *Leisure Studies, 22*, 323–342.

Delle Fave, A., & Massimini, F. (2004). Bringing subjectivity into focus: Optimal experiences, life themes and person-centred rehabilitation. In P. A. Linley & S. Joseph (Eds.), *Positive psychology in practice* (pp. 581–597). London: Wiley & Sons.

Di Caccavo, A., Ley, A., & Reid, F. (2000). What do general practitioners discuss with their patients? *Journal of Health Psychology, 5*, 87–97.

Diener, E. (2000). Subjective well-being. *American Psychologist, 55*, 34–43.

Diener, E., & Suh, E. (1997). Measuring quality of life: Economic, social and subjective indicators. *Social Indicators Research, 40*, 189–216.

Dorner, S., & Elton, A. (1973). Short, taught and vulnerable. *Special Education, 62*, 12.

Engel, G. L. (1977). The need for a new medical model: A challenge for biomedicine. *Science, 196*, 129–136.

Engel, G. L. (1982). The biopsychosocial model and medical education. *New England Journal of Medicine, 306*, 802–805.

Fitzpatrick, R. (2000). Measurement issues in health-related quality of life: Challenges for health psychology. *Psychology and Health, 15,* 99–108.

Friedman, H. S. (Ed.). (1992). *Hostility, coping, and health.* Washington, DC: American Psychological Association.

Glass, R. M. (1996). The patient-physician relationship: JAMA focuses on the center of medicine. *Journal of the American Medical Association, 275,* 147–148.

Gollwitzer, P. M., & Oettingen, G. (1998). The emergence and implementation of health goals. *Psychology and Health, 13,* 687–715.

Gollwitzer, P. M., Wicklund, R. A., & Hilton, J. L. (1982). Admission of failure and symbolic self-completion: Extending Lewinian theory. *Journal of Personality and Social Psychology, 43,* 358–371.

Halle, T. G. (2003). Emotional development and well-being. In M. H. Bornstein, L. Davidson, C. L. M. Keyes, K. A. Moore, & Center for Child Well-Being (Eds.), *Well-Being: Positive development across the life course* (pp. 125–138). Mahwah, NJ: Erlbaum.

Ingstad, B. (1999). The myth of disability in developing nations. *Lancet, 354,* 757–758.

Jackson, J. L., Chamberlin, J., & Kroenke, K. (2001). Predictors of patient satisfaction. *Social Science and Medicine, 52,* 609–620.

Kegan, R. (1994). *In over our heads.* Cambridge: Cambridge University Press.

Kim, U., & Berry, J. W. (1993). *Indigenous psychologies.* Newbury Park, CA: Sage.

Kunnen, E. S., & Bosma, H. A. (2000). Development of meaning making: A dynamic systems approach. *New Ideas in Psychology, 18,* 57–82.

Leedham, B., Meyerowitz, B. E., Muirhead, J., & Frist, M. H. (1995). Positive expectations predict health after heart transplantation. *Health Psychology, 14,* 74–79.

Lombardi M., & Delle Fave, A. (2002). Disability and rehabilitation in Nepal: An example from Bhaktapur CBR. In A. Delle Fave & M. B. Pun (Eds.), *In pursuit of a sustainable modernisation: Culture and policies in Nepal* (pp. 125–143). Milan, Italy: Arcipelago Edizioni.

Majani, G., Pierobon, A., Giardini, A., & Callegari, S. (2000). Satisfaction profile (SAT_P) in 732 patients: Focus on subjectivity in HRQoL assessment. *Psychology and Health, 15,* 409–422.

Marmot, M., & Wilkinson, R. (1999). *Social determinants of health.* Oxford: Oxford University Press.

Massimini, F., Csikszentmihalyi, M., & Carli, M. (1987). ESM and the monitoring of optimal experience: A tool for psychiatric rehabilitation. *Journal of Nervous and Mental Disease, 175,* 545–549.

Massimini F., Csikszentmihalyi, M., & Delle Fave, A. (1988). Flow and biocultural evolution. In M. Csikszentmihalyi & I. Csikszentmihalyi (Eds.), *Optimal experience: Psychological studies of flow in consciousness* (pp. 60–81). New York: Cambridge University Press.

Massimini, F., & Delle Fave, A. (2000). Individual development in a bio-cultural perspective. *American Psychologist, 55,* 24–33.

Mathew, K. M., Ravichandran, G., May, K., & Morsley, K. (2001). The biopsychosocial model and spinal cord injury. *Spinal Cord, 39,* 644–649.

Mendola, R., Tennen, H., Affleck, G., McCann, L., & Fitzgerald, R. (1990). Appraisal and adaptation among women with impaired fertility. *Cognitive Therapy and Research, 14,* 79–93.

Negri, P., Massimini, F., & Delle Fave, A. (1992). Tema di vita e strategie adattative nei non vedenti (Life theme and adaptive strategies in blind people). In D. Galati (Ed.), *Vedere con la mente: Processi cognitivi, affettivi e strategie adattative* (pp. 355–380). Milan, Italy: Franco Angeli.

Nguyen Thi, P. L., Briançon, S., Empereur, F., & Guillemin, F. (2002). Factors determining inpatient satisfaction with care. *Social Science & Medicine, 54,* 493–504.

Nordenfelt, L. (Ed.). (1994). *Concepts and measurements of quality of life in health care.* Dordrecht: Kluwer.

Peterson, C. (1991). Meaning and measurement of explanatory style. *Psychological Inquiry, 2,* 1–10.

Peterson, C. (2000). The future of optimism. *American Psychologist, 55,* 44–55.

Peterson, C., Schulman, P., Castellon, C., & Seligman, M. E. P. (1992). CAVE: Content analysis of verbatim explanations. In C. P. Smith (Ed.), *Motivation and personality: Handbook of thematic content analysis* (pp. 383–392). New York: Cambridge University Press.

Prochaska, J. O. (1994). Strong and weak principles for progressing from precontemplation to action on the basis of twelve problem behaviors. *Health Psychology, 13,* 47–51.

Reed, G. M., Kemeny, M. E., Taylor, S. E., Wang, H.-Y. J., & Visscher, B. R. (1994). "Realistic acceptance" as a predictor of decreased survival time in gay men with AIDS. *Health Psychology, 13,* 299–307.

Ryan, R. M., & Deci, E. L. (2000). Self-determination theory and the facilitation of intrinsic motivation, social development, and well-being. *American Psychologist. 55,* 68–78.

Salovey, P., Rothman, A. J., Detweiler, J. B., & Steward, W. T. (2000). Emotional states and physical health. *American Psychologist, 55,* 110–121.

Saraswathi, T. S. (1992). Child survival and health and their linkages with psychosocial factors in the home and community. *Psychology and Developing Societies, 4,* 73–87.

Scheier, M. F., & Carver, C. S. (1992). Effects of optimism on psychological and physical well-being: Theoretical overview and empirical update. *Cognitive Therapy and Research, 16,* 201–228.

Schulman, P., Keith, D., & Seligman, M. E. P. (1993). Is optimism heritable? A study of twins. *Behaviour Research & Therapy, 31,* 569–574.

Schwarzer, R. (1994). Optimism, vulnerability, and self-beliefs as health-related cognitions: A systematic overview. *Psychology and Health, 9,* 161–180.

Schwarzer, R. (1998). Optimism, goals, and threats: How to conceptualize self-regulatory processes in the adoption and maintenance of health behaviors. *Psychology and Health, 13,* 759–766.

SCN-CBR. (2000). *The rights of the children with disabilities: Mid-term review report.* Kathmandu: SCN-CBR Partners.

Shanafelt, T. D., Bradley, K. A., Wipf, J. E., & Back, A. L. (2002). Burnout and self-reported patient care in an internal medicine residency program. *Annals of Internal Medicine, 136,* 358–367.

Simeonsson, R. J., Lollar D., Hollowell, J., & Adams, M. (2000). Revision of the International Classification of Impairments, Disabilities, and Handicaps: Developmental issues. *Journal of Clinical Epidemiology, 53,* 113–124.

Sodergren, S. C., & Hyland, M. E. (2000). What are the positive consequences of illness? *Psychology and Health, 15,* 85–97.

Tanaka-Matsumi, J., & Draguns, J. (1997). Culture and psychopathology. In J. W. Berry, M. H. Segall, & C. Kagitçibasi (Eds.), *Handbook of cross-cultural psychology: Vol. 3. Social behavior and applications* (pp. 449–492). Needham Heights, MA: Allyn and Bacon.

Taylor, S. E. (1983). Adjustment to threatening events: A theory of cognitive adaptation. *American Psychologist, 38,* 1161–1173.

Taylor, S. E., & Gollwitzer, P. M. (1995). Effects of mindset on positive illusions. *Journal of Personality and Social Psychology, 69,* 213–226.

Taylor, S. E., Kemeny, M. E., Reed, G. M., Bower, J. E., & Gruenewald, T. L. (2000). Psychological resources, positive illusions, and health. *American Psychologist, 55,* 99–109.

Thuriaux, M. C. (1989). The consequences of diseases and their measurement. *World Health Statistics Quarterly, 42,* 110–114

Thuriaux, M. C. (1995). The ICIDH: Evolution, status and prospects. *Disability and Rehabilitation, 17,* 112–118. .

Tripathi, I., & Agarwal, A. (2000). Chronic illness, symptoms and efficacy in children as related to some psychological characteristics of mothers. *Psychology and Developing Societies, 12,* 31–42.

Üstün, T. B., Chatterji, S., Bickenbach, J. E., Trotter, R. T., II, Room, R., Rehm, J., & Saxena, S. (Eds.). (2001). *Disability and culture: Universalism and diversity.* Göttingen, Germany: Hogrefe and Huber.

Veenhoven, R. (2002). Why social policy needs subjective indicators. *Social Indicators Research, 58,* 33–45.

Wallander, J. L., Varni, J. V., Babani, L., Banis, H. T., & Wilcox, K. T. (1988). Children with chronical physical disorder: Maternal reports of their psychological adjustment. *Journal of Paediatric Psychology, 47,* 197–212.

Weinberg, N. (1988). Another perspective: Attitudes of people with disabilities. In H. E. Yuker (Ed.), *Attitudes toward persons with disabilities* (pp. 141–153). New York: Springer.

Werner, D. (1987). *Disabled village children.* Palo Alto, CA: Hesperian Foundation.

Williams, B. (1994). Patient satisfaction: A valid concept? *Social Science and Medicine, 38,* 509–516.

Williams, G. C., & Deci, E. L. (1998). The importance of supporting autonomy in medical education. *Annals of Internal Medicine, 129,* 303–308.

Williams, G. C., Freedman, Z. R., & Deci, E. L. (1998). Supporting autonomy to motivate patients with diabetes for glucose control. *Diabetes Care, 21,* 1644–1651.

Woelk, G. B. (1992). Cultural and structural influences in the creation of and participation in community health programmes. *Social Science and Medicine, 35,* 419–424.

World Health Organization. (1993). *International Classification of Impairments, Disabilities, and Handicaps: A manual of classification relating to the consequences of disease.* Geneva: Author. (Original work published 1980)

World Health Organization. (2001). *International Classification of Functioning, Disability, and Health: ICF.* Geneva: Author.

10

What Works Makes You Happy

The Role of Personal Goals in Life-Span Development

JARI-ERIK NURMI

KATARIINA SALMELA-ARO

W e are not neutral observers of the surrounding world. Rather, some parts of it appeal to us, drive us forward, and make us feel good, whereas other parts arouse anxiety or disgust or just don't have any meaning for us. The kinds of things, activities, people, and environments we like or dislike are bound up with our motivations. Our motives are important because they direct our behavior and the life we live. However, not all people share the same interests or values. In the same situation, some of us choose a path that leads in one direction, whereas others take the opposite route. Individual motivation not only makes people's lives different, but it also helps them to select life paths, contexts, and settings that satisfy their individual needs according to their personal characteristics, earlier experiences, and values. Motivation and related psychological mechanisms are, therefore, among the major concepts that help us to understand why some people succeed in living a happy and satisfying life, while others don't; this is a key topic in positive psychology. What is more, motivational psychology helps us to understand the diversity of life situations, ways of living, and personal commitments that people find satisfying as a route to personal happiness.

Motivation, however, is not only a personal characteristic. It should be understood rather as a relationship between people's needs and values and the environments that satisfy them. Individuals differ not only in what they find appealing or what they value, but also in their life situations, which provide them with options for satisfying their needs and achieving their goals. Being able to create a satisfactory life or a positive developmental trajectory is not so much about the kinds of motivation people have, or the kinds of situations in which they live, but rather how people are able to combine these together. Individual motivation varies according to several personality factors, such as temperament, personality traits, and previous learning history. In turn, people's life situations and related opportunities and constraints are influenced by other factors, such as norms, roles, the demands of a particular stage of life, cultural beliefs and values, society, historical time, and gender roles. As both individual characteristics and life situations vary considerably, it is easy to understand that there are a variety of routes to happiness and positive development, just as there are many paths to unhappiness and negative developmental trajectories. One key notion of this chapter is that motivation and the personal goals that help individuals to adapt to their life situations in ways that satisfy their individual needs is a major route to well-being—what works makes you happy.

Several theoretical frameworks have been used in the history of psychology to understand people's motivated behavior. In psychoanalytic theory, the roots of individuals' behavior, and related problems, were located in unconscious drives, a concept that dates back to a broad notion of sexuality and the importance of early interpersonal relationships (Freud, 1924). Behaviorism looked for the origins of motivation in individuals' learning histories: Positive reinforcement was assumed to lead to an increase in a particular motivated behavior, whereas punishment was expected to decrease the likelihood of a certain behavioral pattern. The humanistic theories early on emphasized the role of self-actualization, autonomy, and spirituality as the possible driving forces of people's behavior (Maslow, 1987; Rogers, 1961). In recent decades, these older frameworks have been complemented by an emphasis on the roles of cognition, self, and social and interpersonal environments in individual motivation (Mischel, Cantor, & Feldman, 1996; Mischel & Shoda, 1995). These approaches have ended up emphasizing the importance of self-constructed personal goals (Karoly, 1993; Nurmi, 1989), projects (Little, 1983), strivings (Emmons, 1986), life tasks, and hoped-for selves (Markus & Nurius, 1986) as "motivational objectives" that guide people's motivated behavior. These theories conceptualize people as forward-looking, self-motivated beings who are capable of determining their own destinies by constructing personally meaningful goals and directing their activities toward attaining these goals. This approach is also used in this chapter to understand how motivation guides people's behavior and development in different life situations and the kinds of consequences it has for their well-being.

In this chapter, we will first introduce some theoretical ideas that provide a basis for the theory of human motivation. Then, a framework for the concept of self-constructed goals and some related empirical findings are summarized. Next, we move on to discuss the life-span theory of motivation, mainly referring to work done by European scholars. Finally, some of the practical outcomes of this research on motivation and personal goals will be discussed.

Basic Notions of Human Motivation

Because the European approach to motivation is based on some theoretical principles that are seldom discussed in the research carried out in North America, they are briefly summarized here.

According to the *relational theory of motivation,* first introduced by the Belgian psychologist Joseph Nuttin (1984) in the early 1960s, motivation is not an inner psychological state that forces a person to act in a certain way. Rather, motivation should be understood as a relation between an internal need and an objective in the external world that satisfies that particular need. In order to understand the development of individual motivation, the dynamics of this relationship should be examined: How do internal needs change in the process of being satisfied by objectives in the surrounding world? Think, for example, of the development of the social motives of a young child. Such motives are typically satisfied in a relationship to a particular person, usually a mother or a father. In order to understand a particular child's social motives, one has to examine the ways in which the child has interacted with his or her parent to satisfy this particular need. Nuttin's theory has important consequences for the research on motivation. It emphasizes the importance of taking into account the context in which motivational objectives are embedded. Interestingly, in many recent frameworks, motivation is measured by coding the contents of people's goals according to the objectives to which they refer, such as leisure activities, education, occupation, family, or self-related issues (Austin & Vancouver, 1996).

Another key principle, suggested by Nuttin and many other cognitive psychologists (e.g., Miller, Galanter, & Pribram, 1960), is that cognition plays an important role in motivation. For example, because an individual's motives refer to objectives in the surrounding world, he or she typically has a cognitive representation of such motivational objectives. This also means that in most cases people know what they are aiming at.

Motivation is also related to cognition in another way, as many cognitive psychologists besides Nuttin have suggested. In order to satisfy a motive, a person needs first to create a set of goals, the attainment of which, step by step, will lead to need satisfaction. These goals are then actualized by means of a variety of plans and strategies. This process has been described in terms of self-regulation (Carver & Scheier, 1998; Gollwitzer, 1990). Consequently, motivational psychology is not only about the kinds of motives people have but also about how they are attained by the deployment of a variety of goals, plans, problem solving, decisions, and strategies.

The next principle that is important for the psychology of motivation, introduced by Lerner (1982) and Brandtstädter (1984), is that not only are people influenced by their previous life histories and learning, but they also select the environments in which they are living and, in so doing, direct their own development in many ways. For example, it is not only that we learn certain kinds of behavior when dealing with our peers, friends, and spouses, but also that we select and intentionally influence the kinds of people with whom we end up dealing (Nurmi, 2004). What is important in relation to the topic of this chapter is that motivation is among the major mechanisms by which people direct their lives and select their environments (Nurmi, 1993). We tend to select friends, hobbies, careers, and spouses that are in accordance with our interests, goals, values, and needs.

The last theoretical notion is that human motivation is a system that consists of several hierarchical levels (Carver & Scheier, 1990; Nuttin, 1984; Sheldon & Emmons, 1995). On the top level of the hierarchy, motivation consists of a variety of basic needs that are typical of all humans as members of the same species. Such motivational tendencies include characteristics that have developed during evolution to improve the fit between individuals and their environments. Besides physiological needs, these include several specific patterns of behavior, such as certain food preferences. Moreover, several cognitive needs, such as curiosity, modeling, competence, and orientation reflex, are included in this level of motivation, as are many forms of social behavior, such as relatedness, certain mating patterns, taking care of offspring, giving preference to kin, and a variety of other forms of social behaviors. The next level of the motivational hierarchy includes individual differences in motivational orientations. These differences originate in individuals' temperamental characteristics and personality traits, on the one hand, and in learning experiences, on the other. Such differences in motivational orientations then provide a basis for the next level of individual motivation, i.e., the kinds of personal goals, projects, and strivings that people construct to actualize their motivational orientations in a particular life situation. The lowest level of the motivational hierarchy consists of a set of subgoals, plans, and strategies by which people actualize their personal goals (Leontjev, 1977; McGregor & Little, 1998).

Personal Goals and Well-Being

Starting in the early 1980s, several researchers in North America and in Europe began to conceptualize human motivation in terms of self-constructed goals. Although many different conceptualizations were used, such as personal projects (e.g., Little, 1983), strivings (Emmons, 1986), future-oriented goals (Nurmi, 1989), and possible selves (Markus & Nurius, 1986), the basic theoretical approach and methodological tools were very similar (Austin & Vancouver, 1996). Motivation was conceptualized as personal goals and life projects, the ways in which people think and feel about these goals, and the extent to which they report progress, attainment, and investment of effort in them. In a typical procedure designed to measure motivation, people are first asked to list the personal goals, projects, and strivings they have in their minds. As the first step in the analysis, these goals are grouped into different categories on the basis of their content, i.e., what life domain they concern (e.g., education, occupation, family, children, self, and leisure activities) or the kinds of basic motives they reflect (e.g., achievement, affiliation, and power). Also, other characteristics of self-constructed goals can be analyzed, such as how abstract versus concrete they are, or how much they are in conflict with other goals. After people have listed their goals, they are typically asked to appraise each of them along several dimensions, such as importance, commitment, progress, attainment, personal control, stress, positive affects, and social support (Austin & Vancouver, 1996). Using these ratings, several scores, such as importance/meaning, attainment/progress, internal versus external control, and stress, can be calculated in order to understand the ways in which people think and feel about their goals and the extent to which they have made progress in their attainment.

Most research in the field, particularly in the United States and Canada, has focused on examining the associations between the ways in which people think and feel about their personal goals and their well-being. This research has shown:

- People who report that their goals are in congruence with their inherent needs report higher well-being than those who report that their goals are incongruent with their needs (Sheldon & Kasser, 1995).
- People who report having intrinsic goals (self-acceptance, affiliation, community feeling) report a higher level of well-being than those who report more extrinsic goals (financial success, materialism, physical attractiveness) (Kasser & Ryan, 1993; Ryan & Deci, 2000).
- People who report high levels of commitment and involvement in their goals (Brunstein, 1993; Cantor & Fleeson, 1991; McGregor & Little, 1998) show a high level of well-being and low distress.
- People who think that they can control the ways in which their goals proceed have higher levels of well-being than those who lack belief in personal control (Heckhausen, 1999).
- People who appraise their personal goals as having progressed well, report high well-being and low stress, whereas those who appraise their goals as having progressed less well report low well-being and high levels of stress and depressive symptoms (Little, 1989; Salmela-Aro & Nurmi, 1996).
- Choosing realistic and feasible goals is associated with well-being (Cantor & Sanderson, 1999). Goal conflict is associated with high levels of negative affect (Emmons & King, 1988), whereas mutual facilitation among goals is related to a high level of well-being.
- People who receive support from significant others (spouses, classmates, supervisors, or coworkers) report higher well-being than those who report less support (Brunstein, Dangelmayer, & Schultheiss, 1996; Ruehlman & Wolchik, 1988).

Overall, these findings suggest that when people have goals that reflect their individual needs, that have progressed well, and that are supported by others, they feel good about themselves and their lives.

Motivation and Life-Span Development

The ways in which people have lived their earlier lives provide a basis not only for their present life situation but also for their well-being and happiness. From this point of view, life-span development and how it is regulated by people's motivation has important consequences for what is meant by positive psychology. While research in North America has focused on the kinds of personal goals that people have and the consequences of these goals on their well-being, European researchers have emphasized the role of motivation and personal goals in people's life-span development (Brandtstädter & Wentura, 1995; Heckhausen, 1999; Nurmi, 1991).

One major idea behind life-span psychology is that individuals experience different developmental environments depending on their age. Just think about the life of a typical college student, and compare it to that of a middle-aged parent involved in working life, or that of an elderly person after retirement. Several theories have described how people experience different developmental environments at different life stages. Some of these theories have described changes in age-related environments in terms of changing normative tasks, demands, and roles. An example of one such theory is that of Havighurst (1948), who used the concept of the developmental task to describe differences in the normative demands and roles that people experience at different periods during their lives. For instance, the typical developmental tasks of adolescence include achieving mature relationships with one's peers, acquiring a masculine or feminine social role, accepting one's physical appearance, achieving emotional independence of one's parents, preparing for marriage and family life, preparing for a career, developing an identity, and achieving socially responsible behavior. By contrast, during middle age, one's developmental tasks focus on assisting children to become happy adults, achieving adult social and civic responsibilities, reaching and maintaining satisfactory performance in one's career, developing leisure activities, relating to one's spouse, and accepting the physiological changes of middle age.

Other scholars, such as Mayer (1986), have emphasized that many institutional structures, such as educational systems, working life, and economics, constitute a variety of "tracks" that direct people's development. An example of such an institutional track is that created by the system of education in a particular society and the related transitional patterns and tracks. Such institutional tracks have also been shown to vary widely across different countries (Hurrelmann,

1994). The reason that these age-related normative and institutional factors are important for individual motivation is that they create an "opportunity space" that channels individuals' motivation and personal goals in a particular stage of life.

Functions of Motivation and Personal Goals

Human motivation has two major functions in the context of life-span development (Nurmi, 2004; Salmela-Aro, Nurmi, Saisto, & Halmesmäki, 2001). The first function is responsible for the *selection* of environments that are in accordance with an individual's needs, which spring from that person's temperamental characteristics and personality traits, on the one hand, and individual learning experiences, on the other. In the course of this selection, people compare their motives to the objectives and opportunities available in their current environments in order to construct realistic goals for their present behavior. The second function of motivation is responsible for people's *adjustment* to their current life situations and the outcomes of previous efforts to attain particular goals. This adjustment process consists of disengagement from previous goals, engagement in a new one, and changes in goal priorities. Such adjustment is important in two kinds of situations. One is when individuals experience substantial changes in their environments, for example, due to experiencing a transition to a new role or a move along an institutional track (Brandtstädter & Wentura, 1995). The other situation is when individuals receive feedback from their previous efforts to attain a particular goal. Particularly, when people have failed to reach a previous goal, they will adjust that goal to cope with their new life situation (Wrosch & Heckhausen, 1999).

The extent to which selection or adjustment dominate in the construction of personal goals will depend on the characteristics of an individual's present life context. This life context can be described in terms of *opportunities* and *constraints* (Heckhausen, 1999). When opportunities exceed constraints, selection will be the dominant mechanism in goal construction: People have several options from which they need to select the one that best fits in with their individual motives (Figure 10.1). By contrast, when constraints exceed opportunities, the adjustment of previous personal goals is needed. In performing adjustment, people need to reconstruct their personal goals both on the basis of the information they have about the environment and according to their possibilities for goal attainment, such as the time required, their personal abilities, and the social support available. Because the number of opportunities and constraints varies across different phases of the life-span, the model can be used conceptualize motivation in life-span development.

Individuals' motivation and their life-span development might be assumed to be associated in three ways. Each of these developmental patterns also has consequences for people's well-being and happiness.

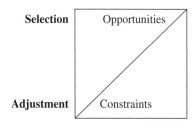

Selection | Opportunities
Adjustment | Constraints

Figure 10.1. Two Functions of Motivation: Selection and Adjustment

Developmental Tasks and Age Constraints
Channel the Construction of Personal Goals

Because people's motives concern objectives in the external world, it might be assumed that the age-related environment—the normative demands, role transitions, and opportunities they are experiencing during a particular life phase—will *channel* the kinds of motives and personal goals they have at different ages (Figure 10.2; Nurmi, 2004). A few studies have sought to examine this hypothesis by comparing different age groups according to their personal goals. The results suggest that people's goals differ and that these differences reflect the developmental tasks, opportunities, and role transitions typical of a particular age phase. For example, when adolescents and young adults are asked about their future hopes and interests, they typically report goals that refer to education, occupation, future family, leisure activities, and self-related topics (Lanz & Rosnati, 2002; Nurmi, 1991). When people move from early to middle adulthood, there are evident changes in their personal goals. For example, Nurmi (1992) found that, while 25- to 34-year-olds often mentioned goals concerning family and self, 35- to 44-year-olds reported goals related to their children's lives and travel; 45- to 54-year-olds mentioned goals concerning health, children's lives, and leisure activities; and 55- to 64-year-olds had many goals concerning health, leisure activities, and world politics. All age groups reported many occupation- and property-related goals. When people moved from middle adulthood to old age, their goals changed again. Cross and Markus (1991), for example, found that elderly people particularly mentioned health- and lifestyle-related topics. Similarly, Smith and Freund (2002) found that very old people's goals often focused on personal characteristics, health, and social relationships.

The life-span theory of motivation assumes that the goals that match the developmental tasks of a particular age are adaptive in directing people's lives and, therefore, should also contribute to their well-being (Nurmi, 1993, 2001). Along with this assumption, it has been shown that young adults who report interpersonal and family-related goals, reflecting the developmental tasks of this age phase, also show a higher level of well-being than do other young people (Emmons, 1991; Salmela-Aro & Nurmi, 1997). Moreover, youths with school-focused goals are at reduced risk of involvement in delinquent activities

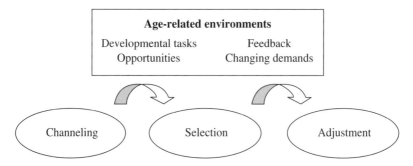

Figure 10.2.   Channeling, Selection, and Adjustment in Age-Related Environments

(Oyserman & Markus, 1990), attain better school outcomes, and feel more connected to school (Oyserman, Gant, & Ager, 1995) than do other adolescents.

By contrast, although thinking about self- and identity-related issues has been
assumed to be a natural part of adolescence and young adulthood (Bosma &
Kunnen, 2001; Erikson, 1959), such goals are associated with low well-being.
It has been found, for example, that people who report self-focused goals also
show low levels of well-being (Salmela-Aro, Pennanen, & Nurmi, 2001) and life
satisfaction (Cross & Markus, 1991). Moreover, an increase in such goals has
been found to lead to an increase in depressive symptoms (Salmela-Aro, Nurmi,
et al., 2001).

The Role of Personal Goals in Directing
Life-Span Development

The life-span theory of motivation also suggests that motivation and personal goals
play an important part in the ways in which people direct their lives and select
different developmental environments (Figure 10.2). Along with this assumption,
Nurmi, Salmela-Aro, and Koivisto (2002) found that the more young adults emphasized the importance of work-related goals and the more they thought they had
progressed in the achievement of those goals, the more likely they were after graduation from vocational school to find work that was commensurate with their education and the less likely they were to be unemployed. Concrete college goals have
also been found to predict subsequent college attendance (Pimentel, 1996). Similar results have been found in interpersonal life domains as well. For example,
young adults' family-related goals predicted subsequent movement toward marriage or cohabitation (Salmela-Aro & Nurmi, 1997).

By contrast, it has been shown that young adults' self-focused, existential-
type goals predict subsequent negative life events, such as the breaking up of an
intimate relationship (Salmela-Aro & Nurmi, 1997). Stattin and Kerr (2001)

showed that adolescents who reported self-focused values (personal satisfaction and enjoyment) were more likely in later life to become engaged in risky behaviors, such as norm breaking, risky sex, smoking, and drinking and to associate with delinquent friends, compared with adolescents who have other-focused values (concern for others' well-being and the common good). One reason that self-focused goals may lead to problems in life is that such goals, if they dominate for too long, do not help people find active ways of dealing with the major challenges and constraints they will experience later in their lives (Salmela-Aro, Pennanen, & Nurmi, 2001). In addition, self-focused goals might be associated with excessive self-reflection, which has been found to have negative affective and cognitive consequences (Ingram, 1990; Nolen-Hoeksema, Parker, & Larsen, 1994; Sedikides, 1992), such as depressive symptoms, negative moods, and negative self-schemas. Finally, self-focused goals also share similarities with identity goals (Gollwitzer, 1990) and abstract goals (Emmons, 1992), which have also been found to be associated with low well-being, possibly because such goals do not specify clear criteria for success and goal attainment (Emmons, 1992).

Adjustment of Personal Goals to the Changing Demands and the Outcomes of Goal Attainment

People sometimes also need to adjust their goals in order to deal successfully with their developmental environment. This adjustment typically occurs in two kinds of situations (Figure 10.2). One situation is when an individual's developmental environment changes. For example, going through certain transitions has been found to affect individuals' personal goals. Salmela-Aro and Nurmi (1997) found that young adults' life situations, such as being married and having children, predicted their subsequent family-related goals. By contrast, being single predicted turning to self-focused goals.

However, people not only construct goals that are in accordance with age-graded normative environments, but they also reconstruct their personal goals to match the specific stages of the particular transition through which they are going. For example, Salmela-Aro, Nurmi, Saisto, and Halmesmäki (2000) showed that women who were facing a transition to parenthood reconstructed their goals to match the specific stages of this transition: The topics of the women's personal goals changed, first from personal achievement to pregnancy, then to deal with the birth of their child, and finally to taking care of the child and being a mother.

It might also be assumed on the basis of the life-span theory of motivation that reconstructing one's goals according to the changing demands of a particular transition has consequences for people's well-being. Salmela-Aro, Nurmi, et al. (2001) found that women who were facing the transition to parenthood and who adjusted their personal goals to match the particular stage-specific demands of this transition, such as goals related to family, spouse, and the birth of the child, showed a decrease in depressive symptoms. By contrast, those who disengaged from such goals showed an increase in depressive symptoms.

Another situation in which people need to adjust their personal goals is when they receive feedback concerning their success and failure in dealing with a particular developmental transition. For example, success in dealing with a certain transition might be assumed to lead to the reconstruction of personal goals in a direction that helps an individual to move to the next stage in a particular developmental trajectory. By contrast, when people fail to cope successfully with a particular transition and actualize their previous goals, they need to adjust their previous goals in order to maintain a positive developmental perspective in later phases of life. This goal adjustment may include revising the standards of goal attainment or disengagement from previous goals and engagement in new ones as a way of coping with the new life situation following the nonattainment of previous goals.

In one study, Nurmi and Salmela-Aro (2002) examined young people who faced a transition from vocational school to working life. Their results showed that young adults who were successful in dealing with the transition from school to work, i.e., who were able to find a job, showed a decreasing interest in personal goals that were no longer adaptive in their current life situation. This was reflected, for example, in their decreasing interest in education-related goals. By contrast, young people who had problems in dealing with the transition to work showed a decrease in their interest in this particular life domain and turned to other types of goals. For instance, among those who were still unemployed 1.5 years after graduation, there was an increase in education- and self-related goals, probably as a way of coping with their life situation.

As might be assumed on the basis of the life-span theory of motivation, goal reconstruction after receiving feedback on previous goal attainment has consequences for individuals' well-being. For example, Nurmi and Salmela-Aro (2002) found that adjusting personal goals to focus on the key demands of the life situation following graduation from vocational school led to a high level of well-being. There was a decrease in depressive symptoms among those who were working on a full-time basis in a profession that did not match their education but who had many work-related goals, whereas those similarly employed but lacking work-related goals reported an increase in depressive symptoms. Among those who had not been able to find a job after graduation but who still reported many work-related goals, there was also an increase in depressive symptoms.

Overall, these results suggest that people adjust their goals when they are facing changing demands and opportunities due to a developmental transition or when they receive information about their success in dealing with a previous life transition. Moreover, such personal goal adjustment also has consequences for people's well-being.

Positive Psychology and Research on Motivation

The present chapter has focused so far on the role that individual motivation plays in the ways in which people direct their lives, on the ways in which they adjust their goals on the basis of their current life situation, and on the impacts that these motivational mechanisms have on people's well-being. Next, the implications of the research on motivation for positive psychology will be discussed in more detail.

Motivation and a Life Worth Living

The theories and empirical findings in the field of motivation and personal goals provide a multifaceted and even complex view of what makes some people evaluate their lives as worth living or even happy and causes others to be dissatisfied with their lives.

First, people who think that their goals are in congruence with their inherent needs report a high level of well-being. Moreover, people who report that they are committed to their goals, who believe that they can control their goals, and who estimate that their goals have progressed well also show higher well-being. In other words, being optimistic about one's possibilities of attaining goals that originate out of one's internal needs provides a basis for happiness.

Second, the life-span approach to motivation suggests that those who have personal goals that help them to deal with the demands and opportunities of the particular life period in which they are living experience well-being and happiness. Moreover, the adjustment of one's personal goals to match the changes in these demands and options owing to either new role transitions or the outcome of an individual's efforts to attain his or her previous goals provide a basis for thinking that life is worth living. However, excessive self-focus is problematic, perhaps because it leads to ruminative thinking. Although we all need sometimes to think about ourselves and evaluate our potential for changing ourselves, continuous self-focus tends to lead to a low sense of well-being.

Third, because people differ not only in their individual motivations but also in the demands and opportunities that face them in their current life situations, one conclusion of our chapter is that there are multiple pathways to happiness or, alternatively, unhappiness. What is more important than individual motives or living conditions is the extent to which people are able to match their motives to the demands and opportunities they are facing. It was also shown in this chapter that one major function of motivation is to adjust one's personal goals in ways that optimize one's possibilities to cope with one's current life context. People who have problems in making this adjustment and are unable or unwilling to change their previous goals may end up feeling unhappy.

Finally, feelings of happiness are also likely to have consequences for the kinds of personal goals that people construct. A high level of well-being can be assumed to increase people's focus on interpersonal goals and their belief in personal control and goal attainment. Low well-being, in turn, is likely to lead to ruminative, self-focused goals. In other words, happiness is likely to lead to the construction of goals that will later contribute to positive feelings about oneself and one's life, thereby laying a foundation for a positive life trajectory. Such a cumulative pattern may explain why some people are able to build a life worth living for most of their lives.

Counseling for a Life Worth Living

People may also benefit in some situations from professional help and guidance when they have to make decisions concerning their future and how to direct their lives (Karoly & Ruehlman, 1995; Little & Chambers, 2003). Such efforts may be helpful, at least in the following situations.

First, in some life situations, people may lack interest in personal goals that would promote their development in the future, or they may lack knowledge of how to attain their goals. A typical example of this kind of situation is presented by young people who, because of a lack of parental advice, role models, or help or because of changing societal opportunities are unable to plan their educations and careers in ways that will promote their adult lives. Counseling in this kind of situation typically aims to help such individuals construct educational plans and vocational goals that are in accordance with their inner needs and that will also match the demands and options they are facing in their developmental environments, as well as match their personal credentials. Moreover, providing young people with information about their future opportunities and nurturing their beliefs in internal control may be important in helping them to develop positive attitudes and beliefs in the attainment of their educational and occupational goals. For example, Wham Marko and Savickas (1998) developed a short intervention procedure to increase high-school and college students' interest in career planning, positive attitudes toward planning, and active goal setting.

Second, people sometimes enter a life situation in which external help and advice will increase their likelihood of finding more satisfactory life prospects. For example, Vuori et al. (2002) developed a job search program (Caplan, Vinokur, Price, & Van Ryn, 1989) for unemployed adults that was designed to increase the participants' self-efficacy beliefs and motivation, to enhance their recognition of personal strengths, to encourage the use of social networks, and to teach them important skills related to finding a job. Vuori et al.'s (2002) results showed that, at the 6–month follow-up, the program had a beneficial impact on the quality of reemployment and also increased well-being among the participants.

To give a further example, Oyserman, Terry, and Bybee (2002) developed an intervention to enhance school involvement among adolescents. They found that a short group-based intervention succeeded effectively in bolstering adolescents' academic goals and improving their engagement with school. Moreover, the intervention helped the young people to articulate specific academic goals, to connect them to specific strategies with which to attain their desired academic selves, to connect them to future adult lives, and finally to develop skills of effective interacting with others in order to attain these academic goals.

Finally, the theory and research on motivation may also be of benefit in situations in which people have ended up feeling dissatisfied with some part of their lives. The problem with such dissatisfaction is that it easily spills over into other life domains. For example, Salmela-Aro, Näätänen, and Nurmi (2000) examined the effectiveness of an intervention program for employees who suffered from severe burnout symptoms. The results showed that the therapeutic interventions led to a decrease in symptoms. Interestingly, it was particularly those participants who reported an increase in the progress of their work-related goals and a decrease in their negative goal-related emotions who benefited most from the intervention.

The present chapter has focused on discussing the roles that motivation and personal goals play in the ways in which people direct their lives and the ways in which they adjust their motives and goals on the basis of their current life situations and the feedback they receive on their previous behavior. Such efforts to direct their lives and to adjust to changes related to their current life situations were also shown to have consequences for people's well-being and for the ways in which they evaluate their lives and themselves. From the viewpoint of the life-span theory of motivation, what works makes one happy.

References

Austin, J., & Vancouver, J. (1996). Goal constructs in psychology: Structure, process, and content. *Psychological Bulletin, 120,* 338–375.

Bosma, H. A., & Kunnen, E. S. (2001). Determinants and mechanisms in ego identity development: A review and synthesis. *Developmental Review, 21,* 39–66.

Brandtstädter, J. (1984). Personal and social control over development: Some implications of an action perspective in life-span development psychology. In P. B. Baltes & O. G. Brim, Jr. (Eds.), *Life-span development and behavior* (Vol. 6, pp. 1–32). New York: Academic.

Brandtstädter, J., & Wentura, D. (1995). Adjustment to shifting possibility frontiers in later life: Complementary adaptive modes. In R. Dixon & L. Bäckman (Eds.), *Compensating for psychological deficits and declines: Managing losses and promoting gains* (pp. 83–106). Mahwah, NJ: Erlbaum.

Brunstein, J. C. (1993). Personal goals and subjective well-being: A longitudinal study. *Journal of Personality and Social Psychology, 65,* 1061–1070.

Brunstein, J., Dangelmayer, G., & Schultheiss, O. (1996). Personal goals and social support in close relationships: Effects on relationship mood and marital satisfaction. *Journal of Personality and Social Psychology, 71,* 1006–1019.

Cantor, N., & Fleeson, W. (1991). Life tasks and self-regulatory processes. *Advances in Motivation and Achievement, 7,* 327–369.

Cantor, N., & Sanderson, C. (1999). Life task participation and well-being: The importance of taking part in daily life. In D. Kahneman, E. Diener, & N. Schwarz (Eds.), *Well-being: The foundations of hedonic psychology* (pp. 230–243). New York: Russell Sage Foundation.

Caplan, R. D., Vinokur, A. D., Price, R. H., & Van Ryn, M. (1989). Job seeking, reemployment, and mental health: A randomized field experiment in coping with job loss. *Journal of Applied Psychology, 74,* 759–769.

Carver, C., & Scheier, M. (1990). Principles of self-regulation: Action and emotion. In E. T. Higgins & R. M. Sorrentino (Eds.), *Handbook of motivation and cognition: Foundations of social behavior* (Vol. 2, pp. 3–52). New York: Guilford.

Carver, C., & Scheier, M. (1998). *On the self-regulation of behavior.* New York: Cambridge University Press.

Cross, S., & Markus, H. (1991). Possible selves across the life span. *Human Development, 34,* 230–255.

Emmons, R. A. (1986). Personal strivings: An approach to personality and subjective well-being. *Journal of Personality and Social Psychology, 51,* 1058–1068.

Emmons, R. A. (1991). Personal strivings, daily life events, and psychological and physical well-being. *Journal of Personality, 59,* 453–472.

Emmons, R. A. (1992). Abstract versus concrete goals: Personal striving level, physical illness, and psychological well-being. *Journal of Personality and Social Psychology, 62,* 3–9.

Emmons, R. A., & King, L. A. (1988). Conflict among personal strivings: Immediate and long-term implications for psychological and physical well-being. *Journal of Personality and Social Psychology, 54,* 1040–1048.

Erikson, E. (1959). *Identity and the life cycle.* New York: International University Press.

Freud, S. (1924). *A general introduction to psychoanalysis.* New York: Permabooks.

Gollwitzer, P. (1990). Action phases and mind-sets. In E. T. Higgins & R. M. Sorrentino (Eds.), *Handbook of motivation and cognition: Foundations of social behavior* (Vol. 2, pp. 53–92). New York: Guilford.

Havighurst, R. (1948). *Developmental tasks and education* (3rd ed.). New York: McKay.

Heckhausen, J. (1999). *Developmental regulation in adulthood: Age-graded normative and sociostructural constraints as adaptive challenge.* New York: Cambridge University Press.

Hurrelmann, K. (Ed.). (1994). *International handbook of adolescence.* Westport, CT: Greenwood.

Ingram, R. E. (1990). Self-focused attention in clinical disorders: Review and a conceptual model. *Psychological Bulletin, 107,* 156–176.

Karoly, P. (1993). Mechanisms of self-regulation: A systems view. *Annual Review of Psychology, 44,* 23–52.

Karoly, P., & Ruehlman, L. S. (1995). Goal cognition and its clinical implications: Development and preliminary validation of four motivational assessment instruments. *Assessment, 2,* 113–129.

Kasser, T., & Ryan, R. M. (1993). A dark side of the American dream: Correlates of financial success as a central life aspiration. *Journal of Personality and Social Psychology, 65,* 410–422.

Lanz, M., & Rosnati, R. (2002). Adolescents' and young adults' construction of the future: Effects of family relations, self-esteem, and sense of coherence. In J. Trempala & L.-E. Malmberg (Eds.), *Adolescents' future-orientation: Theory and research* (pp. 17–34). Frankfurt am Main: Lang.

Leontjev, A. N. (1977). *Toiminta, tietoisuus, persoonallisuus* (Action, cognition, and personality). Helsinki, Finland: Kansankulttuuri.

Lerner, R. M. (1982). Children and adolescents as producers of their own development. *Developmental Review, 2,* 342–370.

Little, B. R. (1983). Personal projects: A rationale and method for investigation. *Environment and Behavior, 15,* 273–309.

Little, B. R. (1989). Personal projects analysis: Trivial pursuits, magnificent obsessions, and the search for coherence. In D. M. Buss & N. Cantor (Eds.), *Personality psychology: Recent trends and emerging directions* (pp. 15–31). New York: Springer.

Little, B., & Chambers, N. (2003). *Personal projects and their clinical usefulness.* Manuscript submitted for publication.

Markus, H., & Nurius, P. (1986). Possible selves. *American Psychologist, 41,* 954–969.

Maslow, A. (1987). *Motivation and personality.* New York: Harper & Row.

Mayer, K. (1986). Structural constraints on the life course. *Human Development, 29,* 163–170.

McGregor, I., & Little, B. (1998). Personal projects, happiness, and meaning: On doing well and being yourself. *Journal of Personality and Social Psychology, 74,* 494–512.

Miller, G. A., Galanter, E., & Pribram, K. H. (1960). *Plans and the structure of behavior.* New York: Holt, Rinehart and Winston.

Mischel, W., Cantor, N., & Feldman, S. (1996). Principles of self-regulation: The nature of willpower and self-control. In E. T. Higgins & A. W. Kruglanski (Eds.), *Social psychology: Handbook of basic principles* (pp. 329–360). New York: Guilford.

Mischel, W., & Shoda, Y. (1995). A cognitive-affective system theory of personality: Reconceptualizing situations, dispositions, dynamics, and invariance in personality structure. *Psychological Review, 102,* 246–268.

Nolen-Hoeksema, S., Parker, L. E., & Larsen, J. (1994). Ruminative coping with depressed mood following loss. *Journal of Personality and Social Psychology, 67,* 92–104.

Nurmi, J.-E. (1989). Development of orientation to the future during early adolescence: A four-year longitudinal study and two cross-lagged comparisons. *International Journal of Psychology, 24,* 195–214.

Nurmi, J.-E. (1991). How do adolescents see their future? A review of the development of future orientation and planning. *Developmental Review, 11,* 1–59.

Nurmi, J.-E. (1992). Age differences in adult life goals, concerns, and their temporal extension: A life course approach to future-oriented motivation. *Journal of Behavioral Development, 15,* 487–508.

Nurmi, J.-E. (1993). Adolescent development in an age-graded context: The role of personal beliefs, goals, and strategies in the tackling of developmental tasks and standards. *International Journal of Behavioral Development, 16,* 169–189.

Nurmi, J.-E. (2001). Adolescents' self-direction and self-definition in age-graded sociocultural and interpersonal contexts. In J.-E. Nurmi (Ed.), *Navigating through adolescence: European perspectives* (pp. 229–250). New York & London: Routledge Falmer.

Nurmi, J.-E. (2004). Socialization and self-development: Channeling selection adjustment and reflection. In R. M. Lerner & L. Steinberg (Eds.), *Handbook of adolescent psychology* (2nd ed., pp. 85–124). Hoboken, NJ: Wiley & Sons.

Nurmi, J.-E., & Salmela-Aro, K. (2002). Goal construction, reconstruction and depressive symptomatology in a life span context: The transition from school to work. *Journal of Personality, 70,* 385–420.

Nurmi, J.-E., Salmela-Aro, K., & Koivisto, P. (2002). Goal importance, and related agency-beliefs and emotions during the transition from vocational school to work: Antecedents and consequences. *Journal of Vocational Behavior, 60,* 241–261.

Nuttin, J. (1984). *Motivation, planning and action.* Hillsdale, NJ: Erlbaum.

Oyserman, D., Gant, L., & Ager, J. (1995). A socially contextualized model of African American identity: Possible selves and school persistence. *Journal of Personality and Social Psychology, 69,* 1216–1232.

Oyserman, D., & Markus, H. (1990). Possible selves and delinquency. *Journal of Personality and Social Psychology, 59,* 112–125.

Oyserman, D., Terry, K., & Bybee, D. (2002). A possible selves intervention to enhance school involvement. *Journal of Adolescence, 25,* 313–326.

Pimentel, E. F. (1996). Effects of adolescent achievement and family goals on the early adult transition. In T. T. Mortimer & M. D. Finch (Eds.), *Adolescents, work, and family: An intergenerational developmental analysis* (pp. 191–200). Thousand Oaks, CA: Sage.

Rogers, J. B. (1961). *On becoming a person.* Boston: Houghton Mifflin.

Ruehlman, L., & Wolchik, S. A. (1988). Personal goals and interpersonal support and hindrance as factors in psychological distress and well-being. *Journal of Personality and Social Psychology, 55,* 293–301.

Ryan, R. M., & Deci, E. L. (2000). Self-determination theory and the facilitation of intrinsic motivation, social development and well-being. *American Psychologist, 55,* 68–78.

Salmela-Aro, K., Näätänen, P., & Nurmi, J.-E. (2000). L'examen des projects personnel au cours d'une psychoterapie destinee aux personnes souffrant d'epuisement professionel (The role of personal project appraisals during group psychotherapy of participants suffering from burnout symptoms). *Revue Quebecoise de Psychologie, 21,* 2–28.

Salmela-Aro, K., & Nurmi, J.-E. (1996). Depressive symptoms and personal project appraisals: A cross-lagged longitudinal study. *Personality and Individual Differences, 21,* 373–381.

Salmela-Aro, K., & Nurmi, J.-E. (1997). Goal contents, well-being and life context during the transition to university: A longitudinal study. *International Journal of Behavioral Development, 20,* 471–491.

Salmela-Aro, K., Nurmi, J.-E., Saisto, T., & Halmesmäki, E. (2000). Women's and men's personal goals during the transition to parenthood. *Journal of Family Psychology, 14,* 171–186.

Salmela-Aro, K., Nurmi, J.-E., Saisto, T., & Halmesmäki, E. (2001). Goal reconstruction and depressive symptoms during the transition to motherhood: Evidence from two cross-lagged longitudinal studies. *Journal of Personality and Social Psychology, 81,* 1144–1159.

Salmela-Aro, K., Pennanen, R., & Nurmi, J.-E. (2001). Self-focused goals: what they are, how they function and how they relate to well-being. In P. Schmuck & K. Sheldon (Eds.), *Life goals and well-being* (pp. 148–166). Lengerich, Germany: Hogrefe & Huber.

Sedikides, C. (1992). Mood as a determinant of attentional focus. *Cognition and Emotion, 6,* 129–148.

Sheldon, K. M., & Emmons, R. A. (1995). Comparing differentiation and integration within personal goal systems. *Personality and Individual Differences, 18,* 39–46.

Sheldon, K. M., & Kasser, T. (1995). Coherence and congruence: Two aspects of personality integration. *Journal of Personality and Social Psychology, 68,* 531–543.

Smith, J., & Freund, A. M. (2002). The dynamics of possible selves in old age. *Journal of Gerontology, 57B,* P492–P500.

Stattin, H., & Kerr, M. (2001). Adolescents' values matter. In J.-E. Nurmi (Ed.), *Navigating through adolescence: European perspectives* (pp. 21–58). New York & London: Routledge Falmer.

Vuori, J., Silvonen, J., Vinokur, A. D., & Price, R. H. (2002). The Tyoehoen Job Search Program in Finland: Benefits for the unemployed with risk of depression or discouragement. *Journal of Occupational Health Psychology, 7,* 5–19.

Wham Marko, K., & Savickas, M. L. (1998). Effectiveness of a career time perspective intervention. *Journal of Vocational Behavior, 52,* 106–119.

Wrosch, C., & Heckhausen, J. (1999). Control processes before and after passing a developmental deadline: Activation and deactivation of intimate relationship goals. *Journal of Personality and Social Psychology, 77,* 415–427.

11

Materialism and Its Alternatives

TIM KASSER

One key feature of contemporary life is the fact that commercialization and consumerism are embedded in almost every aspect of culture. It is well-nigh impossible to avoid messages suggesting that a meaningful, happy life results from the acquisition of wealth and the possessions that convey the right image and high status. We are continually bombarded by commercial messages to this effect on television and in print advertisements, but marketers have recently become increasingly ingenious in the placement of such messages, as they now appear on toilet stalls, in beach sand, and even on temporary tattoos affixed to people's foreheads. Further, commercial messages have made their way into schools and other public places, such as subways, police cars, and sports stadiums. And our governmental leaders continually reinforce the importance of consumerism, placing economic progress and increased consumption at the forefront of public discourse; referring to citizens more often than not as consumers, passing laws that maximize shareholder profits; and even suggesting, after the terrorist attacks on September 11, 2001, that Americans could best help their nation by "going shopping."

In the midst of such an environment, it is not surprising that many of us take on the messages of consumer society, believing that it is of at least some importance to strive for wealth, image, and status. Thus, not only do commercialization and consumerism color our social surroundings, they worm their way into our psyches, leading us to organize some portion of our lives around increasing our salaries and owning more stuff. To one degree or another, all of us adopt a materialistic, or "extrinsic," value orientation (Kasser, 2002) in the belief that "the goods life" is the path to "the good life."

It would be one thing if the messages of consumer society were true, but they are not. It would be another thing if these messages were benign lies, but they are not that either. As it turns out, empirical research documents that there is a high price to pay when people take on the messages of consumer society and organize their lives around materialistic pursuits (Kasser, 2002). Research by a variety of investigators consistently documents that the more people value materialistic aspirations and goals, the less they are happy with their personal lives and the more they act in ways that are socially and ecologically damaging. The purpose of the present chapter is to briefly review evidence supporting this claim and to present some alternatives to the materialistic mindset, lifestyle, and culture.

Before turning to this evidence, it is important for readers to have a basic understanding of how materialism is measured. Two types of strategies are typically used. The *values method* (e.g., Kasser & Ryan, 1993, 1996) asks study participants to rate a variety of different goals or values in terms of how important each is to their own lives. Participants are asked about goals concerning spirituality, relationships, and sensual pleasure, among others, as well as about goals that concern materialism. Some of the sample materialistic goals include "I will be financially successful," "I will keep up with fashions in clothing and hair," and "I will have a lot of expensive possessions." Statistical procedures are then applied to these ratings in order to yield an index of the importance that people place on materialistic values relative to the other things they might care about. The *survey method* (e.g., Belk, 1985; Richins & Dawson, 1992) for measuring materialism is more straightforward, as it asks people how much they agree or disagree with statements like "The things I own say a lot about how I'm doing in life," "Buying things gives me a lot of pleasure," and "My life would be better if I owned certain things I don't have." Although there are other interesting ways to measure materialism (including *subject-generated goals* [Sheldon & Kasser, 1995] and *reaction time methodologies* [Solberg, Diener, & Robinson, 2004]), the values and survey strategies are probably the most widely used.

Having provided this brief methodological backdrop, let us now review some of the research on the personal, social, and ecological costs of valuing materialistic pursuits; readers interested in a fuller exposition are referred to Kasser (2002).

Personal Costs

Throughout history, thinkers in most philosophical, religious, and scientific traditions have warned of the personal difficulties that result from orienting one's life around materialistic pursuits. Even a famous economist responsible in part for our current obsession with economic progress recognized the problems of materialism:

> When the accumulation of wealth is no longer of high social importance . . . the love of money as a possession . . . will be recognized for what it is, a somewhat disgusting morbidity, one of the semi-criminal, semi-pathological propensities which one hands over with a shudder to the specialists in mental disease. (Keynes, 1932, p. 369)

Since the mid-1980s, researchers have begun to provide scientific evidence for such speculation. Studies by Belk (1985), Richins and Dawson (1992), and Kasser and Ryan (1993) measured individual differences in people's materialistic orientations and associated these scores with measures of individual happiness, life satisfaction, and vitality, as well as depression and anxiety. The results consistently pointed toward the conclusion that materialistic people were *less* happy and satisfied with life and that they also reported *more* distress. Thus, the more people "buy into" the messages of consumer society, the lower their levels of personal well-being and the higher their levels of distress.

A growing number of studies have replicated and extended this early research (see Kasser, 2002, for an overview). We now know, for example, that materialistic values are associated with a variety of problems in personal well-being, including more depression, anxiety, and narcissism; less frequent experience of pleasant emotions in daily life and more frequent experience of unpleasant emotions; more problems with substances, such as cigarettes, alcohol, and illegal drugs; and even physical health problems, such as headaches and stomach aches. Similar findings have been reported in children as young as 10 years old (Kasser, 2005) and in adults in their 80s. The problematic associations of materialism and personal well-being have also been replicated in a variety of countries, including Britain, Denmark, Germany, India, Romania, Russia, Singapore, and South Korea. Finally, studies show that materialism is even negatively associated with well-being in samples of entrepreneurs and business students, even though their professional pursuits are assumedly (though not necessarily) focused on the accumulation of profit.

Social Costs

Some people may choose to give up some happiness in order potentially to increase their material wealth and possessions. Such a decision is of course their own choice. The problem, however, is that a materialistic value orientation influences the ways that people act in social contexts and thus affects other people's well-being too. Consider, for example, the recent scandals in which large corporations engaged in unethical and illegal business practices, motivated in part because certain well-paid executives felt they needed more money for their enormous mansions and $6,000 shower curtains. As a means of attaining their materialistic goals, they (allegedly) fixed the books and stole from shareholders, leading to the collapse of their companies and the loss of many employees' jobs and pension plans. Clearly, the materialistic desires of these businesspeople caused untoward consequences for other individuals.

These examples suggest that when desires for profit and wealth become prominent in people's value systems, they become increasingly willing to manipulate other people in ways that might be to their own financial benefit, but that show little concern for the well-being of others. As such, the problems associated with materialism become a social as well as a personal issue.

Research suggests two main reasons why materialism relates to such problematic social behavior. First, some studies show that a focus on materialistic values conflicts with the prosocial values that conduce toward healthy social behavior. For example, materialistic, extrinsic values oppose concerns such as "I will express my love for special people" and "I will help others improve their lives" (Grouzet et al., in press). The cross-cultural research of Schwartz (1996) similarly demonstrates that values for wealth, public recognition, and social image oppose values for benevolence (e.g., being loyal, responsible, and honest) and universalism (e.g., caring about social justice and equality). Such findings obviously are relevant to materialistic choices that detrimentally affect other people.

Second, a strong materialistic value orientation is associated with *objectification,* or the tendency to treat other people as objects to be manipulated rather than as unique individuals with their own desires, needs, and subjective experiences (Kasser, 2002). Focusing on the desire for status and concerning oneself with things apparently leads people to treat others as things. For example, people who are more materialistically oriented are less empathic (Sheldon & Kasser, 1995), less generous (Kasser, 2005; Richins & Dawson, 1992), and more manipulative (McHoskey, 1999). Even their friendships suffer, as extrinsically oriented people have shorter, more-conflictual friendships (Kasser & Ryan, 2001), view their friendships as ways to get ahead in life or to "look cool" (Khanna, 1999), and are more likely to compete and less likely to cooperate with their friends in prisoner's dilemma games (Sheldon, Sheldon, & Osbaldiston, 2000). None of these characteristics bodes well for the ways that extrinsically oriented individuals treat other people.

Ecological Costs

Given that materialistic values are associated with caring less for other people, it should not be surprising that they are also associated with caring less for the Earth and its nonhuman inhabitants. In our quest for ever-escalating levels of consumption and economic growth over the last 200 years, our species (particularly those of us inhabiting the Northern and Western hemispheres of the planet) has inflicted considerable damage on the ecosphere, leading many scientists to be increasingly concerned about the sustainability of our lifestyle, as well as our continued existence (Winter, 2004). The Cree Indians recognized this fundamental tension between materialism and the health of the ecosystem, prophesying:

> Only after the last tree has been cut down,
> The last river has been poisoned,

The last fish has been caught,
Only then will you find
That money cannot be eaten.

Several types of evidence support the idea that materialistic values and goals play their part in ecological degradation. Cross-cultural research shows that materialistic people care less about protecting the environment, having a world of beauty, and attaining unity with nature (Schwartz, 1996). Similarly, materialistic individuals score lower in biophilia, or a general love for living things (Saunders & Munro, 2000).

The environmentally relevant behaviors of extrinsically oriented, materialistic individuals are also problematic. Adults with strong materialistic value systems are less likely to engage in relatively simple but ecologically beneficial activities, such as riding bicycles, recycling, and baking their own bread (Brown & Kasser, in press; Richins & Dawson, 1992); similar results have recently been reported for children in middle and high school (Kasser, 2005). Materialistic individuals also use substantial amounts of resources in social-dilemma games; when they are asked to imagine how much timber they might cut in a national forest, materialistically oriented individuals want to cut more and also report greater feelings of greed (Sheldon & McGregor, 2000). Not surprisingly then, Brown and Kasser (in press) found that materialistic values are associated with higher "ecological footprints" (Dholakia & Wackernagel, 1999), as materialistic lifestyles require the use of significant amounts of resources.

Alternatives to Materialism

Having now documented some ways in which a focus on materialism diminishes our quality of life (as well as that of other species and future generations) and having now probably depressed some portion of the readers of this volume on positive psychology, let us turn to a new question: How can we stop excessive materialism from damaging quality of life now and in the future?

There are many approaches to answering this question, as shown by the many solutions that have been offered over the years by thinkers and activists. Unfortunately, these solutions have thus far not been supported by the powers-that-be, probably because most of the solutions would undermine the status quo and the hold that the power brokers have over society and people. Further, efforts to broadly implement the solutions have been largely uncoordinated, as there exists no central organizing body to bring together those interested in dethroning materialism. Finally, the solutions have not been grounded in a set of empirically supported theoretical principles that could work to conceptually unify the many disparate antimaterialistic activities in which people have engaged.

Over the last few years, however, I have seen increasing cause for hope. There are some people already within the power structures (and others still struggling to enter it) who are succeeding in changing business as usual. A number of groups have formed that are working to bring together people and organizations from across the political spectrum that share the common goal of creating a society that is more personally enlivening, socially just, and ecologically sustainable. And research on issues concerning materialism and consumerism continues to grow as more and more academics in various disciplines begin to understand that this feature of our contemporary world is undermining our quality of life. My thinking of late has been focused on devising a set of theoretical principles which will help to unify and ground the different ways that we might work against the insalubrious influences of materialism. Toward this end, I present below three principles that I hope might help to organize both empirical research and activist efforts that are striving to create healthier alternatives to our consumerist lifestyles and cultures. Each of the three principles can be studied or acted upon in multiple ways, at multiple levels, and from multiple perspectives. Further, each of the principles is, I believe, grounded in solid theorizing and empirical research. After describing each principle and why it is important, I discuss just a few practical solutions that derive from the principle; space limitations preclude a fuller discussion of the many ways that some of these solutions are already being implemented (see Kasser, 2002, 2004, for more on practical solutions).

Principle 1: Decrease the Internalization of and Institutionalized Encouragement for Materialistic Values

This first principle concerns the obvious fact that because we live in a society that so greatly supports materialism through the messages it conveys and the structures it builds, people become increasingly likely to take on, or "internalize" (Ryan, 1995), a materialistic mindset. We are all sponges to some extent, soaking up the messages of society, and when many of those messages promote the idea that happiness can be purchased and that people's worth depends on the size of their pocketbooks, we all, to some extent, believe this and organize our lives around such pursuits. Indeed, the evidence shows that when individuals are frequently exposed to that fount of materialistic messages—television—they are also likely to report higher materialism (Kasser & Ryan, 2001; Sirgy et al., 1998). Research also shows that materialistic values increase when mothers (Kasser, Ryan, Zax, & Sameroff, 1995), friends (Sheldon et al., 2000), and others in one's cultural milieu (Ahuvia & Wong, 2002) value materialistic pursuits. And of course, materialistic values are not only modeled by actors on television and people in our social lives, they are also strongly embedded in many of our social institutions and actively rewarded through governmental policies and laws (e.g., Kelly, 2001).

If we are to decrease the internalization of and institutionalized encouragement for materialistic values, three main pathways are available. First, we can avoid activities and situations where we are likely to be exposed to materialistic messages. Second, we can work to remove materialistic messages from our social environment so that they are less likely to be encountered. Third, we can work to change the laws and policies that support and encourage materialistic pursuits and the proliferation of materialistic messages.

Let us first consider how we can decrease our exposure to materialistic messages. One common strategy is to hit the mute button on the remote control when a commercial comes on the television, but this of course renders us still at the mercy of the many materialistic messages in the subtext of shows like "The Price Is Right," "Who Wants to Be a Millionaire?" and "Survivor." As such, turning off the television is the best option, and Web sites exist to help support ex-viewers during their withdrawal period (e.g., http://www.tvturnoff.org). Happily, recent research suggests that living without television can actually improve the quality of one's life; Hammermeister, Brock, Winterstein, and Page's (2005) study of 385 TV-free families found that only 5% of these children nag their parents about getting products and toys; that the children are more likely to get good grades, read, and play games requiring imagination; and that the family has more minutes of meaningful conversation every week.

We can also work to create commercial-free zones in our environments where propaganda supporting the capitalistic, consumeristic mindset is not allowed. Schools are one environment where "commercial creep" is especially problematic. As the U.S. education system has been increasingly underfunded by the government and citizens, many administrators have turned to corporate "donations" to supplement their budgets. As a result, children in hundreds of school systems watch Channel One, in which they see not only a few minutes of news, but also several advertisements for the latest (often violent) movie and the coolest (often unhealthy) food. Pop machines in schools and exclusive "pouring contracts" also promote not only unhealthy drink choices but commercialism as well (see http://www.commercialalert.org). And corporate-sponsored curricula (e.g., counting with M&Ms) encourage more than just the development of math skills. Many groups have been successful in removing some of these influences from children's schools, but, unfortunately, marketers figure out new and more subtle ways to get their messages out: One recent strategy is to give the "coolest kid" on the playground multiple samples of a new product so he or she can distribute it and start a new craze (Levin & Linn, 2004).

Of course, the reason that commercial creep occurs is that it is supported, even encouraged, by the current structure of our government and business world. The capitalistic economic system, buoyed by governmental officials who are lobbied intensely by corporate representatives, rests on a multitude of laws which move materialism to the forefront of people's behavior. Consider, for instance, that other than not breaking certain laws, the primary legal mandate that corporations must follow is to increase profits and shareholder value. As a result, in their pursuit of profit, many corporations eschew other values and lay off their workforces (to the damage of the communities), pollute (knowing that the fines they will pay are minimal compared to the profits they can make), and pressure employees to work overtime (knowing that it is cheaper and thus more profitable to get more hours from fewer people to whom one must pay benefits). As Kelly (2001) has pointed out, the "corporate aristocracy" is upheld by past legal decisions and could be changed so that businesses and government placed other types of values at the forefront of their decisions. Of course, it is difficult to get lawmakers to change these laws, as they, like others, have taken on the materialistic values of our society and are subject to many pressures encouraging materialism.

Principle 2: Build People's Resistance to Materialistic Actions, Values, and Influences

Avoiding the many materialistic messages in contemporary society while remaining a part of mainstream society is very difficult, and changing the structures and laws that support and encourage a materialistic lifestyle will take years to be successful. Further, there may be elements of our human nature that propel us toward materialistic activities under certain circumstances. Given all of this, another important strategy to pursue is to "psychologically immunize" people to lessen the likelihood that materialistic values will become prominent in their personalities and that they will act in materialistic ways in certain situations. Just as some research suggests that certain "resilient" children can thrive in the face of extreme stress, perhaps there are ways to increase people's resilience to the messages of consumer culture and the inner pressures which propel them toward materialistic actions.

Given that advertising and television messages are so successful in inculcating a materialistic mindset and consumer desire, one popular counterweight is to teach people to approach advertising and other commercial messages in a more critical fashion. Such "media literacy" programs work on the assumption that if people understand the tools of advertising and the ways that ads attempt to manipulate perceptions, feelings, and beliefs, they might be less susceptible to the often automatic processes upon which advertisers capitalize when selling their wares (see http://www.acmecoalition.org). Similarly, Rosenberg (2004) has recently suggested that the cultivation of *mindfulness*, or an open, receptive attention to one's experience, might help to decrease susceptibility to consumerism. Indeed, research shows that mindful people are happier (Brown & Ryan, 2003) as well as better environmental stewards and less materialistic (Brown & Kasser, in press). Happily, just as many programs exist to teach media literacy, validated methods of increasing mindfulness are also present in the literature (Baer, 2003). The resilience built through these perceptual and cognitive approaches might be strengthened through an understanding of the dynamic and emotional processes sometimes involved in materialism and consumption. A variety of theoretical perspectives converge in suggesting that a sense of insecurity or emptiness often causes materialistic values or leads to consumption sprees (Csikszentmihalyi, 2004; Faber, 2004; Kasser, 2002; Rosenberg, 2004; Solomon, Greenberg, & Pyszczynski, 2004), and empirical evidence supports these ideas, showing that feelings of incompleteness (Braun & Wicklund, 1989) or meaninglessness (Chang & Arkin, 2002) and thoughts of death (Kasser & Sheldon, 2000) each increase the likelihood of materialistic activities. Thus, it appears that when people are feeling down, low, or insecure, one of the ways that they try to cope is through the materialistic pursuits that advertisements and cultural myths promise will yield personal benefits. "Retail therapy" is a culturally sanctioned way of dealing with our personal upsets, as it not only distracts people from their inner emptiness (Faber, 2004), but it is good for economic growth!

Materialistic attempts to cope with insecurity seem to do little in the long run, however, to address the underlying concerns that lead to personal upset in the first place. Research on coping styles (Lazarus & Folkman, 1984) could be applied here to help people to learn healthier ways of dealing with insecurity than grabbing their credit card and heading to the mall or typing on their computer the URL for E-Bay. Additional research also suggests that if people are provided with alternative belief systems that help to assuage their underlying fears, they are less likely to act in greedy and materialistic ways (Dechesne, Pyszczynski, Arndt, Ransom, Sheldon, van Knippenberg, & Janssen, 2003). These results are promising in that they suggest that other types of beliefs can help to fill the void and lessen materialistic impulses, even in the face of social pressures to act materialistically.

Thus, another important strategy for increasing people's resilience to materialistic messages is to provide them with healthier values. That is, part of the solution requires building up the values that not only oppose materialistic aims but that conduce toward personal, social, and ecological well-being. Focusing on such healthier values will not only protect against the internalization of materialistic values but will also help people to organize their lives in such a fashion that they have fewer upsets and that, when they do, they will cope in a more adaptive manner.

My colleagues and I call such values *intrinsic* (Kasser & Ryan, 1996), as they are inherently satisfying to pursue in their own right and are linked to the psychological needs whose satisfaction spurs psychological growth and health. Our research has identified three main types of intrinsic values: *personal growth* (e.g., "I will follow my interests and curiosity where they take me"), *affiliation* (e.g., "I will have a committed, intimate relationship"), and *community feeling* (e.g., "I will help the world become a better place"). Research on intrinsic values suggests that they are very promising solutions to the problems of materialism. First, as alluded to above, cross-cultural research shows that intrinsic values generally oppose extrinsic, materialistic aims (Grouzet et al., in press). That is, to the extent that people place a strong value on intrinsic values, they tend to care less about materialistic values. Second, people who place a relatively high value on intrinsic aims report greater psychological well-being, act in more prosocial ways, and behave in a more ecologically sustainable fashion (Kasser, 2002). Thus, part of building resilience to materialism involves increasing the likelihood that people will place intrinsic values at the forefront of what is important to them in life. Unfortunately, we rarely see many advertisements that encourage intrinsic values, unless they are being used to sell something (e.g., "Want to be free? Buy an SUV"; "Want to be loved? Use this shampoo").

Principle 3: Increase the Likelihood That People Will Act Consistently With the Healthier, Intrinsic Values That Oppose Materialistic Values

Building resilience to consumer culture through the internalization of intrinsic values will have the best chance of keeping materialism in check if people's *behavior* is consistent with their intrinsic values. Unfortunately, growth motivations and intrinsic values are rather fragile in the face of the many social pressures that encourage people to act in a more materialistic, extrinsic fashion (Deci, Koestner, & Ryan, 1999; Maslow, 1954; Rogers, 1961) and thus are often overwhelmed in determining one's actual course of action. This point is brought home by the fact that even though most people across cultures rate intrinsic values as more important than extrinsic values (e.g., Schmuck, Kasser, & Ryan, 2000), consumerism and the pursuit of profit seem to dominate our world.

This disjunction between values and behavior suggests that many individuals in contemporary society may be experiencing substantial *cognitive dissonance* (Festinger, 1957), the unpleasant feeling that results when one's actions are out of line with one's ideals. This observation is interesting in two regards. First, it could help to explain the rising rates of depression and anxiety which have been reported in America (Cross-National Collaborative Group, 1992; Twenge, 2000); perhaps people are feeling worse because they frequently behave counter to the values that they hold most dear (and that would provide them with greater health) by going along with our empty, consumerist, hypercapitalistic culture. Second, it suggests that a great reservoir of potential motivation to change our lifestyles may lie not far beneath the surface of the American psyche. That is, just as methodologies based in dissonance reduction have helped people change toward more healthy behaviors (e.g., Aronson, Fried, & Stone, 1991), perhaps similar methods could be devised to help people recognize that their values and behaviors are inconsistent and to nudge them toward acting in ways more congruent with their intrinsic values.

One of the most popular means of helping people disengage from a consumeristic lifestyle seems to rely on these very types of mechanisms in order to increase value-behavior congruence. The Your Money or Your Life program (YMYL; Dominguez & Robin, 1992) involves a series of steps in which people explore what is really most important to them and then rate the extent to which each and every purchase they make actually reflects their values. According to the authors and numerous testimonials, this process helps people to realize that much of their consumption behavior is out of step with their deeper values; the result is that their levels of consumption either significantly decline or undergo important shifts in content. From the perspective of dissonance reduction, this can be explained by the fact that the YMYL program induces people to recognize that their behavior falls short of their ideals. This recognition, in turn, leads to the unpleasant experience of dissonance, which people are motivated to reduce. The clear path to alleviating the dissonance is to change consumption behavior so that it becomes more consistent with one's values.

Intrinsic values can also be better incorporated into economic behavior by changing the computation of national indicators of economic progress. As it currently stands, changes in the Gross Domestic Product (GDP) are the primary way of tracking whether a nation is progressing. From the perspective of the GDP, all economic activity is good, for if people are spending and consuming, the GDP will increase; the economy will be considered to be healthy; and thus, by inference, the nation is prosperous. The problem is that there are many economic activities that increase the GDP but are not particularly beneficial to other facets of national health. A classic example is that, from a GDP perspective, it is worse for the economy if I walk across town and hang out in the park (as no economic activity has occurred) than if I go to a bar and have several drinks ($ = sale of alcohol), drive across town ($ = using gasoline and wearing out my car, which will eventually require maintenance), crash into two other cars ($ = increasing insurance rates and car repair costs), and injure three people ($ = hospitalization costs), one of whom dies ($ = funeral expenses). As this example shows, the GDP only reflects the set of values that concerns the maximization of profit, i.e., materialism. Other indicators of progress and economic activity have been proposed which incorporate other values and correct the GDP by subtracting out economic activity that does not match the types of things that most people believe are worthwhile (Henderson, Lickerman, & Flynn, 2000; http://www.rprogress.org/). Consider the changes in people's behavior and governmental and business policies if nations began attempting to maximize these more intrinsically oriented computations of economic activity, rather than just any economic activity. It is likely that materialism would quickly become only one of many economically encouraged motives, rather than the primary, or even sole, one.

In the same way that it will be helpful to develop national indicators of economic progress that reflect intrinsic values, we also need to develop other models of affluence that reflect intrinsic values. One such model is *time affluence.* Consider that nowadays we are materially affluent but time poverty-stricken. Data show that contemporary Americans work more now than they did 50 years ago and work almost 9 full weeks per year more than Europeans (de Graaf, 2003). In the pursuit of material affluence (i.e., extrinsic, materialistic goals), many people lead hectic, overscheduled lives that allow little time for the pursuit of intrinsic values. It takes time to grow as a person, to connect with family and friends, and to contribute to the community, but time is increasingly too scarce of a resource for such activities. Perhaps what is called for is a rethinking of our national values and reward structures, so that instead of aiming to further increase our wealth, we aim to maximize time so that we can treat ourselves, each other, and the ecosphere with more care. Indeed, recent research shows that people who work fewer hours are more satisfied with their lives and leave smaller ecological footprints (Kasser & Brown, 2003). We can work individually toward increasing time affluence by asking for vacation time rather than raises, and we can work nationally toward time affluence by lobbying for shorter work weeks, more holidays, and job sharing (de Graaf, 2003).

Conclusion

As I hope this brief review has illustrated, recent scientific evidence suggests that the direction our culture is currently taking toward enhanced and ever-present consumerism exacts a considerable cost on people's lives, on the civility of society, and on the sustainability of the ecological resources on which these both depend. Although the forces that encourage and enforce materialism and consumerism often seem to be overwhelming, we might successfully slow materialism's undesirable influences if we work to decrease the internalization of such values, if we build resilience to such values, and if we help people to act more consistently with the healthier values that they may hold. Such efforts hold the promise of a brighter future for ourselves, our children, and other species.

References

Ahuvia, A. C., & Wong, N. Y. (2002). Personality and values based materialism: Their relationship and origins. *Journal of Consumer Psychology, 12,* 389–402.

Aronson, E., Fried, C., & Stone, J. (1991). Overcoming denial and increasing the intention to use condoms through the induction of hypocrisy. *American Journal of Public Health, 81,* 1636–1638.

Baer, R. A. (2003). Mindfulness training as a clinical intervention: A conceptual and empirical review. *Clinical Psychology: Science and Practice, 10,* 125–143.

Belk, R. W. (1985). Materialism: Trait aspects of living in the material world. *Journal of Consumer Research, 12,* 265–280.

Braun, O. L., & Wicklund, R. A. (1989). Psychological antecedents of conspicuous consumption. *Journal of Economic Psychology, 10,* 161–187.

Brown, K. W., & Kasser, T. (in press). Are psychological and ecological well-being compatible? The role of values, mindfulness, and lifestyle. *Social Indicators Research.*

Brown, K. W., & Ryan, R. M. (2003). The benefits of being present: Mindfulness and its role in psychological well-being. *Journal of Personality and Social Psychology, 84,* 822–848.

Chang, L., & Arkin, R. M. (2002). Materialism as an attempt to cope with uncertainty. *Psychology and Marketing, 19,* 389–406.

Cross-National Collaborative Group. (1992). The changing rate of major depression. *Journal of the American Medical Association, 268,* 3098–3105.

Csikszentmihalyi, M. (2004). Materialism and the evolution of consciousness. In T. Kasser & A. D. Kanner (Eds.), *Psychology and consumer culture: The struggle for a good life in a materialistic world* (pp. 91–106). Washington DC: American Psychological Association.

Dechesne, M., Pyszczynski, T., Arndt, J., Ransom, S., Sheldon, K. M., van Knippenberg, A., & Janssen, J. (2003). Literal and symbolic immortality: The effect of evidence of literal immortality on self-esteem striving in response to mortality salience. *Journal of Personality and Social Psychology, 84,* 722–737.

Deci, E. L., Koestner, R., & Ryan, R. M. (1999). A meta-analytic review of experiments examining the effects of extrinsic rewards on intrinsic motivation. *Psychological Bulletin, 125,* 627–668.

de Graaf, J. (Ed.). (2003). *Take back your time: Fighting overwork and time poverty in America.* San Francisco: Berrett-Koehler.

Dholakia, R., & Wackernagel, M. (1999). *The ecological footprint questionnaire.* San Francisco: Redefining Progress.

Dominguez, J. R., & Robin, V. (1992). *Your money or your life.* New York: Viking.

Faber, R. J. (2004). Self-control and compulsive buying. In T. Kasser & A. D. Kanner (Eds.), *Psychology and consumer culture: The struggle for a good life in a materialistic world* (pp. 169–187). Washington, DC: American Psychological Association Press.

Festinger, L. (1957). *A theory of cognitive dissonance.* Stanford, CA: Stanford University Press.

Grouzet, F. M. E., Kasser, T., Ahuvia, A., Fernandez-Dols, J. M., Kim, Y., Lau, S., Ryan, R. M., Saunders, S., Schmuck, P., & Sheldon, K. M. (in press). The structure of goal contents across 15 cultures. *Journal of Personality and Social Psychology.*

Hammermeister, J., Brock, B., Winterstein, D., & Page, R. (2005) Life without TV? Cultivation theory and psychosocial health characteristics of television-free individuals and their television-viewing counterparts. *Health Communication, 17,* 253–274.

Henderson, H., Lickerman, J., & Flynn, P. (Eds.). (2000). *Calvert-Henderson quality of life indicators.* Bethesda, MD: Calvert Group.

Kasser, T. (2002). *The high price of materialism.* Cambridge, MA: MIT Press.

Kasser, T. (2004). The good life or the goods life? Positive psychology and personal well-being in the culture of consumption. In P. A. Linley & S. Joseph (Eds.), *Positive psychology in practice* (pp. 55–67). New York: Wiley.

Kasser, T. (2005). Frugality, generosity, and materialism in children and adolescents. In K. A. Moore & L. H. Lippman (Eds.), *What do children need to flourish? Conceptualizing and measuring indicators of positive development* (pp. 357–373). New York: Kluwer/Plenum.

Kasser, T., & Brown, K. W. (2003). On time, happiness, and ecological footprints. In J. de Graaf (Ed.), *Take back your time: Fighting overwork and time poverty in America* (pp. 107–112). San Francisco: Berrett-Koehler.

Kasser, T., & Ryan, R. M. (1993). A dark side of the American dream: Correlates of financial success as a central life aspiration. *Journal of Personality and Social Psychology, 65,* 410–422.

Kasser, T., & Ryan, R. M. (1996). Further examining the American dream: Differential correlates of intrinsic and extrinsic goals. *Personality and Social Psychology Bulletin, 22,* 280–287.

Kasser, T., & Ryan, R. M. (2001). Be careful what you wish for: Optimal functioning and the relative attainment of intrinsic and extrinsic goals. In P. Schmuck & K. M. Sheldon (Eds.), *Life goals and well-being: Towards a positive psychology of human striving* (pp. 116–131). Goettingen, Germany: Hogrefe & Huber.

Kasser, T., Ryan, R. M., Zax, M., & Sameroff, A. J. (1995). The relations of maternal and social environments to late adolescents' materialistic and prosocial values. *Developmental Psychology, 31,* 907–914.

Kasser, T., & Sheldon, K. M. (2000). Of wealth and death: Materialism, mortality salience, and consumption behavior. *Psychological Science, 11,* 352–355.

Kelly, M. (2001). *The divine right of capital: Dethroning the corporate aristocracy.* San Francisco: Berrett-Koehler.

Keynes, J. M. (1932). *Essays in persuasion.* New York: Harcourt Brace.

Khanna, S. (1999). *Corrosive messages and capitalistic ideology: Well-being, objectification, and alienation from a cross-cultural perspective.* Unpublished honors thesis, Knox College, Galesburg, IL.

Lazarus, R. S., & Folkman, S. (1984). *Stress, appraisal, and coping.* New York: Springer.

Levin, D. E., & Linn, S. (2004). The commercialization of children: Understanding the problem and finding solutions. In T. Kasser & A. D. Kanner (Eds.), *Psychology and consumer culture: The struggle for a good life in a materialistic world* (pp. 213–232). Washington, DC: American Psychological Association.

Maslow, A. H. (1954). *Motivation and personality.* New York: Harper and Row.

McHoskey, J. W. (1999). Machiavellianism, intrinsic versus extrinsic goals, and social interest: A self-determination theory analysis. *Motivation and Emotion, 23,* 267–283.

Richins, M. L., & Dawson, S. (1992). A consumer values orientation for materialism and its measurement: Scale development and validation. *Journal of Consumer Research, 19,* 303–316.

Rogers, C. (1961). *On becoming a person.* Boston: Houghton Mifflin.

Rosenberg, E. (2004). Mindfulness and consumerism. In T. Kasser & A. D. Kanner (Eds.), *Psychology and consumer culture: The struggle for a good life in a materialistic world* (pp. 107–125). Washington, DC: American Psychological Association.

Ryan, R. M. (1995). Psychological needs and the facilitation of integrative processes. *Journal of Personality, 63,* 397–427.

Saunders, S., & Munro, D. (2000). The construction and validation of a consumer orientation questionnaire (SCOI) designed to measure Fromm's (1955) "marketing character" in Australia. *Social Behavior and Personality, 28,* 219–240.

Schmuck, P., Kasser, T., & Ryan, R. M. (2000). Intrinsic and extrinsic goals: Their structure and relationship to well-being in German and U.S. college students. *Social Indicators Research, 50,* 225–241.

Schwartz, S. H. (1996). Values priorities and behavior: Applying a theory of integrated value systems. In C. Seligman, J. M. Olson, & M. P. Zanna (Eds.), *The psychology of values: The Ontario symposium* (Vol. 8, pp. 1–24). Hillsdale, NJ: Erlbaum.

Sheldon, K. M., & Kasser, T. (1995). Coherence and congruence: Two aspects of personality integration. *Journal of Personality and Social Psychology, 68,* 531–543.

Sheldon, K. M., & McGregor, H. (2000). Extrinsic value orientation and the tragedy of the commons. *Journal of Personality, 68,* 383–411.

Sheldon, K. M., Sheldon, M. S., & Osbaldiston, R. (2000). Prosocial values and group assortation in an N-person prisoner's dilemma. *Human Nature, 11,* 387–404.

Sirgy, M. J., Lee, D., Kosenko, R., Meadow, H. L., Rahtz, D., Cicic, M., Jin, G. X., Yarsuvat, D., Blenkhorn, D. L., & Wright, N. (1998). Does television viewership play a role in perception of quality of life? *Journal of Advertising, 27,* 125–142.

Solberg, E. C., Diener, E., & Robinson, M. D. (2004). Why are materialists less satisfied? In T. Kasser & A. D. Kanner (Eds.), *Psychology and consumer culture: The struggle for a good life in a materialistic world* (pp. 29–48). Washington, DC: American Psychological Association.

Solomon, S., Greenberg, J. L., & Pyszczynski, T. A. (2004). Lethal consumption: Death-denying materialism. In T. Kasser & A. D. Kanner (Eds.), *Psychology and consumer culture: The struggle for a good life in a materialistic world* (pp. 127–146). Washington DC: American Psychological Association.

Twenge, J. M. (2000). The age of anxiety? The birth cohort change in anxiety and neuroticism, 1952–1993. *Journal of Personality & Social Psychology, 79,* 1007–1021.

Winter, D. D. (2004). Shopping for sustainability: Psychological solutions to overconsumption. In T. Kasser & A. D. Kanner (Eds.), *Psychology and consumer culture: The struggle for a good life in a materialistic world* (pp. 69–87). Washington DC: American Psychological Association.

12

Getting Older, Getting Better?

Recent Psychological Evidence

KENNON SHELDON

Before I begin with my primary topic, I would like to start with some broader comments about positive psychology, for the benefit of general readers who may be unfamiliar with the potential controversies regarding positive psychology. I would like to consider a question: "Does the positive psychology movement have legs?" This is the title of a skeptical recent article published by Richard Lazarus in *Psychological Inquiry* (2003). Lazarus suggested that positive psychology is just a fad, one that will fade like many other fads in psychology over the years. And indeed, this could well happen.

I think that part of what positive psychology needs to do in order to "have legs" is to demonstrate surprising new findings that might not have come about without the willingness to make more positive, appreciative, and optimistic assumptions about human nature. In some cases, this may mean crossing the unholy line between science and values—being willing to introduce values into one's science. This is something that I run into often, because I study values with the aim of finding out which values might be "best" for people and because I subscribe to a theoretical perspective that makes optimistic assumptions about human nature and people's capacity for positive growth and change—the organismic perspective (discussed further below). Positive psychology, too, is in this somewhat awkward position, with its attempts to understand "the good life" and the nature of human thriving.

Here is one example of flirting with the boundary between science and values—the title of my chapter: "Getting Older, Getting Better?" "Getting better" is a value-laden phrase; it is asking if in some sense we improve as we age, perhaps becoming more moral, good, or virtuous. Maybe I should have used a different title—like "Does Personality Change Over the Lifespan?"—one that doesn't have the value implication. But I decided to keep this title, because it states most clearly the question I'm asking and also the type of questions that positive psychology is asking. I believe that values are inevitable, and it is probably best to state one's assumptions clearly, rather than beating around the bush (Sheldon, Schmuck, & Kasser, 2000). Of course, as scientists, we need to assess the data as objectively as we can, once it comes in. Indeed, we are not permitted to put *too* positive a spin on the data in our research articles, even if we are inclined to do so, because the court of peer review stands as a check.

With that said, let us move on to the primary topic. We all know the phrase "You're not getting older, you're getting better!" It's a funny phrase, because we'd all *like* to believe it, since we're all getting older, seemingly at an increasingly rapid rate. But I think we all share some cynicism about the phrase. When somebody says it, we half-smirk, because we don't really believe it. It seems like wishful thinking. So the question is: Can we come up with any evidence to support the idea that people do get better as they get older?

In fact, there are a lot of potential reasons to think that the phrase is *not* true. First, we're not getting better physically. I'm an avid tennis player and have been playing since I was 9 years old. No matter how much I try, I'm never going to be as good as I was when I was 20. Just making the line calls has become more difficult; I used to see the spot where the ball bounced, but now I see a foot-long blur. Or, if I play a tough match, I'm sore the next day. I don't have the legs I used to.

If we can't have physical improvement as we age, maybe we can have psychological improvement at least? Unfortunately, there are theories that suggest that this isn't true either, theories that emphasize the shrinking perspective of the elderly, their loss of fluid intelligence and creativity, and their struggles to cope with increasing limitations and losses (Herzog, Rodgers, & Woodworth, 1982; Pfeiffer, 1977). Other theorists have gone so far as to argue that the concept of development has no meaning in the latter part of the lifespan. From an evolutionary perspective, once we've reproduced, maybe we should just die and get out of the way.

Still, there are some theoretical perspectives that *do* suggest that people can and do continue to improve over the lifespan, more often than not. George Vaillant (1977) claimed that age brings increased wisdom and less reliance on what he called "immature defense mechanisms." Midlarsky and Kahana's (1994) book argued that people become generally more altruistic and prosocial as they age. Erik Erikson's (1963) psychosocial theory, a very well known perspective on lifespan development, also seems to suggest that there is normative improvement—as we age, we naturally take on larger roles and responsibilities and the task of passing the culture down to the next generation. The organismic philosophical perspective, in which my own work is grounded, also assumes that humans naturally tend toward greater integration and maturity over time, as long as environments are reasonably supportive; this organizational impulse is an essential feature of living systems more generally (Ryan, 1995).

So which is it? Growth or decline? Our very futures hang in the balance. My basic approach to answering this question has been to examine the correlation between chronological age and measures of psychological maturity. This is a simple approach but I think a potentially powerful one.

What are the right measures of psychological maturity to use? In my work, I often use measures of maturity that are based on *personal goals*, that is, the projects and purposes that people are pursuing, which they are able to write down when asked. One of the advantages of this unit of analysis is that it has been little applied in lifespan research, so it can provide a new type of information. A second advantage is that it is an equalizer, a nice unit for comparing people in different phases of a lifespan—*everybody* has goals, no matter what their age. This doesn't mean that everyone is an obsessive list maker; rather, everybody has thoughts about the future and various wishes and intentions regarding the future. Of course, there are large variations in how explicit people make their goals or how committed they feel to them or how hard they try at them—indeed, these are often exactly the variables of interest. Thus, the question for this chapter is: Are variations in important maturity-related goal measures associated with variations in chronological age?

A third advantage of using personal goal measures to study aging is that goals represent people's active intentions. They can tell us a lot about what people are doing, how people are coping, and so on at various phases of the lifespan. Notably, all of the data I will present in this chapter have already been reported elsewhere; some of the relevant tables will be reproduced in this chapter, so that readers can evaluate the evidence for themselves.

The first study I'll present was published in 2001 in the journal *Developmental Psychology*, the top journal in its field, with the most rigorous scientific standards (Sheldon & Kasser, 2001). My collaborator and I employed two different theoretical perspectives on personality development and maturity, to see if age correlates with greater maturity. The two approaches, already mentioned above, were *organismic theory* and *psychosocial theory.* Representing the organismic perspective, we employed Deci and Ryan's self-determination theory, a theory of optimal motivation that has been under development for more than 30 years (Deci, 1975; Deci & Ryan, 1985, 2000). The theory assumes that human beings have a built-in drive or propensity to learn and grow, fueled by "intrinsic motivation," i.e., the desire to do something for its own sake because it is interesting and enjoyable. Much of the early work in self-determination theory was devoted to showing how intrinsic motivation could be undermined by extrinsic motivators, so that a formerly enjoyable task becomes dull and even aversive (Deci, 1975).

In addition to intrinsic motivation and extrinsic motivation, self-determination theory now says that there are two other major forms of motivation (Deci & Ryan, 2000), which lie in a middle zone between intrinsic and extrinsic motivation: *introjected* motivation, in which one is forcing oneself to do something, and *identified* motivation, in which one is doing something that is not necessarily enjoyable but with a full sense of autonomy and internal agreement. The four motivations fall along a continuum of internalization: You can do something because others seem to be forcing you to do it (external, no internalization), because you're forcing yourself (introjected, some internalization), because you choose to even though you don't like to (identified, much internalization), or because you enjoy it for its own sake (intrinsic, most internalization). These four forms of motivation are depicted in Table 12.1.

An example that I like to use is that of a small child. Let's say that a 4-year-old child is being asked to share her candy with a brother or sister. Probably at that age there's not much internalization of the value of sharing, so the only reason this child shares at that point is because her mother makes her (external motivation). What you hope as a parent is that there is a positive socialization process occurring, so that by the time the child is 7 or 8, she might share spontaneously, even if her mother is not there to make her do it. Still, she might only do it out of a sense of inner compulsion or pressure, to avoid guilt (introjected motivation). But hopefully a little later, say by the age of 15 or 16, the person has internalized this important value to the extent that she does it with a sense of wholeheartedness, without resistance or resentment (identified motivation). Eventually, sharing might even become an intrinsic motivation, as the young woman has learned to take pleasure in giving to others and seeing their pleasure.

Here's another example that's more relevant to adults: diaper changing. My youngest child is now 8, but when he was still in diapers, there were times when the only reason I would change him was because I knew it was my turn and my wife would get mad at me if I didn't. That's external motivation. But there were other times when my wife wasn't around, and I made myself do it anyway. But I didn't want to do it, so there was an inner struggle, and sometimes I waited too long. That's introjected motivation. But there were other times when, as soon as I smelled the diaper, I got right up and changed it; for whatever reason, at that moment, I could fully identify with the role of being a good father, and there was no internal resistance. That's identified motivation. But I can tell you, diaper changing never made it to intrinsic, for me.

Table 12.1.   Four Stages on the Road to Mature Motivation, According to Self-Determination Theory's Organismic Perspective

External: Because I have to	Least internalized
Introjected: Because I ought to	
Identified: Because I choose to	
Intrinsic: Because I want to	Most internalized

Notice that self-determination theory has positive directional implications: There's a "better" way to be, such that the more you have internalized your behavior, the more mature you are in doing it. From an existential perspective, you're taking responsibility for your choice; if you're going to do something at all, then get behind it; don't waffle, don't be ambivalent about it. Based on these directional implications, we defined external and introjected as less-mature forms of motivation and identified and intrinsic as more-mature forms. Our primary hypothesis was that chronological age would be associated with the more-internalized forms of motivation.

As a second approach to the question, we applied Erik Erikson's (1963) psychosocial theory. In brief, Erikson said that there are different tasks that we face in our lives, depending on our place in the lifespan. Each task builds on the successful resolution of the task before. In late adolescence, we face the *identity* life task: We have to develop a solid sense of ourselves as a person, persisting over time. After we've formed a reasonably secure identity, the next task is to learn how to relate that sense of self to other selves, i.e., to connect authentically with other adults. This *intimacy* life task needs to be solved during young adulthood, according to Erikson. Then, as we approach middle age, we become more concerned with the next generation and with the thriving of cultural institutions; this is the *generativity* life task. Finally, in the last part of the life span, we encounter the task of bringing it all together to make final meaning of our mortality and the pattern of our lives. This is the *ego integrity* task. These four tasks are depicted in Table 12.2.

Notice that there are positive directional implications for Erikson's theory, just as for self-determination theory: The further along on this list of tasks you are, the more mature you are. Based on this reasoning, we assumed that identity and intimacy are less-mature goal themes to pursue, and generativity and ego

Table 12.2. Four Stages Along the Road to Maturity, According to Erikson's Psychosocial Theory

Identity (late adolescence)	The quest for one's true character and proper role in society (Waterman, 1982)
Intimacy (young adulthood)	The quest for meaningful relations with others and also a life partner (Whitbourne & Tesch, 1985)
Generativity (middle adulthood)	The quest to help the young, create self-defining works, or leave public legacies (McAdams & de St. Aubin, 1992)
Ego integrity (late adulthood)	The quest for ego transcendence or for an understanding of one's place in the ultimate scheme of things (Peck, 1968)

integrity are more-mature goal themes to pursue. Thus, we hypothesized that chronological age should be positively associated with the presence of the latter two themes within peoples' goal systems and negatively associated with the presence of the first two themes.

To summarize: Consistent with the "getting older, getting better" idea, we hypothesized that chronological age would correlate positively with identified goal motivation and intrinsic goal motivation and positively with having goals containing generativity themes and ego integrity themes. Chronological age should correlate negatively with external goal motivation and introjected goal motivation and negatively with having goals containing identity themes or intimacy themes.

We also ventured three other hypotheses. Our second hypothesis was that chronological age would be associated with subjective well-being (SWB: Diener, 1994). This would merely replicate a variety of emerging findings, which suggest that age is modestly associated with at least some measures of well-being (Argyle, 1999). In particular, age tends to be associated with life satisfaction (global approval of one's life) and also with a reduction in negative affect (less-intense negative moods and states). Finding evidence for the age-to-SWB hypothesis in the current data would provide another type of support for the "getting older, getting better" idea, and would also allow us to ask some further important questions, discussed below.

Our third hypothesis was that our measures of maturity themselves would be associated with SWB. This is a well-documented finding in the case of the four forms of motivation studied by self-determination theory, in that more internalized motivations tend to be associated with SWB; thus, we expected to replicate the finding here. Erikson's theory also seems to imply that maturity is associated with psychological well-being, though there is less published data concerning this association. Those oriented toward generativity and ego integrity have succeeded in establishing their identities and in connecting with other identities and are now concerned with meaning making and cultural contribution. Presumably because of this successful adaptation, they are also happier people.

Finally, we ventured a fourth hypothesis, assuming that the first three hypotheses were supported, namely, that increased maturity would *mediate* the relationship between chronological age and psychological well-being. In other words, we hypothesized that older people are happier *because* they are more mature. It seems likely that age itself probably is not causing change; rather, it is other changes, associated with the passage of time, that are doing it (specifically, changes in maturity concerning one's personal goals). Although causality cannot be definitively established with this kind of correlational design, there are statistical techniques which can evaluate whether the data are at least consistent with one's causal assumptions. We intended to employ those techniques here.

The study employed a sample of 108 adults from Columbia, Missouri, ranging from age 18 to 82. We called them at random and offered them two free movie tickets if they participated. We mailed those who consented to participate a questionnaire packet, in which they first rated their general positive affect, negative affect, and life satisfaction (the three measures of well-being we typically use). We combined these into a single measure of SWB (Diener, 1994). They then listed 10 "personal strivings," using Robert Emmons's (1986, 1989) well-validated methodology. Then they rated why they are pursuing each striving, in terms of each of the four reasons focused on by self-determination theory, a method which I have used in many other published studies (e.g., Sheldon & Elliot, 1999; Sheldon & Kasser, 1998). Afterward, we created a relative self-determination score for each participant by adding the intrinsic and identified ratings and subtracting the external and introjected ratings, our typical procedure. We also coded each striving using Erikson's four task categories, that is, we determined whether each striving was an identity, intimacy, generativity, or ego integrity striving and then created a score for participants that summed how many of each type of striving they listed.

Table 12.3 contains the associations of chronological age with the maturity measures and the well-being measures. Supporting our first hypothesis, age was associated with striving self-determination. It was interesting that this effect was driven by the introjected and identified forms of motivation, which bracket the pivot point at which a motive is presumed to become internalized. These findings suggest that older people believe more in what they're striving for and that their strivings are less about trying to appease guilt, compared to younger people. Looking at the Eriksonian categories, three out of four predictions were supported: Older people listed fewer identity strivings and more generativity strivings and ego integrity strivings, on average. The fact that the correlation between age and intimacy striving was nonsignificant suggests that striving for intimacy is equally salient across the lifespan; it's not just young adults who are interested in intimacy.

We also found good support for our second hypothesis, as chronological age was associated with aggregate subjective well-being (see Table 12.3). We also found support for our third hypothesis, that the measures of maturity are themselves associated with subjective well-being (see Table 12.4). Again, this supports the idea that they *are* measures of maturity, as you would expect those in

Table 12.3. Correlations Between Chronological Age and Other Study Variables $(* = p < .05; ** = p < .01)$

	Age		Age
Overall Self-Determination	.23**	# of identity strivings	.20*
External	−.08	# of intimacy strivings	.00
Introjected	−.27**	# of generativity strivings	.39**
Identified	.22*	# of ego integrity strivings	.19*
Intrinsic	−.02	Aggregate SWB	.24**

a better-adjusted or more highly developed state to be happier as a result. However, there was one exception: Although we initially assumed that intimacy striving was representative of *less* maturity and thus should be negatively associated with well-being, based on Erikson's theory, intimacy striving was instead positively associated with well-being in these data. Although Erikson's theory has difficulty explaining this finding, self-determination theory does not, as self-determination theory proposes that humans have a basic need for relatedness, a need that is salient no matter what a person's age (Deci & Ryan, 2000).

Recall our fourth hypothesis, that the association of age with maturity would mediate or help account for the association of age with well-being. To test this, we created an aggregate goal maturity measure by adding up the striving self-determination measure, the generativity measure, and the ego integrity measure and subtracting the identity measure (the measures associated with well-being). A regression analysis showed that the association of age with well-being fell from .24 to .09 when aggregate maturity was included in the model, supporting our general hypothesis. In other words, in this sample, our measures of maturity could account for most of the fact that older people were also happier people.

Now, I will discuss a second study, in which we tried to replicate the basic pattern of results using a somewhat different approach (Sheldon, Kasser, Houser-Marko, Jones, & Turban, in press). Instead of employing a cross-sectional sample of different ages, we instead obtained a matched sample of college students and their parents. These two groups are similar on many factors: They have similar family incomes, genetics, hometowns, histories, and interests. Thus, one can conduct a powerful test by directly comparing a child to his or her parent, to see how they differ. The parents ranged from 38 to 70 in age.

We evaluated the same four hypotheses as in the earlier study. However, we tested them in three different ways. First, we examined the current scores for the parents compared to the current scores for their children. Do parents seems happier and more self-determined now, compared to their children now? Second, we asked parents to think back to what they were like when they were their children's age and compared parents' scores then to parents' scores now. Do parents report feeling happier and more self-determined now, compared to when they were their children's age? Third, we compared younger parents to older

Table 12.4.   Correlations of
Maturity Measures with SWB
(* = $p < .05$; ** = $p < .01$)

	SWB
Striving Self-Determination	.30 **
# of identity strivings	−.23 *
# of intimacy strivings	.23 *
# of generativity strivings	.25 **
# of ego integrity strivings	.17*

parents, using correlational analyses. This third approach was similar to that used in the first study.

Students completed the questionnaire in class for extra credit, and most gave permission for us to contact their parents, in exchange for additional extra credit. Later, we mailed questionnaires to the parents. On the questionnaire, all participants first completed the measures of current well-being, listed their current personal strivings, and rated why they are pursuing those strivings. Next, parents rated their well-being when they were their children's age, then listed and rated the strivings they remember pursuing at their children's age.

Table 12.5 contains the comparisons between parents and children on current well-being and current striving self-determination. As can be seen, both mothers and fathers reported greater well-being than did their children. Mothers reported being more self-determined in their goals than did their children. Fathers were in the predicted direction on self-determination, but the difference was not significant. Still, this first way of testing our hypotheses yielded fairly good support (three out of four).

Table 12.6 compares parents then to parents now. A similar pattern of findings resulted, the one exception being that fathers did not report being significantly happier now, compared to when they were their children's age. However, again, the mean was in the predicted direction, and thus the hypotheses were supported in three out of four cases.

Next, we correlated parental age with parental well-being and parental self-determination, focusing on the contemporary measures only. Again, we found fairly good support: Maternal age correlated .21 with maternal well-being and .26 with maternal self-determination, and paternal age correlated .26 with paternal well-being and .21 with paternal self-determination. Thus, the older parents were both happier at present than were younger parents and more self-determined in their current goals.

Finally, we looked at the mediation question. For mothers, we could account for more than half the variation between age and well-being using the self-determination measure, and for fathers, we could account for about half. In addition to supporting our hypotheses, this result also suggests that there are other, unmeasured factors accounting for the association between age and well-being, besides enhanced self-determination.

Table 12.5. Means for Parents and Children on Current SWB and Goal Self-Determination ($* = p < .05$ and $** = p < .01$ for the comparison with the child's score)

	Child's score	Mother's score	Father's score
SWB	4.52	5.30 **	5.21 **
Self-determination	3.09	3.65 *	3.22

Table 12.6. Means for Parents on the SWB and Goal Self-Determination Measures, Both at the Present Time and at the Child's Age (* = $p < .05$ for the then/now comparison)

	Mother		Father	
	Then	Now	Then	Now
SWB	4.87	5.30*	4.84	5.21
Self-Determination	3.04	3.65*	2.47	3.22*

Now I will present the results of a third study also designed to evaluate the "getting older, getting better" hypothesis. In this study, rather than focusing on personal goals, we instead focused on social duties (Sheldon, Kasser, Houser-Marko, Jones, & Turban, in press). The question is: Why do people perform social duties, such as paying taxes, tipping service people, and voting (the three duties assessed in our study)? Again, according to Erikson's psychosocial theory, people naturally take on more responsibility and accountability as they age. Logically, this should include the doing of important but sometimes unpleasant duties. In terms of the changing-the-diaper example mentioned earlier, the "getting older, getting better" idea suggests that older people should be more willing to change the diaper, i.e., to do what needs doing in order to promote the general welfare.

We tested the same basic hypotheses as before: that age would correlate with a feeling of self-determination in performing duties, that age would be associated with SWB, that self-determination would be associated with SWB, and that self-determination might mediate the age-to-SWB effect. We studied a sample of 160 community adults ranging from age 20 to age 82, who were residents of Columbia, Missouri, and St. Louis, Missouri. They were approached in doctors' offices or retirement homes and were entered into a lottery for a free dinner if they participated. Participants filled out a two-page questionnaire in which they first rated their SWB using the same measures as in the earlier studies. Then, they rated the extent to which they do each of the three duties and also why they do them and when they do them, again in terms of the same four reasons: external, introjected, identified, and intrinsic. We computed an aggregate SWB score for each participant and also computed an aggregate self-determination score for each participant, not only for each duty, but also across the three duties.

Table 12.7 contains the results. As can be seen, our first and primary hypothesis was again supported: Chronological age was associated with aggregate self-determination. Looking at each duty in turn, older people reported voting, paying taxes, and tipping for more self-determined reasons than did younger people. Table 12.7 also shows that self-determination was generally associated with well-being, consistent with the earlier studies and supporting our second hypothesis. However, in these data, there was no association of age with well-being, perhaps because many of the older participants were sampled in retirement

Table 12.7. Associations of Age and SWB With Self-Determination for Duty Enactment (* = $p < .05$; ** = $p < .01$)

	Self-Determination	Type of Duty		
		Voting	Tax paying	Tipping
Age	.23**	.16*	.28**	.19**
SWB	.22 **	.16 *	.16 *	.21**

homes, which can be depressing places. Thus, our third hypothesis was not supported in this sample, and we could not test our fourth hypothesis, that self-determination mediates between age and well-being. But from our perspective, the most important thing was to again show that people feel more self-determined as they become older; in this sense, at least, people seem to consistently "get better" as they age.

Finally, I will present the results of a fourth study, also reported in Sheldon, Kasser, Houser-Marko, Jones, and Turban (in press). One potential criticism of the earlier studies is that they all employed samples from the United States. Thus, it is unclear whether the results would generalize to persons in other nations or cultures. This question is of particular importance because cross-cultural psychologists have recently challenged self-determination theory's claims that autonomy is a universal need and is universally associated with SWB (Markus & Kitayama, 1994; Markus, Kitayama, & Heiman, 1996). We believed that finding an association between self-determined duty enactment and SWB in a non-Western culture would lend further cross-cultural support for self-determination theory's claims (see also Deci & Ryan, 2000). Also, finding an association between chronological age and self-determination would further support the organismic perspective's optimistic assumptions concerning positive personality development in humans.

This study was conducted in Singapore, which is considered to be a collectivist culture. Once again, we focused on social duties, modifying the duties so that they would be appropriate for a collectivist sample. The duties were "helping distant relatives," "obeying authorities (such as teachers, parents, and bosses)," and "staying informed about political issues." There were 213 participants, of ages ranging from 18 to 101, who completed the English-language survey. First, they rated their SWB, using the same measures as before, then rated their reasons for performing the social duties, again using the same measures as before. An aggregate self-determination measure was again computed by averaging across the three duties.

Once again, chronological age was associated with self-determination ($r = .22, p < .01$). This supports Deci and Ryan's (2000) claim that the personality developmental processes posited by self-determination theory should occur within every cultural setting. In addition, self-determination was correlated with SWB ($r = .23$, $p < .01$), supporting Deci and Ryan's (2000) claim that self-determination is a universal psychological need. However, once again, chronological age was not associated with SWB ($r = -.08$), and thus the mediation hypothesis could not be tested. Still, our two most important hypotheses were again supported in this study.

Discussion

These data support the idea that at least some forms of positive psychological change might be normative across the lifespan. That does not mean that the changes occur for everybody; the modest correlations of .20 to .25 between age and self-determination indicate that there are plenty of exceptions, and perhaps you know some of them personally. However, these results do indicate that, more often than not, there is positive change. Here is one way to look at it: In many or most cases, there will be stasis—no change in either direction. When there is change, the question becomes: Which of the two alternatives will dominate—progression or regression? Consistent with the positive psychology perspective, I suggest that there will more often be progression than regression, a trend that would produce the small but significant correlation that we observed. Again, the organismic philosophical perspective would expect this positive bias, given its assumption that living things by nature tend to become more integrated, developed, and organized over time.

Why do we see the positive association of age with self-determination? That is, what is happening to people over time? I suggest that the association arises because, as time goes by, people are paying attention, noticing what makes them happy and what doesn't. They are outgrowing concerns of social approval and the obsession with what others might say. They are becoming aware of the emptiness of some of the more materialistic aspects of our culture, aspects that advertisers try to get us to buy into. As a result, as people get older, they also get better at selecting goals that reflect their deeper interests and identifications, rather than external pressures and compulsions. In the case of duties, people get better at reconciling themselves with the sometimes-unpleasant obligations that help to provide for the common good. I certainly find this to be true in my own life, and perhaps you do in yours.

A different but perhaps complementary perspective on the age-to-self-determination association is that older persons have (on average) been through more crises and traumas, experiences which often bring about self-concept changes and new self-organization (Tedeschi & Calhoun, 1995). Coping with (inevitable) setbacks has helped to teach them what is really important in their lives. Yet another possible explanation for the association is that the normative psycho-social tasks that older people face, such as generativity and ego integrity, are ones which conduce to greater internalization by their very nature or content. For example, these particular tasks may be the most satisfying of the inherent psychological needs (Deci & Ryan, 2000), best promoting the internalization process. Although we cannot distinguish between these potential explanations at present, they provide intriguing directions for future research.

There is an alternative explanation for the age-to-self-determination association, which is worth mentioning. Michael Ross and colleagues (Ross & Wilson, 2003; Wilson & Ross, 2001) have shown the existence of a *present-centered bias*, in which people in general wish to believe in forward personal progress—that their current self is better than their past selves. It may be that the older persons in my studies are most prey to this bias, giving the most exaggeratedly positive answers to the survey questions. It is difficult to rule this out as an alternative explanation. However, we can point to the fact that the finding emerged from multiple methodologies as one mitigating factor. Also, the "most positive way to respond" to the self-determination measures is not necessarily obvious; for example, older people might think that they should be more serious and feel that it is not appropriate to enjoy one's goals, duties, and obligations. As a result, they might downplay, rather than exaggerate, that rating. Still, possible self-reporting biases are an issue that future research in this area will have to address, perhaps using peer or family reports of self-determination and SWB or implicit and indirect measures of self-determination and SWB.

It is also worth briefly returning to the issues which began this chapter. How can positive psychology keep its legs, and also, how can it avoid the pitfalls of taking a somewhat value-laden theoretical approach? Again, I believe that positive psychology will best prove its worth if its studies uncover features of human nature that would not have been found without the more optimistic theoretical perspective (Sheldon & King, 2001). The current research, supporting an uplifting perspective on the aging process, may be a case in point. A rigorous empirical research focus will also help positive psychologists to best cope with the potential pitfalls of their value-laden approach. Data published in the best journals have survived the scientific review process, and thus the articles have presumably not been permitted to exaggerate the effects in which their proponents would like to believe.

Conclusion

Although old age has historically been seen as a time of decline and degeneration (Herzog et al., 1982; Pfeiffer, 1977), the current results concur with more recent and positive views of the aging process which emphasize the remarkable resilience of the human personality (Baltes & Mayer, 1999). Specifically, our results indicate that older persons know clearly what values are most important in life and that they pursue such objectives with a more-mature sense of purpose and ownership. In contrast, the younger persons in our samples were more likely to act out of a sense of guilt or self-division. Thus these findings suggest that a return to the fountain of youth might not be so desirable after all (Ryff, 1989) and that most of us may instead look forward to ever-fuller meanings and satisfactions in our later lives.

References

Argyle, M. (1999). Causes and correlates of happiness. In D. Kahneman, E. Diener, & N. Schwarz (Eds.), *Well-being: The foundations of hedonic psychology* (pp. 353–373). New York: Russell Sage Foundation.

Baltes, P. B., & Mayer, K. U. (1999). *The Berlin aging study: Aging from 70 to 100.* New York: Cambridge University Press.

Deci, E. L. (1975). *Intrinsic motivation.* New York: Plenum.

Deci, E. L., & Ryan, R. M. (1985). *Intrinsic motivation and self-determination in human behavior.* New York: Plenum.

Deci, E. L., & Ryan, R. M. (2000). The "what" and "why" of goal pursuits: Human needs and the self-determination of behavior. *Psychological Inquiry, 11,* 227–268.

Diener, E. (1994). Assessing subjective well-being: Progress and opportunities. *Social Indicators Research, 31,* 103–157.

Emmons, R. A. (1986). Personal strivings: An approach to personality and subjective well-being. *Journal of Personality and Social Psychology, 51,* 1058–1068.

Emmons, R. A. (1989). The personal strivings approach to personality. In L. A. Pervin (Ed.), *Goal concepts in personality and social psychology* (pp. 87–126). Hillsdale, NJ: Erlbaum.

Erikson, E. (1963). *Childhood and society.* New York: Norton.

Herzog, A. R., Rodgers, W., & Woodworth, J. (1982). *Subjective well-being among different age groups.* Ann Arbor: University of Michigan, Institute for Social Research.

Lazarus, R. S. (2003). Does the positive psychology movement have legs? *Psychological Inquiry, 14,* 93–109.

Markus, H. R., & Kitayama, S. (1994). The cultural construction of self and emotion: Implications for social behavior. In S. Kitayama & H. R. Markus (Eds.), *Emotion and culture: Empirical studies of mutual influence* (pp. 89–130). Washington, DC: American Psychological Association.

Markus, H. R., Kitayama, S., & Heiman, R. (1996). Culture and basic psychological principles. In E. T. Higgins & A. W. Kruglanski (Eds.), *Social psychology: Handbook of basic principles* (pp. 857–913). New York: Guilford.

McAdams, D. P., & de St. Aubin, E. (1992). A theory of generativity and its assessment through self-report, behavioral acts, and narrative themes in autobiography. *Journal of Personality and Social Psychology, 62,* 1003–1015.

Midlarsky, E., & Kahana, E. (1994). *Altruism in later life.* Thousand Oaks, CA: Sage.

Peck, R. (1968). Psychological developments in the second half of life. In B. Neugarten (Ed.), *Middle age and aging* (pp. 88–92). Chicago: University of Chicago Press.

Pfeiffer, E. (1977). Psychopathology and social pathology. In J. E. Birren & K. W. Schaie (Eds.), *Handbook of the psychology of aging* (pp. 650–671). New York: Academic.

Ross, M., & Wilson, A. E. (2003). Autobiographical memory and conceptions of self: Getting better all the time. *Current Directions in Psychological Science, 12,* 66–69.

Ryan, R. M. (1995). Psychological needs and the facilitation of integrative processes. *Journal of Personality, 63,* 397–427.

Ryff, C. D. (1989). Beyond Ponce de Leon and life-satisfaction: New directions in quest of successful aging. *International Journal of Behavioral Development, 12,* 35–55.

Sheldon, K. M., & Elliot, A. J. (1999). Goal striving, need-satisfaction, and longitudinal well-being: The self-concordance model. *Journal of Personality and Social Psychology, 76,* 482–497.

Sheldon, K. M., & Kasser, T. (1998). Pursuing personal goals: Skills enable progress but not all progress is beneficial. *Personality and Social Psychology Bulletin, 24,* 1319–1331.

Sheldon, K. M., & Kasser, T. (2001). Getting older, getting better? Personal strivings and personality development across the life-course. *Developmental Psychology, 37,* 491–501.

Sheldon, K. M., Kasser, T., & Houser-Marko, L. (in press). Older but more authentic? Comparing the motivation and well-being of college students and their parents. *Journal of Research in Personality.*

Sheldon, K. M., Kasser, T., Houser-Marko, L., Jones, T., & Turban, D. (in press). Doing one's duty: Chronological age, autonomous duty-enactment, and subjective well-being. *European Journal of Personality.*

Sheldon, K. M., & King, L. K. (2001). Why positive psychology is necessary. *American Psychologist, 56,* 216–217.

Sheldon, K. M., Schmuck, P., & Kasser, T. (2000). Is value-free science possible? *American Psychologist, 10,* 1152–1153.

Tedeschi, R. G., & Calhoun, L. G. (1995). *Trauma and transformation: Growing in the aftermath of suffering.* Thousand Oaks, CA: Sage.

Vaillant, G. (1977). *Adaptation to life.* Boston: Little, Brown.

Waterman, A. S. (1982). Identity development from adolescence to adulthood: An extension of theory and a review of research. *Developmental Psychology, 18,* 341–358.

Whitbourne, S. K., & Tesch, S. A. (1985). A comparison of identity and intimacy statuses in college students and alumni. *Developmental Psychology, 21,* 1039–1044.

Wilson, A. E., & Ross, M. (2001). From chump to champ: People's appraisals of their earlier and present selves. *Journal of Personality and Social Psychology, 80,* 572–584.

13

Afterword

Breaking the 65 Percent Barrier

MARTIN E. P. SELIGMAN

F irst, I want to assert clearly that positive psychology is not remotely intended as a replacement for or competitor to clinical psychology. It is intended as a supplement, another arrow in the quiver of those who treat patients in the clinic. But I have come to have more and more reservations about clinical psychology as it is now practiced. I will contrast the future of positive psychology to the history of clinical psychology to illuminate why I believe that clinical psychology is reaching a dead end—the 65% barrier.

In the United States, because of the exigencies of financing and insurance, psychological treatment of patients confronts restricted budgets. Managed care is one version of that, and in response clinical psychology and psychiatry, as well as their research arms, have come to be professions which are about firefighting rather than fire prevention. The dirty little secret of all of biological psychiatry and much of clinical psychology today is that they have given up the notion of cure. They are almost entirely about crisis management and the rendering of cosmetic treatments.

There are two kinds of medications and, similarly, there are two kinds of psychological interventions. If you take an antibiotic, and you take it long enough, it cures by killing the bacterial invaders. That is, when you're done taking it, the disease does not recrudesce. On the other hand, if you take quinine for malaria, you only get suppression of the symptoms. When you stop taking quinine, malaria returns. Quinine is a cosmetic drug, a palliative, and all medications can be classified either as curative in intention or cosmetic in intention. Palliation is a good thing (I'm wearing a hearing aid right now), but it is not the highest good nor the chief end of interventions. It is—and should be—a way station to a cure.

Every single drug in the psychopharmacopoeia is cosmetic. There are no curative drugs, and biological psychiatry seems to have given up on the notion of cure.

230

I am by no means a Freudian, but one thing that I think was exemplary about Freud is that he was interested in cure. Freud wanted a psychotherapy that was like antibiotics, not a psychotherapy of cosmetics, and palliation is not a significant goal in psychodynamic psychotherapy. The decline of Freudian influence, but much more important the stringencies of managed care, has seduced clinical psychology and psychiatry into working only on symptom relief and not on cures, creating a profession of firefighters.

I've spent a good part of my life measuring the effects of psychotherapy and of drugs. Almost universally, the effects are small to moderate. Depression is typical. Consider two treatments that "work": cognitive therapy of depression and SSRIs (e.g., Prozac). For each, you get a 65% relief rate, along with a placebo effect that ranges from 45% to 55%. The more valid the placebo, the higher the placebo percentage. These numbers crop up over and over, whether you're looking at the percentage of patients who experience relief or at the percentage of relief of symptoms within patients (e.g., Kirsch, Moore, Scoboria, & Nicholls, 2002). Why, I now want to ask, are the effects of almost all of the drugs and the psychotherapies only small to moderate? From the first day that I took up skiing, until 5 years later when I quit, I was always fighting the mountain. Skiing was never easy. In every form of psychotherapy that I know, every psychotherapeutic intervention is a "fighting the mountain" intervention. They don't catch on and maintain themselves. In general, therapeutic techniques share this property of being difficult to do and difficult to incorporate into one's life. In fact, the way we measure their good effects is how long they last before they "melt" after treatment is discontinued.

So that's the first problem of clinical psychology and biological psychiatry: *the 65% barrier.* The second major—I almost want to call it a "moral"—problem, I call *dealing with it,* and it stems in part from the first problem. In the therapeutic century that we've just lived, it was the job of the therapist to minimize negative emotions: to dispense drugs or psychological interventions which make people less anxious, less angry, or less depressed. So the job was minimizing dysphoria. But there is an alternate approach to dysphoria: learning to function well in the face of dysphoria—dealing with it.

This posture emerges from the most important research finding in the field of personality of the last quarter of the 20th century: that most personality traits are highly heritable (e.g., Pinker, 2002). The dysphorias often, but not always, stem from personality traits. As such, I believe that they are modifiable, but not only within limits. So what posture follows from this, which is one of the causes of the 65% barrier, from the likelihood that depression, anxiety, and anger stem from heritable personality traits that can only be ameliorated but not wholly eliminated?

Do you know how snipers and fighter pilots are trained? I'm not endorsing sniping, by the way, I only want to describe how the training is done. It takes about 24 hours for a sniper to get into position. And then it can take another 36 hours to get his shot off. Now that means that typically before he shoots, he hasn't slept for 2 or more days. He's dead tired. Now, let's say we went to a psychotherapist and asked: How would you train a sniper? What the psychotherapist would do is use drugs or psychological interventions that break up fatigue.

That's not how snipers are trained, however. To train a sniper, you keep them up for 3 days, and you have them practice shooting when they are dead tired. That is, you teach snipers to *deal* with the negative state they're in: to function well in the presence of fatigue. Similarly, fighter pilots are selected who are rugged individuals and who do not scare easily. But there are many things that happen to fighter pilots that scare the pants off even the most rugged. Again, you don't call on therapists to teach the many tricks of anxiety reduction, thereby training candidates to become relaxed fighter pilots. Rather, the trainer heads the plane straight for the ground until the pilot is in terror, and the pilot then learns to pull up even when terrified.

The negative emotions and the negative personality traits have strong biological limits, and the best you can ever do with the palliative approach is to get people to live in the best part of their set range of depression or anxiety or anger. But think about Abraham Lincoln or Winston Churchill, two unipolar depressives. They were both enormously well-functioning human beings who dealt with their "black dogs" and functioned beautifully even when depressed. So one thing that clinical psychology needs to develop in light of the stubbornness of the dysphorias is a psychology of dealing with it: developing interventions that train people how to be functional in the presence of their dominant dysphorias.

This is meant to set the stage for talking about positive interventions. So far, I've argued that medications and psychotherapies are almost all cosmetic and that the best they seem to do is to approach the 65% barrier. My hope about positive interventions—and it's just a hope, but it is grounded in a little bit of evidence—is that they may *break* the 65% barrier.

I'm going to discuss three forms of happiness and the identification of strengths and virtues, and then I'll discuss the consequences of using those strengths and virtues in work and love and play and parenting. It's my belief that when you deploy your signature strengths, when you find out, for example, that you're an unusually kind person and you decide to use your kindness more and more in your work, that it maintains itself. It takes hold. It's not fighting the mountain. It's a large effect that gets bigger and bigger. You don't need a therapist to help you much with it; you don't need booster sessions; and it doesn't melt some time after the intervention. The positive interventions may be the buffers against the dysphorias that will lift the clinical psychologist's effectiveness above the 65% barrier.

The Gallup organization and Don Clifton, in particular, worked for years on strengths. Sponsored by the Mayerson Foundation, Chris Peterson has written positive psychology's version of strengths and virtues. The object of this classification (Peterson & Seligman, 2004) is to classify the strengths and virtues, while avoiding some of the obvious errors of the *DSM*—such as the categorical rather than dimensional treatment of entities and its provinciality to North America. Our classification asks: What are the ubiquitous strengths and virtues, the strengths and virtues that almost every culture, every religion, every brand of politics endorses? Of course, when Peterson set out on this venture, our ethical relativist friends told us that there were no such ubiquitous strengths and virtues, that virtue is only a social construction. But what we've found as we've asked the question in many settings is that there seem to be six virtues that almost every religion, culture, and nation endorses, and there exists a set of about 24 strengths nested under those virtues. We have written about the consensual definitions, how you measure these traits, what the sex ratio is, what we know about childhood, what the enabling and disabling conditions are, and what interventions are known to build these strengths.

The first cluster is the wisdom and knowledge virtues, with curiosity, love of learning, judgment, creativity, and perspective as the nested strengths. The second virtue cluster is courage, with valor and perseverance and integrity under that. The third is the humanity and love cluster, which includes intimacy, kindness, sociability, and intelligence. The fourth is justice with the strengths of citizenship, fairness, and leadership. The fifth is temperance, and under that are the strengths of forgiveness, humility, self-regulation, and prudence. The final virtue is transcendence, with appreciation of beauty, gratitude, hope, humor, playfulness, and spirituality nested therein.

To understand the importance of the strengths and virtues, I want to make a distinction among three forms of happiness. American culture's view of happiness has evolved far from what Thomas Jefferson talked about in the Declaration of Independence and what Aristotle meant by happiness. American culture has bought into the Hollywood view of happiness: smiling a lot and feeling a lot of pleasure. Indeed, this is one of the three forms of happiness (Seligman, 2002). This "pleasant life" consists of having as many pleasures as you possibly can and having the skills that amplify those pleasures. The first skill for amplifying pleasure is timing. The pleasures in general, which are all defined by raw feelings—the ecstasies, the raptures, the thrills, the orgasms—all of these have the property of French vanilla ice cream. The first taste is wonderful. The second taste is at about 50%. And by the time you're down to the seventh taste, it's like cardboard. To amplify pleasures, you need to learn how to space them and how to vary them enough to keep them from becoming cardboard. The second set of techniques for amplifying the pleasures are the savoring techniques: sharing them with another person, taking mental photographs, taking physical souvenirs, being very articulate in your description of them. The third are the Buddhist techniques of mindfulness. The pleasant life, which is a perfectly legitimate way to live, consists in having as many of these positive raw feelings as you can and learning the skills to amplify them.

This, however, is not remotely what Aristotle meant by happiness. To introduce Aristotle's notion of *eudaimonia,* the engaged life, I want to tell you about my friend Len. Len was enormously successful in two of the three main realms of life by his mid-twenties. First, in work, he was a multimillionaire, the head of an options-trading company. In play, he was in his twenties a national bridge champion. But the problem about Len was that, unlike Debbie Reynolds, Len doesn't feel positive emotion much at all. In fact, there is a Gaussian distribution of "positive affectivity," and Debbie Reynolds is up at the top, but people like Len are in the bottom 5%, and half of the world's population by definition is in the lower half. These are people who don't smile a lot, who aren't ebullient, and who are not cheerful. I sat across from Len at one of his bridge championships—I'm a bridge player also—and after about 7 days, Len won on the last board. He flashed his full-half smile and ran upstairs to watch "Monday Night Football" alone. This lack of positive emotion wrecked the third great arena of life, his love life. Len dated American women, and American women didn't like Len very much. They told him, "You're not a lot of fun, Len"; "You don't smile a lot"; "You're not much fun to be with"; "Get lost."

Len was wealthy enough to go for 5 years to a Park Avenue psychoanalyst, who looked for the sexual trauma that must have happened to him when he was young to somehow have locked positive emotion inside of him. But there was no trauma. Len grew up on Long Island, and nothing ever happened to him except that he played bridge and watched football. The problem is simply that Len is, biologically, in the bottom range of positive affectivity. Is Len unhappy?

The standard hedonic view, which says that the only form of happiness is the pleasant life, consigns Len (and the entire lower 50% in positive affectivity of humanity) to the hell of being unhappy. Len is, however, one of the happiest people whom I know. Len has abundant *eudaimonia.* When Aristotle talked about the pleasures of contemplation, he did not mean that somehow when we contemplated a philosophical issue that we felt orgasms or that we had any kind of emotion at all. Rather, what Aristotle meant was that we are one with the act, at one "with the music," with what Mike Csikszentmihalyi calls "flow" (Csikszentmihalyi, 1990). Time stops. We feel completely absorbed and immersed in what we are doing. This is what Len has. In work, on the floor of the American Stock Exchange, and in bridge, time stops for Len. Len is in flow often.

What is the relationship of flow to the strengths and virtues? My hypothesis is that the engaged life has a fairly simple formulation. The engaged life consists in identifying your signature strengths (www.reflectivehappiness.com), to use Phil Stone's term, and then using them as much as you can in work, in love, in play, in parenting. What you derive from that is more flow, but not necessarily more pleasure. That is, the engaged life consists in recrafting your life to use these strengths as much as you can. So I hypothesize that the second form of happiness is the engaged life. The engaged life, I want to claim, is vastly less biologically constrained than is the pleasant life. Everyone has strengths and virtues, and the trick is to know what they are and then to be creative enough to deploy them as much as possible.

For bridge players like me, who go into flow when we play bridge, the engaged life doesn't seem to be enough. That is because there's a third kind of life that the human animal craves—a life on which there are no biological constraints at all. That is the meaningful life. I'm not going to be sophomoric enough to try to give you a theory of meaning. But the one thing we know about meaning is that meaning consists in attachment to something larger than you are. And the larger the thing to which you can credibly attach yourself, the more meaning your life has. I believe that we are moral animals, that we are biologically demanding of meaning. The meaningful life is something over and above the pleasant life or the engaged life. With just those two, we often wake up with the gnawing fear that we're fidgeting unto death. Meaning is the antidote to that fear. The third happy life, the meaningful life, consists of identifying your signature strengths and then using them to belong to and in the service of something that you believe is larger than you are.

I've argued then that positive psychology interventions might break the 65% barrier. How so? I will end with three examples of positive interventions that we are now testing empirically. These all emerge from teaching positive psychology. I don't run a clinic and, in fact, I have an educative rather than a clinical model of positive psychology. I teach positive psychology, and one of the lovely things about teaching positive psychology is that there are exercises that you can assign, and you can do them yourself to illustrate and discover the underlying principles. When we teach about the pleasant life, one exercise that we assign is to design and then have a "beautiful day," using the savoring, mindfulness, and timing techniques.

When we study *eudaimonia,* the engaged life, we assign the recrafting of a work task. The students have taken the signature strengths tests, and we then ask them to think of something at work that is tedious. They then recraft this tedious task to do it using their highest strength. One woman was a bagger at the Acme. She hated bagging, which is a tedious, almost meaningless task. Her highest strength was social intelligence, so she decided that she would recraft bagging to make the interaction with her the social highlight of each customer's day. She didn't always succeed, but she transformed the job into an enjoyable one.

When we teach about the meaningful life, we do a "fun versus philanthropy" exercise. The students do something fun, and they contrast this to doing something altruistic. When they do something fun, such as hanging out with friends or masturbating, there is a square wave offset. When it's over, it's over. When they do something altruistic that calls on a signature strength, something very different happens. One of the juniors in our course was phoned by her third-grade nephew in the middle of the week. He needed to be tutored in arithmetic. So she tutored him for 2 hours on the telephone. She said later that, after that experience, the whole day went better: "I was mellower"; "I could listen more"; "People liked me better." One of the business students said that the reason that he had gone to Wharton was to make a lot of money, and the reason he wanted to make a lot of money was that he believed that money brings freedom and happiness. He was astonished to discover that he was happier helping another person than he was shopping.

In conclusion, I want to suggest that positive psychology in the next decade, if we do it well, may invent and validate a group of interventions that bring happiness in all three senses of pleasure, engagement, and meaning. These exercises may be self-accreting and self-maintaining. These will not be interventions in the sense of manipulation; rather, they require a sense of ownership, choice, will, and responsibility. Such interventions are justifiable in their own right, since they will lead untroubled people toward happier lives. When coupled to the interventions that already treat mental illnesses, they may break the 65% barrier.

References

Csikszentmihalyi, M. (1990). *Flow.* New York: Harper.

Kirsch, I., Moore, T., Scoboria, A., & Nicholls, S. (2002). The emperor's new drugs: An analysis of antidepressant medication data submitted to the U.S. Food and Drug Administration. Available: http://journals.apa.org/prevention/volume5/toc-jul15–02.htm.

Peterson, C., & Seligman, M. (2004). *Character strengths and virtues: A handbook and classification.* New York: Oxford University Press; Washington, DC: American Psychological Association Press.

Pinker, S. (2002). *The blank slate.* New York: Viking.

Seligman, M. (2002). *Authentic happiness.* New York: Free Press.

Author Index

Boulton, M. J., 89
Bower, J. E., 94, 170
Brackett, M. A., 108, 109, 110, 111
Bradburn, N. M., 6
Bradley, K. A., 173
Bradley, M. M., 104
Brand, W., 75
Brandstädter, J., 12, 139, 143–164, 184, 187, 188
Branigan, C., 89, 90, 91, 92
Braun, O. L., 208
Bregman, L., 64
Brehm, J. W., 148, 150
Brewin, C. R., 134
Briançon, S., 173
Brickman, P., 149
Brock, B., 206
Brodsky, J., 55
Brooks, K., 134
Brown, A. S., 167
Brown, J. D., 134
Brown, K. W., 76–77, 204, 207, 211
Brown, S. L., 95
Bruner, J., 59
Brunhart, S. M., 169
Brunstein, J. C., 144, 186
Buckingham, M., 33
Buckman, R., 173
Bühler, K., 15, 19, 23, 26–27
Bulkeley, K., 74–75
Buss, D. M., 40
Bybee, D., 195

Cabanac, M., 87, 88
Cacioppo, J. T., 88
Caldwell, N. D., 133
Calhoun, L. G., 226
Callegari, S., 173
Campbell, D. A., 173
Campbell, D. T., 27
Campbell, J., 128
Campbell, K. K., 173
Cantor, N., 183, 186
Caplan, R. D., 194
Caputi, P., 109
Carli, M., 172
Carlson, D., 64
Caro, T. M., 89
Carr, A., 5
Carstensen, L. L., 157
Caruso, D. R., 108, 109, 110

Carver, C. S., 88, 94, 145, 150, 169, 184, 185
Castellon, C., 169
Cawley, M. J., 34
Chamberlin, J., 173
Chambers, N., 194
Chang, L., 208
Changeux, J. P., 26
Chapireau, F., 166
Chatterji, S., 167
Cheek, P. R., 149
Cheung, C., 69, 70
Chomsky, N., 24
Ciarrochi, J., 109
Clifton, D. O., 33
Clore, G. L., 88, 92
Cohen, S., 170
Cohn, M. A., 95
Colby, P. M., 70
Colder, M., 114
Colvez, A., 166
Comte-Sponville, A., 33
Conover, S. A., 167
Conway, A., 95
Cook, M. L., 44
Corbit, J. D., 92
Cosmides, L., 86
Côté, S., 110
Covey, S., 123
Coyle, C. T., 75
Coyne, J. C., 150
Craik, K. H., 40
Cross, S., 148, 189, 190
Cross-National Collaborative Group, 209
Crowne, D. P., 34
Csikszentmihalyi, I., 124, 170
Csikszentmihalyi, M., 3–14, 29, 86, 124, 132, 144, 149, 170, 171, 172, 173, 208, 234
Cuthbert, B. N., 104

Damasio, A. R., 83, 106
Damon, W., 6
Dangelmayer, G., 186
Danner, D. D., 97
Dasen, P. R., 167
Daubman, K. A., 91
Davidson, R. J., 88
Dawson, S., 201, 202, 203, 204
Dechesne, M., 208

Deci, E. L., 52, 170, 173, 174, 186, 209, 217, 222, 225, 226, 227
Deckard, G., 173
de Graaf, J., 211
Delle Fave, A., 12, 51, 139, 165–181
Dember, W. N., 91
Dennett, D., 26
Derryberry, D., 91
de St. Aubin, E., 219
Detweiler, J. B., 170
Deutsch, W., 25
Devlieger, P. J., 168
Dholakia, R., 204
Di Caccavo, A., 173
Dickerson, S. S., 130, 135
DiClemente, C. C., 133
Diener, C., 88
Diener, E., 6, 85, 88, 98, 124, 146, 165, 201, 220, 221
Dilthey, W., 24, 25, 26
Dilts, R., 123
Dittmann-Kohli, F., 157
Dixon, R. A., 146, 148
Dolhinow, P. J., 89
Dollahite, D. C., 64
Dominguez, J. R., 210
Dorner, S., 167
Doyle, W. J., 170
Draguns, J., 167
Duval, T. S., 152

Easterbrook, J. A., 107
Eckhauser, F. E., 173
Edelman, G. M., 26
Ekman, P., 86
Elder, G., 146
Eliade, M., 65
Elkins, D. N., 64
Elliott, A. J., 221
Ellis, A., 43
Elton, A., 167
Emmons, R. A., 12, 16, 62–81, 124, 144, 183, 185, 186, 189, 191, 221
Empereur, F., 173
Engel, G. L., 166
Enright, R. D., 75, 76
Epstein, M., 51
Erikson, E., 4, 31, 190, 216, 219, 220, 221, 222, 224
Erikson, M. J., 64
Estrada, C. A., 91

Faber, R. J., 208
Fagan, P. J., 122
Fahey, J. L., 170
Faust, D., 134
Fava, G., 124
Feist, G. J., 115
Feldman, S., 183
Felser, G., 154
Ferriss, A. L., 62
Festinger, L., 209
Field, D., 173
Fireman, P., 170
Fitness, J., 111
Fitzgerald, R., 168
Fitzpatrick, R., 165
Flaste, R., 52
Fleeson, W., 155, 186
Flynn, P., 210
Folkman, S., 94, 96, 208
Fowler, J. W., 4
Frank, J. D., 134
Frankl, V., 50
Fredrickson, B. L., 12, 83, 85–103, 124, 157
Freedman, S., 75
Freedman, Z. R., 173
Freud, S., 183
Freund, A. M., 153, 189
Fried, C., 209
Friedman, H. S., 170
Friesen, W. V., 97
Frijda, N. H., 86, 88, 104
Frist, M. H., 168
Fromm, E., 55

Galanter, E., 184
Gall, M., 112
Gallup, G. G., Jr., 152
Gardner, H., 6, 105
Gardner, W. L., 88
Garfield, S. L., 134
Gasper, K., 92
Gatz, M., 154
Giardini, A., 173
Gilbert, D. T., 153
Glaser, R., 114
Glass, R. M., 173
Glober, G., 173
Glück, J., 4
Gohm, C. L., 124
Goldman, S. L., 114

Pfeiffer, E., 216, 227
Phillips, F. L., 122
Piedmont, R. L., 67–68
Pierobon, A., 173
Pimentel, E. F., 190
Pinel, E. C., 153
Pinker, S., 24, 231
Pitts, R. C., 30
Pléh, C., 12, 15, 16, 19–28
Poll, J., 62
Pollack, S. D., 113
Pomerantz, E. M., 94
Popper, K. R., 26
Power, M., 134
Pribram, K. H., 184
Price, R. H., 194
Priester, J. R., 88
Prigogine, I., 57–58
Prochaska, J. O., 168
Prochaska, O., 133
Pyszczynski, T. A., 157, 208

Rand, K. L., 124
Ransom, S., 208
Rathunde, K., 4, 5, 149
Ravichandran, G., 174
Reed, G. M., 94, 170
Reed, M. B., 94
Reid, F., 173
Reker, G. T., 156
Renner, G., 145, 153
Rican, P., 64, 66
Rice, C. L., 112
Richards, T. A., 96
Richins, M. L., 201, 202, 203, 204
Ris, M. D., 91
Roberts, R. C., 73, 74
Roberts, R. D., 110
Robin, V., 210
Robinson, G. F., 91
Robinson, M. D., 201
Rodd, Z. A., 152
Rodgers, W., 216
Roese, N. J., 152
Rogers, C., 209
Rogers, J. B., 183
Romer, D., 35
Rose, N., 120
Rosellini, R. A., 152
Rosenberg, E., 207, 208
Rosenberg, E. L., 87

Rosenblatt, A., 157
Rosenzweig, A. S., 91
Rosenzweig, M. R., 25
Rosnati, R., 189
Ross, L., 152
Ross, M., 227
Rothbaum, F., 154
Rothermund, K., 145, 146, 147, 148, 149, 150, 151, 152, 153, 154, 155, 156
Rothman, A. J., 170
Rubin, M. M., 110
Ruehlman, L. S., 184, 194
Ruzzene, M., 111
Ryan, R. M., 76–77, 170, 174, 186, 201, 202, 205, 207, 208, 209, 216, 217, 222, 225, 226, 227
Ryff, C. D., 34, 143, 228

Saile, H., 154
Saisto, T., 155, 188, 191
Salmela-Aro, K., 12, 140, 155, 182–199
Salovey, P., 12, 83, 104–119, 124, 170
Sameroff, A. J., 205
Sanders, G. S., 62
Sanderson, C., 186
Sandvik, E., 85
Saraswathi, T. S., 167
Sartorius, N., 167
Saunders, S., 204
Savickas, M. L., 194
Schefft, B. K., 91
Scheier, M. F., 88, 145, 150, 169, 184, 185
Schmitz, U., 154, 155, 156
Schmuck, P., 6, 209, 216
Schooler, J. W., 134
Schulman, P., 169
Schultheiss, O., 186
Schultheiss, O. C., 144
Schulz, R., 145, 153, 154
Schure, E., 86
Schutte, N. S., 108
Schütz, A., 111
Schwartz, S. H., 203, 204
Schwartz. N., 6
Schwarz, N., 107
Schwarzer, R., 169
SCN-CBR, 172
Scoboria, A., 231
Scott, A. B., 65

Seagal, Z., 130
Sedikides, C., 191
Seewald-Marquardt, A., 64
Segall, M. H., 167
Seidlitz, L., 67
Seligman, M. E. P., 5, 6, 7, 12, 15, 16,
        29, 30, 35, 36, 37, 38, 41, 46, 49,
        50, 59, 74, 86, 96, 124, 132, 140,
        143, 146, 147, 157, 169, 230–236
Sellin, I., 111
Sen, A., 143
Shaffer, L. F., 114
Shanafelt, T. D., 173
Sharp, L. K., 114
Sheldon, K. M., 6, 12, 140, 185, 186,
        201, 203, 204, 205, 215–229
Sheldon, M. S., 203
Sherman, E., 157
Sherrod, L. R., 90
Shoda, Y., 183
Sifneos, P. E., 106
Sigmon, D. R., 124
Silvia, P. J., 152
Simeonsson, R. J., 166
Simon, H. A., 107, 143
Simons, C. J. R., 90
Singer, B., 34, 143
Singer, J. L., 90
Sirgy, M. J., 205
Sitarenios, G., 109
Skinner, E. A., 145
Skoner, D. P., 170
Slade, M. D., 97
Smith, C., 64
Smith, H. L., 146
Smith, J., 189
Smith, P. K., 89
Smith, R. P., 24, 42
Smith, T. B., 62
Snowdon, D. A., 97
Snyder, C. R., 5, 124
Snyder, S. S., 154
Sodergren, S. C., 168
Solberg, E. C., 201
Solley, C. M., 59
Solomon, R. D., 73
Solomon, R. L., 92
Solomon, S., 157, 208
Sonnad, S. S., 173
Spranger, E., 25, 26
Stanton, J., 68

Stattin, H., 190
Staudinger, U. M., 5, 146
Staw, B. M., 150
Stein, N. L., 96
Stengers, I., 58
Stern, C., 24, 25
Stern, W., 15, 19, 23, 24, 25, 26, 27
Sternberg, R. J., 41, 105
Steward, W. T., 170
Stifoss-Hanssen, H., 66
Stiles, W. B., 134
Stock, H. S., 152
Stock, W. A., 146
Stone, J., 209
Stone, T., 73
Straus, R., 109
Streng, F. J., 72
Suh, E. M., 124, 146, 165
Susser, E. S., 167
Swank, A. B., 66
Szasz, T. S., 37

Tanaka-Matsumi, J., 167
Tarakeshwar, N., 66, 68
Tatarkiewicz, W., 144
Taylor, G. J., 106, 113
Taylor, S. E., 32, 94, 130, 134, 135, 152,
        169, 170
Teasdale, J., 130
Teasdale, J. D., 169
Tedeschi, R. G., 226
Tehrani, K., 69, 70
Tennen, H., 96, 152, 168
Terry, K., 195
Tesch, S. A., 219
Tesser, A., 152
Thierman, S., 64
Thompson, R., 107
Thompson, S. C., 149
Thuriaux, M. C., 166
Tobin, S. S., 146
Tolley-Schell, S., 113
Tooby, J., 86
Trabasso, T., 96
Trépanier, L., 155
Trinidad, D. R., 110
Tripathi, I., 167
Trope, Y., 94
Tsang, J., 72
Tucker, D. M., 91
Tugade, M. M., 92, 94–95, 96

Subject Index

child abuse and emotional intelligence, 113–114
clinical psychology, 139–140, 230–232
cognitive-behavioral psychotherapeutic approach, 121–123, 133–135
cognitive dissonance and materialism, 209–210
cognitive processes
  in dual-process model, 150–153, 155–156
  in emotional intelligence model, 107
  and health quality-of-life, 167–170
  in motivation theories, 184, 185
  in multiregulation personality model, 56, 58–59
  and positive emotions, 90–97
commercial-free zones, 206
commercialism. *See* materialism
compensation and aging, 148
complacency, as love of learning disorder, 45
conformity, as disorder of creativity, 41
connectedness, in Spiritual Transcendence Scale, 67–68
consciousness, self-reflective, 8–12
constraints and motivation, life-span development, 188–190
consumerism. *See* materialism
contentment
  response tendency, 89, 91–92
  and undo hypothesis, 93–94
contiguity, in utilitarianism, 20–21
convergence theory, 24–25
courage virtue
  defined, 30, 32
  disorder continuum, 39
  and well-being, 129
creativity
  disorders of, 41–42
  and emotional intelligence, 115
  and positive emotions, 89–90
critical thinking, disorders of, 43–44
cross-cultural studies
  age-subjective well-being, 225–226
  functional optimism, 139
  health and quality-of-life, 167, 172
  materialism, 202, 203, 204, 209
  quality-of-life, 139
  spirituality, 68, 76
  well-being strategies, 127–131
cultural mediation, 59

curiosity disorders, 42–43
cynicism, as critical thinking disorder, 44

daring, as well-being strategy, 129
defensive ideas of happiness, 144
defensive optimism, 169
depression
  and *DSM* classifications, 40
  and emotional intelligence, 112–113
  and goals, 144–145, 148, 149–150
  and materialism, 209
  positive intervention potential, 231–232
  treatment effectiveness, 231
  and well-being strategies, 129, 132–133
development theories, commonality, 4–5
differential psychology, 23–26
disinterest, as curiosity disorder, 42
dispositional optimism, 169
disposition logic, 53
drive gratification logic, 53
drug treatments, 230–231
DSM classifications, 30, 37, 40
  See also VIA Classification of Strengths
dual-process model
  overview, 139, 145–146, 157–158
  accommodative processes, 148–150
  aging implications, 153–157
  assimilative processes, 147–148
  information processing, 150–153

eccentricity, as disorder of creativity, 41–42
ecological costs of materialism, 203–204
ego integrity task, 219–220, 226–227
emancipation stages, 55–57
emotional intelligence
  overview, 83–84, 104, 115–116
  benefits, 110–114
  concept development, 105–106
  four-branch model, 106–108
  maladaptive potential, 114–115
  measuring, 108–110
Emotional Quotient Inventory (EQ-i), 108
emotions, spiritual, 71–77
engaged life, 124, 234–235
epigenetic laws, 25
EQ-i (Emotional Quotient Inventory), 108
Eriksen, Erik, 219
ethology, 26–27
eudaimonia, 15, 234

external motivation, 217–219

extrinsic values and materialism, 202–203, 211

fear
and meaningful life, 235
response tendency, 86, 91–92
FGA (Flexible Goal Adjustment), 153, 158*n*
fighter pilot example, 231–232
Flexible Goal Adjustment (FGA), 153, 158*n*
flow, 124, 234–235
Flow Questionnaire, 171–172
forgiveness, 75–76, 111
freedom
mediation's role, 58–59
in Mill's perspective, 22
and responsibility, 56–57
as social meme, 11–12
Freudian psychology, 231
functional optimism, 139, 169
fun *vs.* philanthropy exercise, meaningful life, 235–236

GDP (Gross Domestic Product), 210
generativity life task, 219–220, 226–227
goals, personal
in aging-psychological maturity model, 217–220, 223
in dual-process model, 147–150
with health constraints, 168–169
in life-span development model, 187–192
and meaning, 144–145
and spirituality, 69–71
and well-being, 139, 185–187, 193–195
See also motivation
gratitude, 71–73
Gross Domestic Product (GDP), 210
groupthink, 43
gullibility, as critical thinking disorder, 44

habit logic, multiregulation personality model, 53
habits, in ethology, 26–27
Hamlet, 58
happiness
historical perspectives, 15, 20–21
types of, 144, 233–236
See also well-being *entries*

health and quality-of-life
biopsychological model benefits, 165–166, 174–175
India study, 167
optimal activities impact, 170–172
professional worker experiences, 172–174
psychological opportunities, 167–170
health benefits, emotional intelligence, 112–114
historical perspectives
overview, 15, 27
of consciousness, 9–11
Mill's work, 19–23
Stern's theorizing, 23–26
utilitarianism model, 20–21
humanistic psychotherapeutic approach, 121–123

ICF (International Classification of Functioning), 166
identified motivation, 217–218
identity life task, 219–220
immanent errors, defined, 24
immunization principle, avoiding materialism, 207–209
India, quality-of-life study, 167
individuality
in Mill's perspective, 21–22
Stern's approach, 24–26
and survival instincts, 9
information processing
about health conditions, 167–170
in dual-process model, 150–153
See also cognitive *entries*
ingenuity disorders, 41–42
insight, as well-being strategy, 132–135
instincts, in ethology, 26–27
intelligence testing, 24
interest
disorder of, 42–43
response tendency, 89, 90
International Classification of Functioning (ICF), 166
intimacy life task, 219–220
intrapersonal intelligence, defined, 105
See also emotional intelligence
intrinsic motivation, 217–218
intrinsic values and materialism, 202–203, 208–211
introjected motivation, 217–219

job performance and emotional intelligence, 111–112
joy
  response tendency, 89, 91–92
  and undo hypothesis, 93–94
judgment, disorders of, 43–44
justice virtue, 30, 33, 39

know-it-all-ism, as love of learning disorder, 45
knowledge, Mill's perspective, 21, 22–23
knowledge virtue
  defined, 30, 32
  disorder continuum, 39–45
Korea, spirituality research, 68

language acquisition, 24
learned habit logic, 53
LEAS (Levels of Emotional Awareness Scale), 108–109
Len (friend), 234
Levels of Emotional Awareness Scale (LEAS), 108–109
life satisfaction. *See* well-being *entries*
life-span development model
  counseling implications, 194–195
  motivation's role, 187–194
  See also aging *entries*
life tasks, Eriksen's theory, 219–220
Life Theme Questionnaire, 171–172
life world logic, 53
logics of behaviors, 53–55
love
  Mill's perspective, 21, 22–23
  response tendency, 89
love of learning, disorders of, 44–45
love virtue, 30, 32, 39

MAAS (Mindfulness Attention Awareness Scale), 76–77
management branch, emotional intelligence model, 107
materialism
  alternatives to, 204–210
  costs of, 140, 200–204
Mayer-Salovey-Caruso Emotional Intelligence Scale (MSCEIT), 109–111, 112, 115
meaning emancipation stage, 56

measurement systems
  character strengths, 34–35
  coping processes, 153
  emotional intelligence, 108–110
  materialism, 201
  optimal experiences, 171–172
  psychological maturity, 217
  See also spirituality
media literacy programs, 207–208
mediation
  and aging-psychological maturity model, 220, 222, 223
  and personality development, 58–59, 125, 135
MEIS (Multifactor Emotional Intelligence Scale), 109, 112
mental health benefits, emotional intelligence, 112–114
metabrain, 8–9
Mill, John Stuart, 19–23
mindfulness
  and materialism, 207–208
  and pleasure, 233
  and spirituality, 76–77, 125
  as well-being strategy, 125, 130, 135
Mindfulness Attention Awareness Scale (MAAS), 76–77
moods *vs.* positive emotions, 87–88
morbid interest, as curiosity disorder, 42
mortality and positive emotions, 97
motivation
  overview, 182–185
  ethology's principles, 26–27
  European principles, 184–185
  and life-span development, 187–195
  Mill's perspective, 22–23
  and self-constructed goals, 185–187, 189–192
  self-determination theory, 217–219
  utilitarianism model, 20–21
  See also goals, personal
motor emancipation stage, 56
MSCEIT (Mayer-Salovey-Caruso Emotional Intelligence Scale), 109–111, 112, 115
Multifactor Emotional Intelligence Scale (MEIS), 109, 112
multiregulation personality model
  overview, 15, 59–60
  behavioral logics, 52–55

emancipation stages, 55–57
mediation's role, 57–59

negative emotions
  cognitive effects, 90–92
  positive intervention potential, 231–232
  research dominance, 85–89
  undo hypothesis, 92–95
Nepal, quality-of-life study, 172
Nikki principle, defined, 49
NOS diagnosis, VIA Classification's
    advantages, 37
nosiness, as curiosity disorder, 42–43
nun study, 97

offensive ideas of happiness, 144
ontological mediation, 59
opportunities and motivation, life-span
    development model, 188–190
optimal experience, defined, 170
  See also health and quality-of-life; well-being entries
optimism, and health goals, 139, 169–170
originality disorders, 41–42
orthodoxy, as love of learning disorder,
    45

pain, in utilitarianism, 20–21
pedanticism, as love of learning disorder,
    45
personal goals. See goals, personal
personalism, 25–26
personality development
  behavioral logics, 53–55
  emancipation stages, 55–57
  mediation's role, 57–59
  Mill's theory, 20–23
  multiregulation model, 52–55
  Stern's theory, 24–26
  See also aging entries; dual-process model
philanthropy vs. fun exercise, meaningful
    life, 235–236
physical activity, as well-being strategy,
    128–129, 130, 135
physical emancipation stage, 55–56
play, functions of, 89–90
pleasant life, 233–235

pleasure
  as happiness category, 233
  positive emotions compared, 87
  in utilitarianism, 20–21
positive emotions, broaden-and-build
    theory
  overview, 83, 88–90, 97–98
  cognitive functions, 90–92
  and psychological resilience, 94–97
  research review, 85–88
  thought-action functions, 90–92
  undo hypothesis, 92–95
  well-being effects, 96–97
positive psychology, overview
  focus of, 3–5
  as paradigm shift, 5–7
  potential intervention benefits, 84,
    140–141, 230–236
  theoretical framework challenges, 6,
    49–52, 215–216
  See also specific topics, e.g., emotional
    intelligence; health and quality-of-life; well-being entries
possibilities logic, 53–54
prayer fulfillment, in Spiritual
    Transcendence Scale, 67–68
present-centered bias, 227
psychobiological therapeutic approach,
    121–123
psychodynamic therapeutic approach,
    121–123
psychography, 24
psychosocial theory, Eriksen's, 219–220
  See also aging-psychological maturity
    model
psychotherapeutic therapies
  treatment effectiveness, 230–232
  as well-being strategy, 120–123, 131–136

quieting the mind, as well-being strategy,
    128, 130, 135

rationality
  and emotional intelligence, 105–106
  in ethology, 26–27
reflection and reframing, as well-being
    strategy, 129, 130
regulation of behavior. See
    multiregulation personality model

relational theory of motivation, 184
religion, defined, 64
   See also spirituality
Religious Commitment Inventory, 68
resilience
   in dual-process model, 149–150
   and materialism resistance, 207–209
   and positive emotions, 94–97
response tendencies and emotions, 86–88
responsibility and freedom, 56–57
retail therapy, 208
reverence, 73–74

sacred. *See* spirituality
salutogenesis approach, 168
schools and commercialism, 206
selection function of motivation, 184–
   185, 188–190
self-determination theory, 217–219
   See also aging-psychological maturity
   model
self-efficacy and health quality-of-life,
   168–169
self-focused goals, life-span theory, 190–
   191, 193–194
self-help, as well-being strategy, 123
self-perfection goal, in Mill's perspective,
   21
self-reflective consciousness, 8–12
Self-Report Emotional Intelligence Test
   (SREIT), 108
semiotic mediation, 59
shortage economy theory, 22–23
Singapore, social duties study, 225–226
sniper example, 231–232
social costs of materialism, 202–203
social duties studies, 224–226
social norms logic, 53
social relationships
   emotional intelligence benefits, 110–
   111
   life satisfaction correlation, 124, 186
   as well-being strategy, 129, 130, 135
spirituality
   defining, 16, 63–66
   emotion level, 71–77
   personal goal level, 69–71
   research approaches generally, 62–63
   trait level, 66–68
   as well-being strategy, 124–125
Spiritual Transcendence Index, 67

Spiritual Transcendence Scale (STS), 67–
   68
sporadic human being concept, 52
   See also multiregulation personality
   model
SREIT (Self-Report Emotional Intelligence
   Test), 108
Stern, William, 23–26
stimuli response logic, 53
strengths and happiness, 232–236
   See also VIA Classification of Strengths
structural mediation, 59
STS (Spiritual Transcendence Scale), 67–68
student-parent study, 222–224
subjective well-being (SWB) hypotheses.
   See aging-psychological maturity
   model
survey method, materialism
   measurement, 201
survival instinct and self-reflection, 8–10
SWB (subjective well-being hypotheses).
   See aging-psychological maturity
   model
systemic group approach, 121–123

talk therapy, 120–123, 133
television, 42–43, 205–206
temperance virtue, 30, 33, 39
Tenacious Goal Pursuit (TGP), 153, 158*n*
thought-action repertoires and positive
   emotions, 90–97
time affluence, 211
Trait Meta-Mood Scale, 111
transcendence, as spirituality measure,
   67–68
transcendence virtue, 30, 33, 39
transgradient errors, defined, 24
triteness, as disorder of creativity, 41

ultimate understanding logic, 54
understanding branch, emotional
   intelligence model, 107
undo hypothesis, broaden-and-build
   theory, 92–95
un*DSM*. *See* VIA Classification of
   Strengths
universality, in Spiritual Transcendence
   Scale, 67–68
unreflectiveness, as critical thinking
   disorder, 43–44
utilitarianism, 20–23

value emancipation stage, 56
values
    and materialism, 201, 209–210
    scientific legitimacy, 3–6
VIA Classification of Strengths
    overview, 15–16, 30–34, 232–233
    clinical advantages, 35–38, 45–46
    continuum of disorders, 38–40
    measurement approach, 34–35
virtues, overview, 30–36, 37–38, 232–
    233
    See also VIA Classification of Strengths

well-being
    behavioral correlations, 124
    and character measurements, 46*n*
    and materialism, 201–202
    and personal goals, 182–185, 193–
        194
    positive emotions' effects, 96–97
    See also aging-psychological maturity
        model; health and quality-of-life

well-being, strategies for achieving
    overview of clinical implications, 84,
        135–136
    and cognitive style, 132–135
    comparisons, 125–126
    and life-span development model,
        194–195
    psychotherapeutic, 120–123, 131–132
    self-help, 123
    self-report studies, 126–132
    spirituality, 124–125
wisdom virtue
    defined, 30, 32
    disorder continuum, 39–45
wonder, 73–75
work benefits, emotional intelligence,
    111–112
work exercise, engaged life, 235
World Health Organization, 166

yogas, 125
Your Money or Your Life program, 210